THE HOLLYWOOD STARS

BASEBALL IN MOVIELAND
1926 - 1957

THE HOLLYWOOD STARS

BASEBALL IN MOVIELAND
1926 - 1957

BY RICHARD E. BEVERAGE

Author of
"The Angels – Los Angeles in the Pacific Coast League"
Member of the Society for American Baseball Research

THE DEACON PRESS
Placentia, California 92670

Library of Congress Catalog Card No. 84-070556
ISBN 0-940684-01-2

All book orders and other correspondence pertaining to
this publication should be directed to the author, Richard E.
Beverage, c/o Deacon Press, 1244 Brian Street, Placentia,
CA 92670.

TABLE OF CONTENTS

Gilmore Field and surroundings. Gilmore Stadium is left of center while the Pan-Pacific Auditorium is just above Gilmore Field.

Gilmore Field during its heyday.

PREFACE

The year 1983 saw the former Brooklyn Dodgers and New York Giants complete their twenty-sixth season as residents of the Pacific Coast. Twenty-six years is a generation in Biblical terms and truly, a generation of baseball fans has grown up in the West, cheering for the now Los Angeles Dodgers and San Francisco Giants as well as those teams which came after them. This is major league baseball at its finest. Has the West ever been anything but major league?

It may surprise the younger reader to learn that the Dodgers and Giants were not the originators of baseball in the West. For over half a century when baseball was discussed, it was discussed in reference to the Pacific Coast League. The PCL, representing all of the major cities in California and the Pacific Northwest, was nominally a minor league. In reality it was never that. The league had acted as a breeding ground for the major leagues for years. At first, the clubs signed their own talent, developed their stars and subsequently sold them to the Eastern clubs at substantial profit. Hall of Fame members Joe DiMaggio, Ted Williams, Harry Heilmann, Lloyd and Paul Waner, and Earl Averill began their careers in the West, as did other greats, just a shade below this level – Ernie Lombardi, Babe Herman, Charlie Root, Tony Lazzeri, Wally Berger among others too numerous to mention. In later years the PCL acted as the finishing school for the major leagues. The independent clubs had been supplanted by the farms of the majors. It was in this role that such future stars as Irv Noren, Billy Martin, Ernie Broglio, Al Rosen, Gus Zernial and Ferris Fain received their final seasoning before attaining major league stardom.

This book is an effort to tell the story of one of the PCL's important clubs, the Hollywood Stars. The Stars came into existence in 1926, then after a pause in 1936-37, began anew in 1938. The club became an important part of the Los Angeles sports scene after World War II when it had its greatest success, and interest remained high until the 1957 season when the transfer of the Dodgers to Los Angeles appeared imminent.

The story of the Stars is really one of two separate teams. The first began operations in 1926 and ended in 1935 when owner Bill Lane transferred the club to San Diego, to become the Padres. The second version began in 1938 when the Mission club of San Francisco was shifted to Southern California. The two entities had entirely different characteristics and perhaps should not be linked together. But I have arbitrarily chosen to do so to give impact to the continuity of Hollywood as a baseball entity. The purist may not agree with this approach, but I think it makes a better story.

A history of a baseball club needs ample statistics and I have provided enough to satisfy the most avid figure buff. The yearly leaders in the major offensive categories are listed as well as the important pitching records. In addition I have compiled the all time won-lost records of all Stars pitchers who had a pitching decision with the club along with a reconstruction of the basic lineup of each year. An index of all Hollywood players is also included. I am hopeful that this information will bring back some memories to the Stars fans and provide a resource to the baseball historian.

I feel very fortunate to have been able to speak to and correspond with many former Hollywood Stars and wish to thank them one and all—Mickey Heath, Johnny Kerr, Chuck Stevens, Roger Bowman, Bob Kahle, Rugger Ardizoia, Babe Herman, Dan Crowley, Jim Baxes, Dick Smith, George O'Donnell, Eddie Erautt.

Many thanks to Cece Carlucci, the greatest umpire in the Pacific Coast League, for his valuable comments on the Great Riot of 1953. Also, I wish to thank Ron Kaluzok for providing his computer capabilities in developing some of the statistical information.

I hope that you, the reader, enjoy this book, which has been a labor of love. I wish that my good friend, Randy Wiseman, could have lived to read it.

INTRODUCTION

The Pacific Coast League celebrated its eighty-first year in 1983. Eight-one years is by far the longest period of operation of any minor league in the West and it is only surpassed by the International League, which began its long history in 1884.

The makeup of the league is very different from what it was in its first season of 1903. Of its original cities, only Portland remains. The league now extends from Albuquerque to Honolulu and on up into Canada. It is now essentially a talent feeder to the major leagues; only the Hawaii franchise is locally owned.

The original membership consisted of San Francisco, Oakland, Los Angeles, Sacramento, Portland and Seattle. The PCL grew directly out of the California State League, which was operating in 1902. These leagues were not the beginning of professional baseball in the West, of course. Western baseball, as it is played today, dates back at least to 1868 when the first organized game was played in San Francisco. There were many professional teams during the balance of the 19th century, and the California State Leagues began in the late 1890's. Many of these teams were no more than town teams, but they all played a part in creating a thriving baseball climate in California.

During its first year of operations, the PCL was an

"outlaw" league—that is, it was not a member of the National Association of Professional Baseball Clubs, which had been founded the year before. In 1903 the league competed head to head with the Pacific Northwest League, which had been outraged by the PCL's placing of franchises in Seattle and Portland. Clubs were placed in California cities by the PNL, which then adopted the name of Pacific National League. After a bitter fight during the 1903 season, the latter league gave up, leaving the Golden State to the PCL.

Peace terms were achieved between the outlaws and the National Association in February, 1904, and the PCL became a respected member of Organized Baseball, as it has been ever since. During the next several years, the PCL battled with another outlaw California State League for fan support, and there were teams from each league in some cities. But by 1909, the PCL had won the struggle, and from then on until the arrival of the National League in 1958, it was the predominant baseball organization in the West.

The league frequently shifted its franchises during the early years. Tacoma was temporarily a member in 1904 and 1905, replacing Sacramento. This franchise was shifted to Fresno in 1906, then dropped along with Seattle in 1907 when the league shrank to four teams at the height of the war with the California State League. In 1909, Sacramento was readmitted along with Vernon, a small industrial city on the outskirts of Los Angeles. The Vernon team, which was owned by the Maier meat packing family, was shifted in 1913 to the suburb of Venice on the other side of town, where the club remained through the 1914 season.

In 1915, Salt Lake City came into the league as a replacement for the Sacramento franchise, which had become a ward of the PCL. The league maintained the same group of cities until 1918 when the Portland club was transferred to Sacramento. That city remained without baseball for only the one season and returned to the PCL along with Seattle in 1919. That same year, the league expanded to eight teams for the first time.

The Salt Lake club is the direct antecedent of the Hollywood Stars, with which we are concerned here. The Sacramento franchise had been transferred to San Francisco in September of 1914 as a bankrupt operation and was run by the PCL for the balance of that season. But the league was not in the business of running ball clubs and let it be known that the franchise was for sale. An angel appeared in the person of H. W. "Bill" Lane, who had owned the Salt Lake club in the now defunct Union Association. He bought the franchise and players at a nominal sum, moving the club to the Utah capital in time for the 1915 season. This began an association with the PCL that was to last for twenty-four years.

Lane was a very interesting individual. He was born in 1860, spent part of his youth as an Indian fighter in the West, then made a small fortune as a miner in Alaska and the Yukon territory around the turn of the century. He moved to Utah where he became active in state politics, then got into baseball when the Union Association began operations in 1911.

Lane spoke with a harsh gravelly voice, which was due in part to his years in the mines. He had a diffident air about him and was frequently discourteous to people he didn't like. A lifelong bachelor, Lane was to contribute much to the PCL. He didn't do it for altruistic reasons. At his death in 1938, it was estimated that Lane had taken over a million dollars out of baseball.

The Salt Lake Bees finished in second place in 1915, five games behind the champion San Francisco Seals. That was as close as Lane's club would come to a pennant in Salt Lake. The Bees had another second place finish in 1925, but were 12½ games behind another Seal champion. For the most part, the club finished around the .500 mark during its eleven years in the league.

Salt Lake City had its share of good players. Tony Lazzeri is perhaps the best known. He joined the Bees in 1923 as a rookie off the San Francisco sandlots, was farmed to Lincoln of the Western League in 1924, and then took over at shortstop in 1925. There he had one of the finest seasons in baseball history. Lazzeri hit 60 home runs, an all time

PCL record, while driving in 222 runs, also the league standard. Lazzeri was sold to the Yankees after that season, where he starred at second base for over a decade.

Other fine players were first baseman Earl Sheely and Bunny Brief; infielders Eddie Mulligan, Johnny Kerr and Morrie Rath; outfielders John Tobin, Johnny Frederick, Bill Rumler and Paul Strand. Lefty O'Doul played two years in Salt Lake as a slugging outfielder after earlier success as a pitcher with San Francisco. Truck Hannah was the best known of the catchers.

The Bees were notable for their hitting prowess. During their eleven years in the PCL, the club averaged .298 and led in team batting nine times. They reached their pinnacle in 1924 when the Bees averaged .327, the highest mark ever achieved in the higher minor leagues or in the majors for that matter. The club belted 204 home runs in 1923, a PCL standard for thirty-five years.

Individual performances bordered on the unreal. Paul Strand was the league's leading hitter in 1922 and 1923, hitting .384 and .394. During that 1923 season, he had 325 hits. No one in the long history of the PCL, with its very lengthy seasons, would exceed that mark. Other players had years almost as great. Rumler .362 in 1919; Sheely .371 in 1920; Manager Duffy Lewis .403, as a part-time player, in 1921, then .392 in regular duty in 1924; O'Doul .375 in 1925.

The Bees played in tiny Bonneville Park, which helped to inflate some of the hitting totals. Games played there were often slugfests. The most outrageous affair was a 35-11 contest won by the Vernon Tigers in May, 1923. In that game, Pete Schneider of the visitors hit five home runs, drove in 14 runs, and narrowly missed a sixth homer in his last time at bat.

Pitching was generally a problem for Bee teams. They often had one or two good pitchers, but were weak in second line hurling. The best record was compiled by Claude Williams, who posted 33 victories, along with 294 strikeouts, in 1915. He went on to major league success with the Chicago White Sox before being caught up in the

Black Sox scandal of 1919. Other Salt Lake pitchers who produced fine records were Paul Fittery, 29-19 in 1917; Ralph Stroud, 26-13 in 1921 and Bill Piercey, 21-11 in 1925. Rudy Kallio was a steady winner for the Bees during the 1920's and was a long time performer for other PCL clubs. Hollis Thurston spent three seasons at Salt Lake just before beginning his long successful major league career in 1923.

The Bees never prospered in Salt Lake City, and Lane made most of his money by selling players to the major league clubs. His biggest coup was the sale of outfielder Paul Strand to the Philadelphia Athletics in 1924. Strand had been a hitting demon in the PCL, but failed in the American League and was soon on his way back to the minors. Lane was $40,000 richer after that transaction, much to the chagrin of Connie Mack.

By 1925, other PCL owners were complaining about the high cost of railroad travel to the Utah capital. Travel was a large component of operating expense in those days, and clubs were not especially eager to play in Salt Lake City in front of small crowds. It was clear to Bill Lane that something would have to be done. His personal profit situation in Salt Lake City appeared to be limited by the size of the park, as well as that of the metropolitan area. Salt Lake City was a small city in those days, and Lane was dubious that it would ever properly support PCL baseball.

At the winter meetings of 1925, opportunity presented itself. The Maier family wanted out of the Vernon operation. The club had fallen on evil days after its three championships of 1918, 1919 and 1920 and was now up for sale. In November, 1925, a San Francisco group purchased the Tigers and located the club in the Bay city, where it would be known as the Mission Club of San Francisco. This change left the Los Angeles territory available for a second club, and Lane was quick to take advantage of it. He knew that four other PCL clubs were in favor of his move to Southern California and on January 11, 1926, the league officially gave Lane permission to shift the Salt Lake franchise to Los Angeles.

The Hollywood Stars were about to be born.

The home of the Hollywood Sheiks, 1926-35.

Dedication ceremonies at Wrigley Field, January 15, 1926. Judge Kenesaw M. Landis, Commissioner of Baseball, was the speaker.

1926 – A NEW TEAM IN TOWN

HOLLYWOOD! THE NAME EVOKES GLAMOUR today – just as it did sixty years ago when Hollywood was becoming the center of the motion picture industry. It is ironic in view of its later hedonistic image that the village of Hollywood was founded in 1887 by a group of temperance reformers. By the turn of the century the movie pioneers had discovered that its climate and sunshine made Hollywood an ideal location for camera work. The city of Los Angeles annexed Hollywood in 1910. As the years went by the two blended together so much as to become indistinguishable from each other.

The Hollywood Chamber of Commerce was delighted when Bill Lane announced that his team would be known as the Hollywood baseball club. When the players assembled at old Gilmore Park for the opening of spring training, all of the important Hollywood dignitaries were present and gave Lane and his boys a rousing welcome.

Naturally, the club would be called the Hollywood Stars. "Nonsense" said Lane. "Bees they are and Bees they shall remain." During the training season the players wore uniforms with the old Bee emblem. But shortly before the club was ready to head north for the season opener at San Francisco, Lane agreed – the team should be called the Stars. But he never officially recognized the name and during the early Hollywood years, the club was usually called the Sheiks.

The Stars/Sheiks would not play in Hollywood proper. There was only one suitable facility in Los Angeles – Wrigley Field, located in the south-central portion of the city and a substantial distance from the Hollywood district. It was hoped that the club would play an occasional game there, but that would not occur during the Lane days.

Wrigley Field had opened in September, 1925 and was pronounced by all to be the finest park in America. While this may be slight exaggeration, Wrigley Field was a lovely ball park. It seated somewhat more than 20,000 with capacity listed at various times as 20,451 and 20,857. Rarely was this capacity to be taxed while the Stars made Wrigley Field their home.

The park was ideal for hitting. Although the dimensions appeared formidable enough – 340 feet to left field, 412 feet to dead center field and 339 feet to right – the power alleys were very shallow, a mere 345 feet to both right and left center. In addition a steady breeze blew out to right field, and this frequently conveyed high fly balls into the bleachers. Games at Wrigley were often slugfests. Such sluggers as Steve Bilko, Gene Lillard and Max West of the Angels were to thrive there. The Stars would soon acquire their own muscle men to beat a tattoo on the Wrigley fences.

Lane thought he had a very potent club in the spring of 1926. Returning from the second place Bees was a fine nucleus of players – first baseman Roy Leslie, second baseman Johnny Kerr, outfielders Johnny Frederick, Les Sheehan and Joe Connolly, along with catcher John Peters. Pitchers Dick McCabe, Hank Hulvey, Sheriff John Singleton, and Harry O'Neill would form a very representative pitching staff. And Manager Oscar Vitt would begin his second year as manager of the club after leading Salt Lake to its runner up position in 1925.

Vitt would become a Hollywood fixture as the years went on. He was born in San Francisco in 1890 but was an Oakland resident by 1925. His major league career was spotty; joining Detroit in 1912 after two years with the San Francisco Seals, ol'Os enjoyed ten years as a major league third baseman. His lifetime average with the Tigers and Boston Red Sox was a modest .238. Sold to Salt Lake City in 1922 he spent four years there as the regular third baseman. He became a playing manager in 1925 and showed that the extra burden had a positive effect on his play as he hit a career high .345 and sparkled in the field.

The major weapons in the 1925 Salt Lake arsenal were not in training at Hollywood in 1926. The great Tony Lazzeri had been sold to the New York Yankees for $50,000 and three players while Frank O'Doul was in training with the Chicago Cubs at Catalina. Still, Lane felt that his club would do about as well as the previous year.

Of the players obtained from the Yankees a youngster from Toledo, Mack Hillis, would take over Lazzeri's short-stop position with Leslie, Kerr and Vitt at the other infield spots. Each had hit over .300 in 1925.

Frank Zoellers, a speedster up from Atlanta, took over in center field while Frederick was in left and Sheehan in O'Doul's spot in right. Fritz Coumbe, a pitcher turned out-fielder, and Joe Connolly would provide relief in the outfield while Howard Lindimore would serve as utility infielder. Each of these men had hit well in similar roles at Salt Lake.

The pitching was strengthened by the addition of Curtis Fullerton from the Yankees. A righthander, Fullerton had won fifteen at St. Paul in 1925, and he would join Singleton, McCabe, and O'Neill as regular starting pitchers. But the most significant addition to this staff took place in March after spring training had begun when Lane traded holdover Rudy Kallio to Sacramento for Frank Shellen-back. It was the best trade Lane ever made.

It was only fitting that Shellenback was the first player

3

the Stars obtained after moving to Southern California, for Frank was a local boy, a graduate of Hollywood high school. His is one of the great "might have been" stories of baseball. Shellenback had a brief trial with the Los Angeles Angels in the spring of 1916 but was released and played semi-pro ball for the rest of the summer. He was impressive enough to be signed by the Chicago White Sox and after a year of minor league experience made his major league debut in 1918. It was in Chicago that Shellenback learned the spitball from the famous Eddie Cicotte. The pitch would serve Shellenback well for many years.

At the end of the 1919 season Shellenback was sent to the Vernon Tigers for more experience. It was here that fate intervened and consigned Frank to the PCL for the remainder of his playing career. During the winter meetings that year both major leagues outlawed the spitball with exception of those pitchers on major league rosters at that time. If a pitcher came up from the minor leagues after that, he would not legally be able to use the pitch.

Frank had a good year at Vernon in 1920, winning 18 games, and might have been able to return to the majors without the spitter. After all, he was only twenty-two. But in 1921 he suffered a chipped bone in his elbow, and it appeared that his career might be at an end. He missed most of the 1922 season before having an operation which proved to be successful. But he no longer possessed the fine fast ball he once had and was forced to rely on the spitball. After two more seasons at Vernon, Shellenback was traded to Sacramento in 1925.

Mickey Heath and Johnny Kerr advise me that the spitball must be thrown with the first two fingers placed on the saliva between the stitching. The ball is thrown overhand with the fingers sliding off the ball at delivery. This gives the pitch its breaking potential and you can break it inside or out or more often straight down. It will have the velocity of a fast ball most of the time.

Shellenback threw the pitch almost two thirds of the time and his efforts produced a large number of ground balls. In one memorable game at San Francisco in 1932 Shellenback allowed only one fly ball, his infield producing 18 assists to go along with 8 strikeouts. He was usually easy to hit, but his infield turned many of those ground balls into rally-ending double plays.

Frank was a big man. In an era when most pitchers were 5'11" or less, Shellenback stood 6'3" and was often the tallest player in the league. He was a good hitter, and this ability kept him in games where lesser pitchers would have been relieved. His career average at Hollywood was .277 and only five players—Frank Kelleher, Mickey Heath, Dave Barbee, Ray Jacobs and Cleo Carlyle—surpassed his total of 61 home runs as a Hollywood Star.

The addition of Shellenback strengthened the pitching staff immensely and when O'Doul was returned by the Cubs for obscure reasons, both Vitt and Lane were certain that Hollywood would be a prime contender for league honors.

The PCL was a very formidable league in 1926. After the shifting of the Salt Lake and Vernon franchises at the winter meetings, the lineup of clubs consisted of the San Francisco Seals, Los Angeles Angels, Oakland Acorns, Seattle Indians, Portland Beavers—or Ducks, as they were often called—and the Sacramento Senators along with Hollywood and the Mission team. Each was locally owned with the exception of the Angels, who were owned by William Wrigley, Jr. of Chicago. Mr. Wrigley was also the majority stockholder of the Chicago Cubs, and the National League club had a very close relationship with the Angels during this era.

Along with the Los Angeles franchise, San Francisco was probably the strongest during these years. The PCL owners made the most of their profits by signing young players at nominal salaries, developing them over several years and then selling their contracts to the major leagues at handsome returns on their initial investments. There were also many veterans on each club who were on their way down from the majors. The rosters were very stable with many players remaining for several years. The era of the farm system and chain store baseball had not yet penetrated the Pacific Coast.

When the Hollywood Stars broke training camp en route to San Francisco for the opening of the 1926 season both Bill Lane and Oscar Vitt thought they had a pennant contending team. The pitching was definitely stronger than the 1925 staff and although Lazzeri would certainly be missed, Hillis appeared able to make the plays at shortstop. Kerr had been impressive during the training period and looked ready for a fine season.

In 1926 the Pacific Coast League began play on April 6, well before the start of the major league season. This was customary at that time. The PCL usually began its season several weeks before the major leagues and continued well into October. The league policy for many years was to schedule weeks of play, rather than specific numbers of games between each team. Each week would consist of a seven game series which began on Tuesday and concluded with a Sunday double header. Monday was traveling day. Occasional Monday games were sprinkled throughout the season, and doubleheaders were always scheduled for the holidays. A twenty-eight week schedule was drafted for 1926, about average for the 1920's, when the clubs played around 200 games a year.

Torrential rains in the Bay Area delayed the start of the 1926 season for three days, but the Stars won their very first game ever on April 9, 4-3 behind Dick McCabe. The next day Frank Shellenback made his Hollywood debut, pitching the first of his twenty-four shutouts in a Sheik uniform, 2-0. And when the club swept the Sunday doubleheader behind Singleton and Fullerton, who also hurled a shutout in his first Hollywood game, Lane was ecstatic. After all, the Seals were defending champions.

The opening game at Los Angeles drew 10,000 fans to witness the beginning of the long Angel-Hollywood rivalry and the Stars won this one 6-2 on the strength of O'Doul's home run with two on in the first inning. Unfortunately, the high point of the 1926 season had been reached by the Stars. Los Angeles took the rest of the series to even the Hollywood record and the club was never to be much better than .500 for the balance of the year.

The league race was very tight during the first two months of the season with the Angels the early leader threatened by Oakland. Hollywood stayed at or near .500 through May, but the club experienced a very poor June and fell into last place in early July. The club rallied after that, reaching fifth place in early August where it remained through the middle of September before settling into sixth place for the balance of the season.

Hillis was not able to do the job at shortstop and was sold outright to New Haven in mid May when Hollywood purchased Dudley Lee from the Boston Red Sox. This was a fortunate acquisition. Lee took over the shortstop position as his very own and would stay there through 1932. He would be an important part of future Hollywood successes.

Dudley Lee was a little fellow, only 5'6" tall, but with arms that had the texture of bridge cables and that seemed to hang down to his ankles. He had been considered the best shortstop in the minor leagues while at Tulsa in 1923, and was acquired by the Red Sox in 1924. He played on a part time basis in Boston for the next three years before being shipped to Hollywood.

Never much of a hitter, Lee was a fine fielder who covered a lot of ground. His fielding average was never particularly high, but he tried for everything and made a lot of errors on plays he shouldn't have attempted. According to Mickey Heath, "Lee put buckshot in his glove to keep it low to the ground. That way he didn't miss many ground balls."

The big difference between the 1925 Bees and 1926 Stars was offense. Salt Lake led the league in batting; Hollywood finished last. The Stars scored 600 fewer runs than the last Bee edition. It wasn't simply the loss of Lazzeri; all of the returning Bees were well below their 1925 performances.

7

O'Doul dropped from .375 to .338, Vitt from .345 to .252, Kerr from .330 to .272, Fritz Coumbe from .331 to .250. The team hit a mere 80 home runs. Vitt was beside himself through most of the year, trying to wring out more base hits from the dormant Hollywood bats.

The pitching carried the Sheiks some of the way but couldn't carry the team very far. Shellenback led the way with sixteen wins and a sparkling 2.97 ERA. He pitched seven shut outs, his personal high. McCabe and Singleton pitched well but never seemed to get enough runs and both lost more than they won. Fullerton did well at the beginning of the season but was very ineffective at times and won only ten games. He was especially terrorized by the champion Angels, losing five times to Los Angeles without a win. Hank Hulvey won his first seven games but was then injured and finished 13-10. An eighteen year old free agent from Oakland, George Hollerson, was impressive and won nine games.

At the annual stockholders meeting held in November 1926, Lane announced that his Hollywood club had lost $15,000 during its first year in Southern California. The club had drawn a satisfactory 273,000 fans, a substantial increase over 1925 in Salt Lake. He was hopeful of improvement in 1927.

1926 STANDINGS

	W	L	PCT.
Los Angeles	121	81	.599
Oakland	111	92	.547
Mission	106	94	.530
Portland	100	101	.498
Sacramento	99	102	.493
HOLLYWOOD	94	107	.468
Seattle	89	111	.445
San Francisco	84	116	.420

Lefty O'Doul, spring training, 1925.

9

Johnny Kerr in 1932.

Mr. Kerr in 1982.

1927 – MORE OF THE SECOND DIVISION

THE 1927 EDITION OF THE STARS WAS LITTLE different from the 1926 team. Once again the club finished in sixth place and was last in team batting. Unlike the previous year when the Sheiks gave a good account of themselves through May, the 1927 team started out slowly and were in last place until the fourth of July. They played better after that and managed to work their way to fifth place for a time but settled into sixth for the last month of the season.

It was obvious at the end of the 1926 season that the Hollywood Sheiks were not the hard hitting Salt Lake Bees any longer, and Lane was determined to improve the offense. He went about it in a very peculiar way, however. First, he got rid of his best hitter, Lefty O'Doul, selling him to San Francisco for a very nominal sum. Although O'Doul had hit a satisfactory .338 in 1926, that was a far cry from his marks in Salt Lake City. Lane thought that Lefty wasn't hustling at times and voiced his displeasure quite vigorously. O'Doul didn't appreciate the comments and let it be known that he didn't like playing or living in Los Angeles anyway. So when the opportunity came to unload the slugger, Lane quickly took advantage of it.

The trade was a bad one for the Sheiks. O'Doul was so glad to be back in his hometown that he socked a resounding .378 with 33 home runs and led the Seals to a second place finish. At season's end Charlie Graham peddled his prize to the New York Giants for $20,000. O'Doul was a solid success in the National League this time. He hit .398 in 1929 and stayed in the league through 1934. This was unquestionably one of the worst player moves Bill Lane ever made.

Other Sheiks were removed from the roster during the winter. Big John Peters was sold to Kansas City of the American Association, leaving a big gap at the catching position while Coumbe, Leslie and Zoeller were also shipped out. None of these players had performed especially well in 1926.

As replacements, the Sheiks acquired first baseman Jim McDowell and catcher Denny Murphy from the Mission club. Neither of these players were strangers to Los Angeles fans, both having graced the Vernon roster for several years. A .250 hitter, Jim was a very agile fielder and led all PCL first basemen in assists in 1926. Murphy was a pretty good hitter but not in the class of Peters as a workman behind the plate.

Oscar Vitt had decided to call it quits as a player that spring and the club scurried around to find a replacement at third. Rookie Tom Holley, signed off the Long Beach sandlots as a free agent, and National League reject Cotton Tierney split time during the spring, but Holley was very inexperienced and Tierney was through. Both were gone by mid-June. Charlie Gooch, a reserve during the past two years, played the position most of the year. His fielding was adequate but he hit a weak .252 with only one home run.

Hollywood did not impress anyone during spring training, and the consensus was that the club would finish seventh. The Sheiks started out on a miserable note, losing the opener at Sacramento 10-1 and then proceeding to drop the next five games. There was virtually no hitting. Johnny Frederick, who was counted on to carry much of the offensive load, got off to a horrendous start and no one else picked up the slack. The club returned to Los Angeles, won two games from the Angels, then dropped another six straight. It looked to be a long year.

Help was obtained when youngster Jim Sweeney was purchased from Sacramento, and the veteran Clarence "Babe" Twombley was signed as a free agent after his release by Jersey City. Twombley had played for the Angels and was a fine hitter although with little power. These two sparked the attack and for a time the club rallied.

The pitching held up remarkably well in view of the anemic batting attack. Shellenback was the leader along with Fullerton who won three well pitched games in April. Hulvey pitched well, too, as a regular starter this year. And Vitt was pleased with the performance of young Bill Murphy. Signed as a free agent in 1926, the Arizona native had seen little action that year. He impressed Vitt with several strong relief appearances in the spring and won his first starting assignment, 2-0 from the Seals. He was a regular after that, winning 14 games.

The Sheiks remained in last throughout May with little hope of improvement. In those days when the farm system was in its infancy, the independent minor league owner relied on friendships with other clubs for player help. Lane had good rapport with Colonel Ruppert of the Yankees, especially after Tony Lazzeri had worked out so well at New York, and he was also on good terms with Frank Navin at Detroit. Over the next several years these sources were to provide a number of good players to Hollywood.

During the first week of June, Lane acquired the first baseman he had been looking for. Mickey Heath was a youngster under contract to Toronto but actually Detroit property. He had hit .335 for the Maple Leafs and sparkled afield as Toronto won the International League pennant in 1926. This year he had not started off well and when the Tigers sent the hard hitting Dale Alexander to Toronto, there was no room for Heath. So Lane was able to acquire him in a rather shady transaction, on a "loan" basis. Mickey

13

remained at Hollywood through the 1930 season. He was to contribute much to the club's success during those years.

Outfielder Pat McNulty was acquired from Cleveland at about the same time and was installed in center field. With the acquisition of these two the offense was strengthened immensely, although Heath went hitless in his first fourteen times at bat with the club before breaking out with a rash of hits. The Sheiks played .500 ball from the middle of June for the balance of the season. They moved out of last by winning six straight from the Angels during early July and even made a move towards the first division before falling back.

The club finished last once again in team batting. McNulty led with a rather low .312 average and the other outfielders, Twombley and Frederick, were the only other Sheiks to crack the magic .300 mark, at .309 and .305, respectively. Kerr was the leading home run hitter with 18 as no other Sheik was in double figures. Johnny also stole 41 bases while fielding his position almost flawlessly. He and Lee were rapidly becoming a fine double play combination.

The pitching corps was much improved over 1926. Shellenback had a fine year at 19-12 and a 3.05 ERA. Included in his victory total were four shutouts, one being a one-hitter at San Francisco on April 27. Hulvey was a solid 17-14 and not far behind was young Bill Murphy at 14-8. A young lefthander, Bud Teachout, was signed after graduation from Occidental College in June by Detroit and in another of those peculiar transactions so common in those days was loaned to Hollywood for the balance of the 1927 season. Teachout had been a real standout in the college ranks in 1927 with an amazing 60 wins to his credit. He threw very hard and had a very good curve ball for a youngster. The collegian produced six wins for the Sheiks that year. Curt Fullerton after a good start faded during mid-season and finished with 13-19. He would have done better had he not been required to face Sacramento, losing

14

seven times to the fourth place Solons without a win.

Oakland won its first PCL championship in fifteen years in 1927. The Acorns breezed to the pennant by 14½ games over second place San Francisco, and the race was virtually decided by late July. Attendance fell off rapidly throughout the league after that. The owners were worried and to create more interest for the 1928 season voted to play a split season. The first place clubs of each half would then meet in a post season championship series. Lane was against the plan, fearing it would appear too bush league, but was outvoted. The split season would be a regular part of PCL baseball for the next few years.

1927 STANDINGS

	W	L	PCT.
Oakland	120	75	.615
San Francisco	106	90	.541
Seattle	98	92	.516
Sacramento	100	95	.513
Portland	95	95	.500
HOLLYWOOD	92	104	.469
Mission	86	110	.439
Los Angeles	80	116	.408

(From the collection of Dick Dobbins)

Mickey Heath.

(From the collection of Dick Dobbins)

Frank Shellenback.   Johnny Frederick

1928 – THE BATS ARE BOOMING

THE FORTUNES OF HOLLYWOOD BASEBALL improved sharply in 1928. From what was a rather non-descript second division club during the previous two years the Sheiks became a bona fide pennant contender almost overnight. In the first year of the PCL's experiment with a split season Hollywood finished a strong second during the first half, five games behind the Seals, and then led most of the way in the second half. A slump in late September dropped the club to third, only three games behind the Seals and the Sacramento Solons who finished in a tie. In a playoff series the Seals defeated the Solons, four games to two and were proclaimed champions of the league for the year.

The 1928 Sheiks were vastly better offensively. They hit .289, fourth best in the league, scored 137 more runs than they had in 1927 and hit 111 home runs. The fans responded well to this team and turned out 411,000 strong. Interest was high throughout the PCL cities, and all clubs except Seattle showed a profit.

Lane strengthened the club immensely during the off-season. He tried to fill the third base gap by persuading Colonel Ruppert of the Yankees to send Julie Wera to Hollywood. Wera, whom Babe Ruth called "Flop Ears," was a reserve on the great 1927 Yankee team and it

17

was felt that he could improve by everyday play in the minors. An aggressive player, Wera was a pretty good hitter although just an average fielder.

Outfield help was secured from the Boston Red Sox in the person of Cleo Carlyle. A Georgian, the twenty-five year old Carlyle had spent an indifferent 1927 season with the tail end Red Sox after several fine years at Toronto. He was a good left handed hitter who seemed at his best in the clutches. As an outfielder, there were few better. He patrolled center field for the Sheiks over the next six years, and while not as spectacular as his local rival, Jigger Statz, Carlyle caught many a ball that seemed out of his reach. He moved very gracefully and possessed a fine throwing arm. A slender fellow, Carlyle was not as durable as other players and suffered frequent injuries.

As important as Carlyle was to be for the Stars, the prize catch that year was the acquisition of catcher Johnny Bassler from Detroit. Here was perhaps the finest catcher in PCL history. Bassler handled his pitchers well, had an exceptional throwing arm and was an outstanding hitter, although with little power. He remained at Hollywood through the 1935 season and had a lifetime average of .332 in a Sheik uniform.

Bassler was not new to the PCL by any means, having made his debut with Los Angeles in 1916. After a fine season with the Angels in 1920, he was sold to Detroit where he remained for the next seven seasons. Bassler was thirty-three years old in 1928, at the top of his game. He was just what the Hollywood pitching staff needed that year and together with the veteran Sam Agnew formed the best catching staff in the league. It is no coincidence that Frank Shellenback was to enjoy his best years with Bassler as his battery mate.

The club seemed very strong in spring training that year. The facilities at Santa Monica were poor and a rock hard diamond caused many minor leg injuries, but the Sheiks were ready to go when the season began. Vitt opened with an infield of Heath, Kerr, Lee and Wera. Mickey was beginning to get the feel of the PCL and hammered out many a line drive in training. Just as camp broke, Carlyle fell ill with a kidney ailment and was forced into the hospital. He was out a month and in his place Vitt used Babe Twombley with McNulty in left and American League veteran Bobby "Braggo" Roth in right. An early day power hitter, he was well past his best years and was let go in June after hitting .283 in 67 games with only one home run.

The pitching staff was led by Shellenback with Hank Hulvey, Dick McCabe, Curt Fullerton and Bill Murphy as returning starters. The club picked up Walter Kinney, a rotund left handed knuckle ball pitcher from Portland, and the little veteran was to win 17 games that year.

The most pleasant surprise was a twenty year old from the University of Utah, Gordon Rhodes. He had been signed as a free agent by Vinegar Bill Essick, the old Vernon manager, who was now working for Hollywood as a coach and part time scout. Rhodes had a fine fast ball and an explosive curve ball which earned him many strikeouts. He began the season in relief and after several impressive appearances, received his first start against San Francisco on May 6. Rhodes responded with a ten inning 1-0 victory and was a regular starter after that. He won 17 games in 1928, including four shutouts, and he led the Sheiks with 129 strikeouts. Rhodes might have won twenty games that year had he not come down with tonsilitis in August. He was weakened by the illness and missed several starts.

Hollywood opened at Oakland and won the first four games before losing in Kinney's debut. The Sheiks stayed in the lead through most of April and early May. The hitters did not get off well, and only the fine pitching of Shellenback, McCabe and Hulvey kept Hollywood on top. A slump during early May saw the club drop out of the lead, but the Sheiks regained first place on June 6. They remained there for a week before falling behind the Seals for good. Injuries to Shellenback and Wera hastened the decline, and Carlyle had not hit well after returning from his illness. Lane tried to restore some punch to the lineup

19

by trading Pat McNulty to Columbus for outfielder Walt Rehg. The forty year old Rehg had played in the National League as far back as 1912, but was still a good hitter. The Sheiks had become top heavy with lefthanded hitters and Rehg provided more balance. The grayhaired veteran hit .306 in 78 games.

It was about this time that Bill Lane received a startling ultimatum. Notice was served by the Angels that at the end of the 1928 season Hollywood would have to leave Wrigley Field. The letter was written by President Joe Patrick and had its origins in the Angels' policy regarding Ladies Day. Mr. Wrigley had begun to let ladies in free to Chicago Cub games and the practice was very successful. Wrigley naturally spread the idea to Los Angeles where Patrick adopted the idea wholeheartedly. The trouble was that ladies were being admitted free to *all* games at Wrigley Field, both Angels and Sheiks. Lane simply couldn't afford it and wanted Los Angeles to pay 32½ cents for every female admission.

The controversy raged for the balance of the summer with Wrigley periodically threatening Hollywood with immediate eviction and Lane vowing to move his ball club to Phoenix or Berkeley, whichever would have him. A compromise was reached at season's end when Wrigley agreed to confine Ladies Day to certain days of the week and paid the Sheiks a portion of the lost revenue. The incident was the first rift in the relationship between Wrigley and Bill Lane.

The Sheiks were hot in July as the second half of the season began and led the league through most of the month. They suffered a loss when the Yankees transferred Wera to St. Paul, but the club recalled young Leo Ostenberg from Boise and he filled in very nicely at third, hitting .294 over the balance of the season.

The Sheiks were finally knocked out of the lead during the first week in August by their nemesis, the Angels. Hollywood could not beat Los Angeles that year, losing 19 out of the 28 games between the clubs. Vitt shook the club up after losing five straight and falling behind Sacramento. Curt Fullerton was traded to Portland for veteran out-fielder Elmer Smith and pitcher Johnny Couch. Smith had led the PCL with 46 home runs in 1927 and moved into right field immediately. The change helped. Smith hit 14 home runs over the last two months of the season and the club went on a tear to move back into first place on August 23.

When Hollywood returned home two games ahead of Sacramento, it appeared that the club would be able to win. But it was not to be. Rhodes had been severely weak-ened by his illness and was only a shadow of his former self. McCabe, a sensation during June and July, also slumped badly at this time, leaving too much of the burden on the shoulders of Shellenback and Kinney. Although the Sheiks remained in first place through September 11, they lost the first four games of a critical series to Sacramento to fall two games behind on September 15. A brief rally saw the Sheiks gain a tie for first on September 23, but once again, losses to the Angels dropped the club to third place for the last two weeks of the season.

In spite of the September disappointment, 1928 had been an exciting year. The defense sparkled all season long. Johnny Kerr and Dudley Lee had fine seasons afield. Lee had one stretch of thirty-four games where he played error-less ball. Kerr was the best second baseman in the league and outplayed the more publicized Jimmy Reese that year. Johnny also hit .301 and showed good power with 16 home runs. The left field wall was an inviting target for the peppery little infielder. "I uppercut the ball a lot," he says, "and those walls weren't really that far away." Lane enter-tained many offers for Kerr's services but declined them all. He paid for it when the White Sox drafted Johnny for only $4,000. Kerr played in the American League through 1935 and was a member of the 1933 champion Washington Senators.

Other Stars had fine years. Mickey Heath came on strong that year, hitting .307 with a team leading 19 home runs. A change in his batting stance improved his power, and Heath was to send many a baseball over PCL fences before he left Hollywood.

Babe Twombley hit .314 to lead the regulars, while Sam Agnew hit .321 in a part time role. Johnny Bassler hit an even .300 and was brilliant behind the plate. He had an amazing 125 assists in 127 games, a remarkable feat in an era when base stealing was not attempted as much as it is today.

The pitchers were led by Frank Shellenback, who won 23 games and had a sparkling 3.13 ERA. Frank had a terrific year at the plate also, hitting .325 with 9 home runs. He won three of his games with homers and was frequently used as a pinch hitter. McCabe made a fine comeback after two losing years and finished at 16-10. He was perhaps the club's best pitcher during the first half of the year.

Hank Hulvey pitched well, both as a starter and in relief. He was especially fearsome to the Mission Bells, winning seven games with only one loss. The only pitching disappointment was Bill Murphy who slumped to 5-6. He suffered a broken jaw in May and missed much of the season.

If the Sheiks had been able to handle Los Angeles as well as the other PCL teams, there would have been no race. But the Angels had a hex on Hollywood that year and at one point won 13 of 15 games played. In contrast, the Sheiks took the season series from both San Francisco and Sacramento and took 19 out of 24 from Mission.

Vitt did well managing this team. He didn't have an especially good outfield and had problems at third base. But he juggled his lineups well, seemed to know who was going to have a hot streak and had his club hustling all the way. He was a few years away from being an active player now, and he seemed more sure of himself as a manager this year.

The 1928 Hollywood team created a bit of history by becoming the first professional team to fly to its destination. The Sheiks were in Seattle on July 15 for a double header where it was learned that they would not be able to make train connections to Portland in time to catch the Cascade Limited to Los Angeles. The trip from Portland to Southern California took almost two days in 1928 and as a result, the Sheiks would not make it to Los Angeles in time for a Tuesday game.

Lane persuaded about half the club to remain in Seattle for the Sunday double header and then fly to Portland right after the games. The rest of the players went south on Saturday along with all the equipment trunks. It was a real gamble on Lane's part, for air travel was risky in those days. But the plane arrived in Portland with no trouble, and the train connection was made. It would be many years before air travel became a regular part of the baseball scene.

1928 STANDINGS

1st HALF

	W	L	PCT.
San Francisco	58	34	.641
HOLLYWOOD	53	39	.576
Sacramento	50	42	.544
Mission	49	43	.533
Los Angeles	48	44	.522
Oakland	40	52	.435
Portland	37	55	.402
Seattle	33	59	.359

2nd HALF

	W	L	PCT.
Sacramento	62	37	.626
San Francisco	62	37	.626
HOLLYWOOD	59	40	.596
Oakland	51	48	.515
Mission	50	49	.505
Portland	42	57	.424
Los Angeles	39	60	.394
Seattle	31	68	.313

(From the Collection of Dick Dobbins)

Dudley Lee

25

(From the Collection of Dick Dobbins)

Hank Severeid

1929 – THE SHEIKS ARE CHAMPIONS

HOLLYWOOD BATS BOOMED LOUDLY IN 1929. The club achieved its highest average ever, .311, and exploded for 153 home runs. Once again the Sheiks scored runs in droves, leading the league with 1233 tallies, over six a game. Thirty-eight times that year Hollywood scored ten or more runs, including a 20-1 slaughter of Portland and an 18-2 shellacking of Seattle. Oscar Vitt had four regulars who batted .345 or better and alternate catcher Hank Severeid hit .415 in 79 games.

The era of the big sock had begun in earnest. The Stars' average placed them third behind Mission and San Francisco. The Bells hit .319 that year, the highest PCL average since Salt Lake City had been in the league and not to be surpassed until Albuquerque hit .325 in 1981. The two San Francisco teams also paced the league in home runs, the Seals with 182 and the Bells with 170. Six clubs bettered .300 and the league as a whole hit .302.

The Stars expected to be a stronger club when they assembled for spring training. Johnny Kerr would be missed as would Gordon Rhodes, who had been sold to Lane's Yankee friends for a nice profit, but Vitt thought his third base problem would be solved with the acquisition of Russ "Red" Rollings from the Red Sox. He took over at the beginning of training and impressed everyone with his hitting. Mike Maloney, a youngster purchased from Boise, was given Kerr's second base job.

The outfield was composed of Carlyle, Joe Bonowitz and Bill Albert at the beginning. Bonowitz was picked up from Fort Worth where he had been a fine hitter, but he was returned to the Panthers in May after failing to impress. Albert, a youngster obtained from Springfield of the New England League held down right field most of April but played sporadically after. His career ended tragically during the off season when he was killed in an automobile accident.

The Sheiks received an unexpected bonus during the winter of 1928 when Sheriff Bill Rumler was restored to the good graces of Organized Baseball. Rumler had been suspended late in the 1920 season for his involvement with gamblers. Although he was cleared of any wrongdoing, Rumler remained out of baseball for the next eight years. He remained on the Hollywood reserve list all that time as ineligible to play. When Rumler was pardoned, Lane invited him to spring training. The powerfully built out-fielder had been a fine hitter during his previous stint in the PCL and proved during spring training that he had not lost his batting eye even though he was thirty-seven years old. "I'll use him against left handers only" said Vitt. Old Os' had to eat those words when Rumler began to hit so well. The Sheriff played in 140 games in 1929, hitting .386 to finish third in the batting race behind Ike Boone and Smead Jolley. That is the highest mark in Hollywood history.

The pitching staff looked to be improved. Shellenback was, of course, the ace of the staff and the best pitcher in the league. He was joined by two new faces, Augie Johns, a left hander obtained from Fort Worth, and Buzz Wetzel, who had joined the club in September 1928. George Hollerson was back after a year in the Utah-Idaho League and was much improved. These four along with Walt Kinney and Hank Hulvey did most of the pitching that year. Dick McCabe was still around, but he was released to

28

Fort Worth in June.

The PCL directors had not been pleased with the split season of 1928 and prepared a twenty-eight week straight schedule. However, the Missions jumped into an early commanding lead and the owners, fearing a repeat of 1927 when Oakland ran away with the championship, met hurriedly and voted to split the season again. The first half ended on July 3 with Mission declared the first half winner.

This was a stroke of luck for Hollywood. The Sheiks had played rather poorly through the first three months of the season in spite of all that hitting. There were numerous soft spots in the lineup. Maloney was unable to do the job at second base, and he was replaced by veteran Howard Burkett, signed after his release by the Angels in May. The son of Hall of Fame outfielder Jesse Burkett, Howard was not nearly as good as his famous father. Burkett hit only .245 and his play afield was just average.

The outfield remained unsettled through much of May. Bonowitz and Albert were tried and found wanting while the ancient Wally Rehg played on a regular basis. Then Lane found the outfielder he had been looking for. The Yankees sent the speedy Elias Funk from St. Paul to complete the Rhodes deal, and he joined the club in May. Liz, as he was called, had hit .304 for the Saints in 1928. He was a fine fielder with a pretty good throwing arm. Funk took over in left field, and that problem was solved. In 150 games he finished right behind Rumler at .384. Lane realized a fine profit on this transaction when Funk was sold to Detroit in September for $40,000 and two players.

The second half opened with the Sheiks routing Sacramento 15-1, and the club won its first five games. A sweep of a series with Seattle vaulted Hollywood into first place on July 14, and the Sheiks remained in contention thereafter.

The race was very close. Portland and San Francisco seemed improved over the earlier part of the season while the Missions tailed off slightly. The lead changed hands among these four clubs through August with the Angels also making a surprising run for it. Only Sacramento and Seattle were really out of contention.

In mid July Hollywood made a fortunate acquisition when catcher Hank Severeid was signed after his release by Sacramento. A long time member of the St. Louis Browns, Severeid hit .289 in fifteen American League seasons. He was just what the Stars needed. Bassler was having a bad year after his great play in 1928 and was in the throes of a hitting slump. The other catcher, Rowdy Sypher, was more widely known for his fighting prowess than his ballplaying ability. Severeid joined the club in Portland and moved right into the lineup for a few games. He then shared the duty with Bassler until August 11 when Johnny broke his thumb. Severeid caught almost every game after that. His big bat was smoking. During his first month in a Hollywood uniform Severeid hit .435 and many of his blows were game winners.

The race continued to be close through August and September as the Stars moved in and out of the lead. As late as September 19 the distance between first and fifth place was only two games. The Stars were tied with the Seals for the lead on that date. But San Francisco faded after that, and Hollywood dealt a crushing blow to the Angel hopes by taking a doubleheader on September 22 behind Shellenback and Wetzel.

Both the Mission Bells and the Sheiks played .500 ball for the last two weeks, allowing Hollywood to ease into the second half championship. In a way the club backed into the title, when the two teams each lost a season ending doubleheader. The Missions were playing at last place Seattle and blew the championship by losing both games to that incredibly weak team. Meanwhile, at Wrigley Field Johnny "Junk" Walters of Portland pitched and won both games from the Stars, 4-1 and 9-2. The teams were tired and looked it that day.

A playoff series for the league championship was now necessary, and Mission was a strong favorite. But in a surprising turn of events the Stars took the Bells four games to two to win their first PCL championship. After losing the first two games at San Francisco's Recreation Park, the Sheiks took the next four contests.

This was Frank Shellenback's series. He won the third game 11-5 and drove in three runs with a home run and two singles. Returning to Los Angeles, Frank's pinch homer in the ninth tied the fourth game and the Stars won it 4-3 in ten innings. After Augie Johns defeated Bert Cole, the Missions' best pitcher, 6-3 to give Hollywood a one game lead, Shellenback came back to win the finale, 8-3. Before 15,000, the spitballer once again homered. The Stars won this game with five runs in the eighth inning. It was a great climax to an exciting year.

As befitting a championship team, there were many fine performances. Mickey Heath was the most valuable player. He hit a rousing .349 and led the club with 38 home runs and 156 runs batted in. He had three homers in a 20-1 shellacking of Portland and included an inside the park homer in the final game of the championship series. In the field Heath demonstrated a wizardry that hadn't been seen in the PCL since Hal Chase was a member of the Angels.

Rollings hit .324 and had 239 hits, an all time Hollywood record. He was drafted by the Boston Braves that winter. Lee hit only .262 but was better than ever in the field. He had to be, for Rollings wasn't very mobile.

The outfield was simply awesome that year. In addition to the heroics of Funk and Rumler, Carlyle hit a resounding .347 and was well over that before a late season slump. Oddly enough, his brother, Roy, hit .348 at Oakland that year. This was Cleo's best year. He drove in his personal high of 136 and played a fine center field.

Severeid's contribution may have been the key to the championship. The veteran hit .415 in 79 games and drove in 72 runs. Vitt had him batting fourth during the August and September stretch, and Severeid responded well. He added additional hitting strength when the club needed it most.

The pitchers were battered around through much of the season. Shellenback was consistent throughout the season and won 26 games, his best year so far. But Frank was hit hard on many occasions and his ERA was a high 3.97. His hitting kept him in many games when he wasn't sharp. Shellenback hit 12 home runs that year, to go with a fine .322 batting average.

Johns finished at 17-10 and was the only other Sheik with an ERA below four. He was especially effective against the two San Francisco teams, winning seven of eight decisions from them. It was his 3-1 win over the Bells on September 29 that put Hollywood in first place to stay.

Young George Hollerson won ten games during the second half and finished 13-13. Only twenty-one, Hollerson appeared to have a long career ahead of him, but this proved to be his best year. Wetzel was extremely valuable, winning 17. He was most effective against the Seattle and Sacramento teams. Hank Hulvey worked long and often and had a 14-11 mark although his ERA was a high 6.07.

Oscar Vitt was very proud of this club as he had every right to be. From the middle of July it was the best in the league. Another pitcher or two and the race wouldn't have been close. Lane was determined to do something about that shortcoming before the next season.

1929 STANDINGS

1st HALF

	W	L	PCT.
Mission	63	35	.643
San Francisco	59	39	.602
Oakland	56	43	.566
HOLLYWOOD	52	47	.525
Los Angeles	47	52	.475
Sacramento	46	53	.465
Seattle	39	60	.394
Portland	33	66	.333

2nd HALF

	W	L	PCT.
HOLLYWOOD	61	42	.592
Mission	60	43	.583
Los Angeles	57	46	.554
Portland	57	46	.554
San Francisco	55	48	.534
Oakland	55	48	.534
Sacramento	39	64	.379
Seattle	28	75	.272

Mickey Heath (L) and Bill Murphy

This offer expires April 1st, 1930

(From the Collection of Dick Dobbins)

Bill Rumler

Jim Turner

(Both from the collection of Dick Dobbins)

Buzz Wetzel

The 1930 Champion Sheiks

Top Row, Left to Right – Frank Shellenback, Hank Severeid, Emil Yde, Bill Rumler, George Hollerson, Jim Turner, Eddie Leishman, Gordon Jones, President Bill Lane, Buzz Wetzel, Cleo Carlyle, Vance Page, Dave Barbee, Hank Hulvey. *Bottom Row, Left to Right* – Augie Johns, Lou Catina, Mickey Heath, Harry Green, Otis Brannan, Mike Gazella, Dudley Lee, Les Cook, Johnny Bassler, Manager Oscar Vitt, Jess Hill.

1930 – NIGHT BASEBALL AND ANOTHER PENNANT

THE 1930 SEASON WAS ONE OF THE MOST EXCIting PCL seasons in Los Angeles. The Stars repeated as league champions with perhaps their finest team in history. As in 1929, Hollywood finished in second place during the first half, won the second half and then easily won the championship playoff from the Angels. For the first time Los Angeles and Hollywood had the best teams in the league, and the long bitter rivalry between these teams began in earnest that year.

Along with the excitement of the pennant race, night baseball came to Los Angeles in 1930. The fans loved it. They turned out in droves to watch the Angels and Stars, even though the first effects of the depression were beginning to be felt that summer. The two clubs combined drew better than 850,000 customers that year. That was more than two teams could attract for major league baseball in St. Louis. A big series in September, when the Angels were challenging the Stars for the lead, drew 79,941.

The Stars appeared to be stronger than ever when the club opened training at San Diego that year. Once again Lane had called upon his Yankee friends for aid. This time he secured third baseman Mike Gazella from New York to replace the departed Red Rollings. This was a fine move, for Gazella was a good fielder and he proved to be a pretty good hitter in 1930, hitting .303 with 94 runs batted in. A graduate of Lafayette College, the thirty-four year old Gazella had been a member of the 1927 Yankees, as had Julie Wera of the 1928 Stars.

Second base was immensely strengthened when the club acquired Otis Brannan from the St. Louis Browns. He had been the regular second baseman for St. Louis in 1928, fielding well, but hitting only .244. That was not sufficient to hold his job in 1929, and Brannan sat on the bench most of that year. He was on his way to Hollywood at the end of the season where he would remain through 1933. Brannan was a fine second baseman. He ranged far and wide for balls hit in his direction, covered more ground than any second baseman in the league and helped Lee on the double plays. With a spitballer like Shellenback on the mound it was essential to have a good infield behind him to handle all the ground balls that he served up. Gazella and Brannan fit nicely with holdovers Heath and Lee to give Hollywood the best infield in the league.

Lane had reached into the Piedmont League for pitching help during the winter and came up with two right handed prizes in Jim Turner and Vance Page. Turner was by far the better of the two. He was not quite twenty-seven that spring and had pitched professionally since 1923. Although he had good records, he had never appeared above class B until Lane bought him for Hollywood. Page was twenty-four and like Turner, he relied on good control and a sinking fast ball to get the hitters out. Page was bothered by a sore arm for most of 1930 and was not much help that year. Turner looked good from the start and before long was taking his turn as a regular starter.

Oscar Vitt fairly bubbled over with optimism that spring. "We've got the best infield in the league," he said "and our catching is the best too. Gazella and Brannan should hit .300 and Lee will be better. He won't have to cover as much ground as he did in 1929. All we need to insure the pennant are two more outfielders."

The outfield did appear to be the weak spot. Although Carlyle was back, a lot of the offense was missing with Funk gone to Detroit, and there was some question about Rumler's durability. Harry Green, a youngster who had played occasionally in 1929, looked very good in spring training and would see a lot of action during the year. Other outfielders were Frank Wetzel from San Antonio and Al McNeeley, a San Diego boy who had played at Tucson in his first professional season in 1929.

Outside of Page and Turner the only other new pitcher of note was left hander Emil Yde, down from Detroit in the Funk trade. Yde proved to be very useful that year both as a pitcher and pinch hitter, but he is probably best remembered for losing a game without throwing a pitch. In a game at Oakland Yde came in to relieve Page with the bases loaded and the score tied in the last of the ninth. While going into his initial wind up, Yde committed a balk, allowing the winning run to score.

In spite of the additional strength, the 1930 Sheiks started out badly and were in the second division through the first two months of the season. Shellenback had a horrible spring. He complained of arm trouble as the season began and missed several starts. When he did see action, he was battered rather freely and did not win his first game until May 17. He was still not right even then. Vitt decided to let him work his way out of it and left him in games long after other pitchers would have been relieved. Frank staggered through several games for victories including one in San Francisco where he allowed 18 hits but still won, 11-6.

At the end of May the club began a losing streak that reached nine before Hollerson defeated the Angels 6-3 on June 5. The Stars had fallen to seventh place and did not remotely resemble the fine team of the year before. Things were getting pretty desperate.

It was then that the Stars turned the entire season around. First, they signed the outstanding all around athlete from the University of Southern California, Jesse Hill. Next, the club acquired the slugger that Vitt had been looking for all spring in the person of outfielder Dave Barbee from Seattle. Finally, the Yankees returned pitcher Gordon Rhodes to the Sheiks for additional seasoning. These three, all arriving in early June, transformed Hollywood into a championship team.

Hill was one of the greatest athletes in USC history. A three sport letterman, Hill was a regular on the 1929 Trojan football team that played in the Rose Bowl, set an IC4A broad jump record in the winter and hit over .400 as a member of the 1930 baseball team. Coaching was to be his real vocation, and he signed to coach football at Riverside City College upon his graduation in May. But Hill loved baseball and thought he could play in the majors. He signed a Hollywood contract during graduation week and made his first appearance on June 4 against Los Angeles.

Hill's debut was unreal. Entering the game in the seventh inning, the rookie hit Berlyn Horne's first pitch over the left field wall. The next day Hill was posted to right field and led off the batting order as the Stars ended their nine game losing streak. He hit well from the start, batting .407 for his first two weeks of action. When Barbee arrived from Seattle, Hill shifted to left field where he played with the skill of a ten year veteran. Fast and possessing a fine throwing arm, Hill strengthened the defense considerably. Vitt shifted him to center field when a left hander was on the mound, using Rumler in left and leaving Carlyle on the bench.

Barbee was a twenty-five year old North Carolinian who had played briefly with the Philadelphia Athletics in 1926. He came to the PCL in 1928 with Portland but was traded to Seattle in mid-season. Although the Indians had a terrible team, Barbee found a home there, hitting .327 in 1928 and .316 in 1929 with 22 home runs. But Seattle was in bad financial shape and after another poor start in 1930, the Indians unloaded some of their better players. Barbee was available and Lane grabbed him.

Barbee joined the Sheiks on June 18 and homered in an 11-7 loss to the Missions. He took over in right field and batted fourth. Barbee was made for Wrigley Field. A strong pull hitter, Barbee was a terror to the opposition pitchers in Los Angeles. He hit five home runs in his first ten games there and always hit better at home. A happy-go-lucky fellow, Dave didn't think too much of manager Vitt's training rules, and the two frequently had words over the player's failure to abide by them.

The Stars were sixth when Barbee arrived, seven games below .500. They took three of five from Mission, then began a twelve game winning streak against Sacramento. The Senators came into Wrigley Field leading the league, but Hollywood knocked the Capitol City club out of first place by taking seven straight. The Sheiks then took five games from Oakland before losing on July 5. They were now in the thick of the pennant race.

But it was too late. The Stars took four of seven at Sacramento to move into second place by one half game but were 3½ games behind the Angels when the first half of the season ended on July 14.

The second half was all Hollywood. The club began auspiciously with a 13-7 win over their Portland nemesis, Junk Walters, and went on from there. Shellenback had improved after his slow start and was 7-7 after suffering a 5-4 loss at Seattle on July 23. He would not lose again in 1930. The Stars took over first place for good on July 27.

The coming of night baseball almost overshadowed the excitement of the Stars' fine showing. The Great Depression was beginning to settle over the country after the Stock Market crash of 1929, and there was a considerable drop in minor league attendance during the spring of 1930. Night baseball was looked upon as a possible solution to the problem. Lee Keyser, owner of the Des Moines club of the Western League, sought and received permission from his league to play night games at his park; and on May 2 the first regularly scheduled professional night game was played. It was a great success, drawing over 10,000 spectators, including many minor league club owners. Within a matter of weeks light towers were installed in such cities as

Buffalo, Indianapolis, Omaha, San Antonio and Jersey City with similar results.

The first night game in the PCL was played at Sacramento on May 22. Shortly afterwards, all clubs except the two San Francisco teams announced plans for night baseball. Lane was not really intrigued with the prospect, but he was willing to go along with William Wrigley, who boasted that he would install the finest system that money could buy.

The Angels played the first night game in Los Angeles on July 22 before 17,000 fans and the Stars made their after-dark debut on August 5. Only 4,935 turned out to see the Seals blast Jim Turner and the Sheiks, 8-2. The next night, however, 13,688 were in attendance and 11,495 paid their way in to the third game. It was obvious that the fans liked night baseball, and secretary Spider Baum announced that for the rest of the season all week day games would be played at night. A pattern was set in Los Angeles which has endured to this day.

The Sheiks were winning almost two out of every three games played but were only 2½ games ahead on August 30. They then launched an eight game winning streak against the Mission Reds to pull 6½ games ahead of Los Angeles before beginning a crucial series at Wrigley Field with the Angels on September 9.

It was the biggest series between the two clubs up to that time. 79,941 fans were in attendance as the Angels and Stars split eight games. The Sheiks split the Admission Day double header, then won 4-1 behind Turner and 15-4 behind Shellenback to pull 8½ games ahead. Those games effectively decided the pennant race. 13,391 saw Hollywood split the Sunday double header to remain 6½ in front. The Stars played .500 ball for two weeks, then won ten straight to settle the issue. The pennant was officially clinched on October 11.

A playoff was necessary to determine the league championship once again, and it was felt that the Angels had a chance to dethrone the Sheiks. After all, Los Angeles had taken the season series from Hollywood rather handily. But in a tremendous display of offensive power Hollywood easily defeated the Angels four games to one to repeat as PCL champions.

All of the games were slugging contests, and in 1930 the Stars could outslug them all. The first game went to Hollywood, 9-8, as the Stars scored four runs in the eighth inning to win. The next day it was Hollywood again, 14-12, as pitcher George Hollerson homered with two on in the eighth to decide the issue.

The Angels took the third game, 11-10, as the Stars blew an eight run lead, but the last two games were all Hollywood. Jim Turner bested the Angels, 22-4, as Ed Baecht and four Seraph pitchers were unable to stop the Hollywood onslaught. Mickey Heath had two home runs in this game and drove in nine runs while Turner also homered and had six RBI's. In the final game Shellenback went the distance to beat the Angels, 8-4, behind home runs by Barbee and Brannan.

The series was dominated by Barbee who went 12 for 19 with 4 home runs. The Stars hit .360 against what was thought to be a pretty good Los Angeles pitching staff.

Lane was ecstatic over the Stars that year. This was the pinnacle of his success in Los Angeles; for Hollywood fortunes would take a decisive downturn in the next few years. But he had every reason to be proud of the 1930 club. It scored 1205 runs, an average of 6½ per game and hit a resounding 182 home runs. Both figures led the league and are also the all time Hollywood records. The club sported a .309 average and boasted ten regular players over the .300 mark. Hank Severeid continued his remarkable hitting of the previous year by leading the Stars with a .367 mark in 129 games. Bassler was right behind him at .365. Has there ever been a more potent catching staff? Hill was at .356 and the venerable Bill Rumler hit a remarkable .353. At the advanced age of forty-two Rumler was having a fine season platooning with Carlyle and Hill when he broke his ankle on August 29. That ended Rumler's career with the Stars. In 1931 he was back in Lincoln in the Nebraska State League.

Barbee led the PCL with 41 home runs that year, just edging out Mickey Heath who had 37. Dave drove in 115 runs in a Hollywood uniform in only 100 games. He was merely getting ready for the 1931 season which would prove to be his best.

Heath started out very badly but finished well to close at .324. For a time in June Mickey was benched in favor of Harry Green, but he had three home runs in a June 15 double header at Mission and was back in the lineup to stay. He set a PCL record during a series against the Reds when he stroked 12 consecutive hits. That record was tied in 1954 by another Star, Ted Beard, but has never been bettered in the major leagues or the minors. Heath led the Stars with 136 runs batted in.

The most valuable player of this Hollywood aggregation was Otis Brannan. He was easily the best second baseman in the league that year, hitting .307 and driving in 130 of his mates. In the field there was no infielder who could touch him. He led the league in total chances and while his average wasn't particularly high, he always seemed to make the big play when it was needed.

The pitching staff was led by Turner who had a fine 21-9 record, but others had good seasons too. Shellenback made a remarkable about face after his early season miseries and finished with 12 straight wins. He was especially effective against Sacramento and Mission, winning four games each without a loss to these clubs. Rhodes was very valuable during June and July but experienced arm trouble in early August and was of little use thereafter. Still, his record of 9-2 was enough to merit another chance with the Yankees in 1931.

The staff had remarkable depth. In addition to the big three, Emil Yde and Buzz Wetzel pitched well as starters and in relief with each winning 13 games. Hollerson was 13-10 while Augie Johns checked in at 12-11 and Hank Hulvey was 11-10. Only Vance Page had a losing record, but that was due to arm trouble more than anything else.

The ERA's on this staff weren't especially low, but they couldn't have been in 1930 when the offense was at its peak.

The 1930 Stars were one of the finer teams in PCL history and are often rated as the best of all Hollywood teams. Depth is what distinguished this team from others. Vitt juggled his players to perfection and seemingly got the most out of every man. While perhaps not in the class of the 1934 Angels the 1930 Hollywood Stars could have held their own against virtually all others.

1930 STANDINGS

1st HALF

	W	L	PCT.
Los Angeles	57	42	.576
HOLLYWOOD	54	46	.540
Sacramento	53	46	.535
Oakland	52	48	.520
San Francisco	52	48	.520
Mission	48	52	.480
Seattle	44	56	.440
Portland	39	61	.390

2nd HALF

	W	L	PCT.
HOLLYWOOD	65	35	.650
Los Angeles	56	42	.571
San Francisco	49	50	.495
Sacramento	49	50	.495
Seattle	48	51	.485
Oakland	45	55	.450
Portland	42	56	.429
Mission	43	58	.426

(From the collection of Dick Dobbins)

Mike Gazella

(From the collection of Dick Dobbins)

Johnny Bassler

1931 – THREE IN A ROW IS TOO MUCH

THE STARS THOUGHT THEMSELVES ON THE verge of a dynasty in the spring of 1931. The team that had closed the previous season in such fine fashion was virtually intact. Both Vitt and Lane predicted another championship. They were half right. Hollywood easily won the first half pennant chase but stumbled badly in the second half season and fell to fifth place. They then lost the playoff series to San Francisco in four straight games. Clearly, the Hollywood dynasty was not at hand.

Oscar Vitt greeted a very formidable team when spring training began that March. Only Heath was absent from the group of regulars who had made short work of the Angels in the 1930 championship series. Mick was finally getting his well deserved big league chance with Cincinnati, where he would open the 1931 season as the Reds' first baseman. The Heath story is an interesting one and is typical of those less regulated times.

Mickey Heath had joined Hollywood in the spring of 1927, ostensibly on option from Detroit by way of Toronto where he had spent 1926 and part of 1927. He spent the balance of that year as well as 1928, 1929 and 1930 at Hollywood. At no time was he recalled by Detroit nor was he eligible for the draft, since his contract was held by a major league club.

At the end of 1929 Mickey fully expected to be in Detroit or on the roster of another major league club in 1930. But once again he was passed up in spite of his .349 average and a growing reputation as a fine fielder. Heath spent 1930 at Hollywood where he again enjoyed a fine year. But the draft went by another time without Heath being selected.

Mickey was disturbed enough this time to do something, and he wrote a letter to Judge Landis, outlining his problem. The commissioner was interested and replied to Heath, asking for all of the details. But Mickey never answered for he had been sold to the Reds for two players, outfielder Marty Callaghan and infielder Pat Crawford. Did the word get out that Landis was looking into the problem? How did Hollywood end up with two players when Detroit owned Heath's contract? We will never know for certain. But it appears that the rules of baseball were violated in this instance.

Heath's career in the major leagues was a short one. He opened as the regular Cincinnati first baseman, but broke his arm in his ninth game. While recuperating, he contracted a case of rheumatic fever which severely weakened him; and he was never quite the same player again. After a brief period with the Reds in 1933, he was returned to the minors where he finished his playing days. Fate was against Mickey Heath. With a little bit of luck he would have enjoyed a fine major league career.

One other familiar face was not there in 1931. Hank Hulvey was sold to Chattanooga during the winter. He had joined the club while it was in Salt Lake City and had enjoyed some good years in Hollywood. Hank won 69 games as a member of the Sheiks, a figure surpassed by only Frank Shellenback and Pinky Woods of the latter day Stars. He was a good hitter, too and was frequently used as a pinch hitter by Vitt.

Of the two players received from Cincinnati Crawford refused to report. Hollywood was too far away, he said, and the Reds sent him to Columbus instead. Callaghan was a fine fielding outfielder who hit well but with little power. He had spent the 1930 season with Cincinnati, hitting .278 in a part time role after seeing earlier PCL duty with Seattle.

The Reds owed the Sheiks a player when Crawford wouldn't report and fulfilled that obligation by sending first baseman Jack Sherlock to Hollywood. This proved to be beneficial to the Stars. Sherlock was a fine fielder and as a right handed thrower was very versatile, playing at third or shortstop when the occasion called for it. He specialized in catching errant throws from other infielders. Sherlock hit .324 for the Phillies in 1930 and while not quite that good at Hollywood, proved to be a timely hitter, driving in many an important run.

With Sherlock at first the Sheiks were a better balanced club in 1931 with one more right handed hitter. The pitching staff was virtually identical to the 1930 club with the only important addition being a young right hander, Elmer Bray, from Winston Salem in the Piedmont League.

League scribes picked Hollywood to repeat as champions in 1931. The club opened on the road as usual and after a so-so month of April caught fire in early May. The Stars were in seventh place on May 7, but then proceeded to win 36 out of the next 48 games to take a commanding lead. They were 8½ games ahead in late June when the directors abruptly voted for the split season again. The first half ended on July 5 with Hollywood 5½ games ahead of second place Portland.

The second half was a completely different story. The club experienced one injury after another and started slowly but rallied to within a game of first place in September. They then hit their worst slump of the year when everyone stopped hitting and lost nineteen of twenty-eight games to end up in fifth place, 11½ games behind San Francisco.

A playoff was necessary to decide the league championship and the Seals made short work of the Stars, defeating them in four straight. Hollywood was handicapped by the illness of pitcher Frank Shellenback who appeared in only one game, but it is doubtful that he would have made a great deal of difference. The Seals ace, Sam Gibson, won two of the four games, after having defeated the Stars four times during the regular season.

1931 belonged to Frank Shellenback and Dave Barbee, who had superb years. The veteran spitballer was virtually invincible. He had finished 1930 with twelve straight wins, won two in the championship series, then won his first five starts in 1931, before tasting defeat. After losing 2-0 to Phil Page of Seattle on May 3, he then went on to win his next fifteen decisions before losing 9-3 on August 8 to the Seals. A string of thirty-four wins in thirty-five decisions! That is remarkable pitching.

Shellenback's nineteen straight over a two year period was a record at the time – it was subsequently broken in 1933-34 by Fay Thomas of the Angels, who won twenty-two. The fifteen straight in one season was second to Frank Browning's sixteen in a row in 1909.

Several of the games Shellenback pitched in his most successful year were masterpieces – a 1-0 three hitter against Sacramento, 6-0 with only four hits at Oakland, a 3-0 six hitter against the Angels. Only once all year was he removed from a game because of ineffective pitching. His 27 wins are the all-time high for Hollywood. He added to his stature by hitting 9 home runs to go along with a .293 average. Three of those circuit clouts won ball games.

Barbee had a marvelous season. Suspended for the first three games of the season for breaking training, he belted a towering home run in his first game back and went on from there. His 47 home runs easily led the PCL and he had 166 RBI's as well. Both are Hollywood records. Dave's .332 average was the Sheiks' best in 1931.

During the season there was much speculation as to where Barbee would go at year end, but Lane couldn't make an acceptable deal and he was forced to let Dave go in the draft to Pittsburgh. Barbee saw part time duty with the Pirates in 1932 but hit only .257. He was sent to

Toronto of the International League in 1933 and never reappeared in the majors. An easy going fellow, Dave's training habits were not the best and that probably prevented him from making his mark in the major leagues.

Injuries and pitching weakness doomed the Stars' chances in 1931. Brannan and Hill were frequently absent as were Carlyle, Lee and Gazella. Sherlock saw a lot of action at third and shortstop while young Lou Catina replaced Brannan at second. Harry Green filled in at first while Sherlock was elsewhere and Marty Callaghan appeared in 112 games in the outfield. But outside of Callaghan's .304, none of the reserves hit much and the defense was weakened as well. Most of the injuries took place during the second half and the Stars were not really the same club.

The pitching was very inconsistent. Turner had sparkled in 1930 but was hit hard at the beginning of 1931. He managed to win 17 but was erratic until late in the year. Buzz Wetzel pitched well in the early season but then slumped and was released in early August when the Stars acquired Lou McEvoy from the Yankees. This was a move Vitt regretted. McEvoy, a big winner at Oakland a few yers back, won only four games, while Wetzel caught on with Los Angeles and had three wins over Hollywood during the last month of the season.

Vance Page recovered from his 1930 arm miseries and showed a lot of promise. His 17-8 record was exceeded only by Shellenback's 27-7. Rookie Elmer Bray pitched well in April and May, then lost his last nine decisions. Emil Yde was 14-16 while George Hollerson disappointed at 4-4 and was sent to Beaumont in July.

The Depression was beginning to tighten its grip on the country as the 1931 season ended. Although the PCL had experienced a satisfactory year, the directors were fearful of the future. For the next several years, economy would be the focal point of the league's activities.

1931 STANDINGS

1st HALF

	W	L	PCT.
HOLLYWOOD	57	34	.626
Portland	50	38	.568
San Francisco	48	42	.533
Mission	45	47	.489
Los Angeles	43	47	.478
Seattle	41	46	.471
Sacramento	41	48	.461
Oakland	31	54	.365

2nd HALF

	W	L	PCT.
San Francisco	59	38	.608
Los Angeles	55	42	.567
Oakland	55	47	.539
Portland	50	49	.505
HOLLYWOOD	47	49	.450
Sacramento	45	53	.459
Seattle	42	58	.420
Mission	39	56	.411

(From the collection of Dick Dobbins)

Dave Barbee

Cleo Carlyle

1932 – DEPRESSION TIMES

THE STARS WERE DETERMINED IN 1932 TO recapture the championship which had eluded them the previous year. Lane had improved the club during the off-season, he thought, and both he and Oscar Vitt were full of enthusiasm when spring training began.

Jess Hill had been sold to the Yankees during the 1931 season and was in training at Newark this year. In his place the Sheiks had acquired outfielder George Quellich from the Yankee chain. An Oakland resident, Quellich had been a steady power hitter in the International League for several years, achieving a high of .347 with 31 home runs at Reading in 1929. He was given the left field job as Barbee's replacement.

Young Al McNeeley took over in right field that spring. McNeeley had signed with the Stars out of high school in 1930 and had seen limited action with Hollywood in 1931. He was fast and had a good arm but not much power. Carlyle was back in center field while Marty Callaghan returned as a capable reserve. The outfield was Vitt's biggest concern that spring, but by the close of training he felt good about the situation.

The infield returned intact from 1931 and a capable young reserve, Alan Strange, from Durham of the Piedmont League looked good. Bassler would do most of the catching with Hank Severeid gone to Wichita Falls as the Spudders' manager.

The pitching had been strengthened considerably with the signing of veteran Tom Sheehan as a free agent. Big Clancy had been released by Baltimore at the end of 1931. He was thirty-eight years old and had pitched in the American League as far back as 1916. He had enjoyed his greatest years in the American Association, winning a high 31 games at St. Paul in 1923. Sheehan was past his prime in 1932 but he still possessed his old cunning. Vitt planned to use him in relief but he was so effective coming out of the bullpen that Oscar moved him into the starting rotation.

Myles Thomas was the other notable pitching addition. He had been sent to Hollywood along with Quellich in the Hill transaction. A graduate of Penn State, Thomas had enjoyed several fair years with the Yankees. He relied on the screwball and an occasional knuckle ball, having only an average fast ball. Thomas had spent the 1931 season at Newark, winning 18 for the Bears.

Thomas joined Frank Shellenback, Vance Page, Jim Turner and Johnny Miljus as starting pitchers. The latter had been acquired from Seattle and was the epitome of a "junk" pitcher. The crafty Serb threw several off-speed pitches, including perhaps baseball's first blooper ball. He bothered the hitters plenty when he was right. Carl Dittmar, the longtime Angel shortstop, called Miljus the toughest pitcher he ever faced.

Vitt's relationship with Bill Lane hit an all-time low that spring when the owner signed Wade Killefer as a coach. A former manager of the Angels, Killefer was very popular in Los Angeles and was signed as a coach for spring training only. His duties were ill-defined, however, and when the season began, Killefer remained as a special assignment scout and adviser to Lane. There was much speculation that he would replace Vitt at the close of 1932 and naturally, this did not sit well with Oscar. However, Killefer subsequently was hired as manager of Indianapolis later that summer.

The minor leagues were greatly affected by the depression in 1931 and during the winter meetings the National Association established a salary limit as well as reduced playing rosters of all the teams. But the PCL would have none of it. Led by Angel president Joe Patrick, the owners refused to abide by the restrictions. Their position was very logical. Each club wanted to put the best players it could afford on the field even if it meant paying higher salaries to some. A lower salary base would lead to inferior play and eventually lower attendance. The league retained its roster limit of twenty veterans and five rookies during 1932. But during the year many clubs tried to reduce expenses by cutting expensive veteran players.

Portland and Los Angeles were expected to contend for the championship with the Stars picked for third. Hollywood started well and moved into first place on May 15. They remained there for the next month with Portland providing the chief competition.

The lineup had undergone several changes. Quellich had opened in left field, but was a great disappointment. He was unable to get going and was finally benched on May 7 in favor of Marty Callaghan. Callaghan immediately began to hit and took over the position for the rest of the year. Quellich was released on May 30. At the same time the Stars signed Bob Meusel, the former Yankee great. Out of the game for most of 1931, Meusel soon proved that he had not lost his batting eye as he hit .407 in his first 17 Hollywood games. He was hitting .329 when the Stars released him in September as an economy move. Gazella had slowed up greatly and wasn't hitting, so Vitt began to give rookie Strange some playing time at third. The youngster played well in the field, but had to move to shortstop for a period while Lee was out with an injury. Eventually, Strange went back to third on a permanent basis when Gazella was released on September 6.

Hollywood fell out of first place when the club lost a July 4 doubleheader to Sacramento. The Stars were unable to regain the lead for the balance of the year. After a slump in

August and September that saw them drop nine games behind Portland on Labor Day the Stars took six of eight games from the Beavers in their only visit of the year to Wrigley Field. That cut the lead to five games and for the rest of the season the Stars remained in hot pursuit. They cut the lead to two games entering the last week of the season and had a chance. But Yde lost to the Angels 3-2 and Page was beaten 4-3 in ten innings to end any hope the Stars had. The Beavers finished five games ahead of the Stars. It was the first Portland championship in eighteen years.

Offensively, the club did well in 1932, hitting .291, but the power that had characterized Hollywood teams of the recent past was not there. Otis Brannan led the team with 17 home runs. Carlyle had 16, with McNeeley and Jack Sherlock the only other Stars in double figures.

Bassler and Carlyle had exceptional years. The veteran catcher was behind the plate in 156 games and hit his career high of .357 to lead the Hollywood hitters. Johnny had 120 assists to go along with his fine hitting, and he ended a personal drought with a home run against Portland on September 11. It was Bassler's first homer since 1928.

Carlyle had one of his finest years also. Always injury prone, the graceful Carlyle played virtually the full schedule for the first time and hit .346 with 106 runs batted in. He was now gaining recognition as a fine fielder and indeed he was. Mickey Heath was especially high on Carlyle's ability and calls him one of the better centerfielders he has ever seen. "Carlyle wasn't as spectacular as some but he got to balls that most outfielders wouldn't have come close to." That was certainly true in 1932.

The pitching was led as usual by Frank Shellenback. At the very zenith of his career, the big spitballer had another remarkable year. Shellenback won 26 games with a fine 3.14 ERA. He started 36 games and went the distance in 35 of them. In the 322 innings he pitched that year only once was Shellenback charged with a wild pitch. Considering the erratic nature of the spitball that has to be a record! Frank was virtually invincible at Wrigley Field with a record of 19-3. He was especially vexing to the Angels, winning seven games without a loss. Several of his games were masterpieces—a 3-1 decision over San Francisco on May 6 in which Shellenback allowed only three hits and served up 18 ground balls; a 6-2 win at Sacramento with seventeen ground balls and only three balls hit to the outfield. For a time during 1932 there was a rumor that Connie Mack was trying to acquire Shellenback for the Philadelphia Athletics and had spoken to Judge Landis about an exception to the spitball rule. But nothing ever came of it.

As great as Shellenback was during that season, he was almost upstaged by Clancy Sheehan. The crafty veteran baffled the PCL hitters in his first exposure to the West and finished with a record of 13-6. He won his first seven decisions and would probably have finished with an even more impressive record had he not been injured in an auto accident in early May, causing him to miss three weeks of action. Sheehan led the PCL with seven shut outs including three 1-0 games.

The rest of the staff had mixed reviews. Miljus was released after several unsuccessful starts while Turner continued his decline from his fine debut in 1930. The Tennessee milkman finished 11-10 and was at the bottom of the staff with a 4.61 ERA. Myles Thomas was inconsistent and finished 14-18 while Vance Page posted a 13-19 record and was especially ineffective during July and August. Augie Johns had sparkled during spring training and was counted on for a big year, but he lost his life savings when a Texas bank failed in April and that ruined his spirit. Johns was released to Fort Worth in July. The veteran Emil Yde came out of the bullpen in July to join the starting corps and finished 17-9, his best record in a Hollywood uniform.

The Sheiks were just a little shy of championship caliber in 1932. Another starting pitcher may have put them over the top, but perhaps another power hitter would have been more useful. The club was an exciting one, however, and drew 297,000 paid admissions in that depression year. Lane enjoyed a profitable year at Wrigley Field in 1932. He would not enjoy another.

1932 STANDINGS

	W	L	PCT.
Portland	111	78	.587
HOLLYWOOD	106	83	.561
Sacramento	101	88	.534
San Francisco	96	90	.516
Los Angeles	96	93	.508
Seattle	90	95	.486
Oakland	80	107	.428
Mission	71	117	.378

(From the collection of Dick Dobbins)

Otis Brannan

Oscar Vitt

1933 – THE BIG FOUR AND A CLOSE CALL

THE FORTUNES OF HOLLYWOOD BASEBALL began to turn downward in 1933. Although the Sheiks were in strong contention for most of the year, they lost a critical series to the Angels during the first week of September and fell out of the lead, eventually finishing in third place. The club was caught up in the general economic malaise of the era and failed to show a profit for the first time since 1926. Paid attendance fell alarmingly, to less than 180,000. Perhaps worst of all, the hated Angels finished on top of the PCL and attracted most of the attention in Los Angeles.

Lane had taken major steps to beef up the Hollywood attack over the winter. First, he acquired the veteran outfielder, Cedric Durst, from St. Paul. No stranger to Los Angeles, the thirty-six year old Durst had starred as an Angel in 1924 before beginning a five year major league career spent mostly as a reserve with the Yankees. Durst had been a fine outfielder in his prime, but he had slowed down considerably. Still a good hitter, he had hit .314 for the Saints in 1932.

Two former Angels were picked up via the free agent route when first baseman Ray Jacobs and third baseman Fred Haney agreed to terms just as spring training was about to begin. In Jacobs, Lane found the power hitter he

had been looking for. The veteran had spent five successful years in Los Angeles, hitting a total of 114 home runs in
a Seraph uniform. While not usually a high average hitter,
Ray had hit .332 in 1929 and was versatile enough to play
the other infield positions also.

The release of Haney by the Angels in September, 1932
was one of the many economy moves in the PCL at that
time, for the peppery third baseman had a lot of good
baseball left in him. A .300 hitter in 1932, Haney would
provide some badly needed speed for the Sheiks.

Lane's friend, Wade Killefer, was now at Indianapolis
and this triggered a series of transactions between the
Indians and Stars which saw outfielder Doug Taitt and
pitcher Archie Campbell come to Hollywood in exchange
for Jim Turner, Marty Callaghan and Dudley Lee. In Taitt,
the club was getting a more powerful hitter than Callaghan
while Campbell was a hard working veteran who could
start or relieve. Both Vitt and Lane had been disappointed
with Turner after his fine rookie season of 1930 and felt
that Campbell would be of more value to the club. They
were sorry to see the popular Lee go. Deadly Dudley had
served the Stars well during his tenure at shortstop. As
good a fielder as there was in the PCL during those years,
Lee would long be remembered by Hollywood fans. He
played more games in a Hollywood uniform than anyone
else in history.

Alan Strange took over at shortstop, leaving Otis Brannan as the only survivor of the 1932 infield. Carlyle was
back in center field with Durst and Taitt on either side of
him. Johnny Bassler was once again counted upon to do
the bulk of the catching with assistance from Herman
Franks, an eighteen year old making his professional
debut.

The pitching was a little thin. Although Sheehan, Shellenback and Page would join Campbell as starting pitchers,
there was little else. Emil Yde had been counted upon
again this year, but he resisted the pay cut that Lane
offered and refused to sign. The veteran lefty was finally

dealt to St. Paul in June. Vitt persuaded Buzz Wetzel to come out of retirement, and the thirty-eight year old veteran looked surprisingly good in training. Other pitchers were Dick Schultze, a Pasadena boy with a fine curve ball, Pete Donohue, a twenty game winner for Cincinnati in the past and Dan Crowley, the only left hander on the staff.

The club trained at Long Beach, and that proved to be a bad choice for a devastating earthquake severely damaged their hotel and playing facilities. Lane quickly moved the headquarters to Sawtelle field in west Los Angeles. The team looked good in exhibition games against the major league clubs, and Vitt thought he might have a winner.

The depression was much worse in 1933, and owners cut expenses wherever they could. This year the player limit was restricted to twenty-three, but most clubs operated with no more than twenty at any given time. Salary cuts were imposed. Both Bassler and Shellenback, the highest paid Sheiks, saw their paychecks slashed by more than 50% and Vitt took a sizable cut, too.

There was little money to buy talent, and free agents were the usual source when a club needed a player. Ticket prices were reduced along with everything else. That year the Stars charged 85 cents for a box seat, 60 cents for the grandstand, and 25 cents for bleachers.

Hollywood started out slowly but then played well to move into first place on May 11. The race was very close in 1933 with first Portland, then Sacramento, taking the lead and Hollywood never very far behind. The Sheiks stayed in or around first through the next month. The attack was paced by Ray Jacobs, who got off to a resounding start. He had nine home runs in April and hit his twentieth on May 25, a torrid pace. Doug Taitt and Ced Durst were right behind him while Fred Haney was proving to be a speed demon on the base paths. And the big four of the pitching staff were performing in yeoman-like fashion with Campbell especially impressive.

But injuries began to take their toll. First, Bassler was out with a sore heel, leaving the catching to the green Herman Franks and weak-hitting Lloyd Summers. Strange missed a month, and in June Taitt sprained his ankle, ruining his season. Joe Berkowitz filled in well in the infield, and the Stars signed Vince DiMaggio after his release by San Francisco as a replacement for Taitt.

The injuries and the overwork of the pitching staff caused the club to fall back, and by mid-August the Stars were in fourth place. Suddenly the team turned around, won two consecutive series against Portland and Oakland, and was back in the thick of things.

Hollywood then suffered the most bitter blow of the season when Ray Jacobs was forced out of action on August 26 with a broken wrist. He had hit his 36th home run the day before to help Sheehan to a 5-1 win. There was no experienced replacement for the slugger, and in desperation Vitt turned to young Dan Crowley.

Crowley was a Los Angeles boy who had performed briefly as a pitching hopeful earlier in the year. He was not impressive on the mound, and the Stars released him in June. But in late July, Hollywood was in need of replacement pitchers and signed Crowley again at the princely sum of $150 a month. Dan was used as a relief pitcher in a few games and worked out as a first baseman as well. When the chance came to play regularly, the young Irishman out of Loyola High School made the most of it.

The Stars were only one game behind Los Angeles when they began a series against Sacramento on August 29. A Crowley home run in the last of the ninth gave Hollywood a 3-2 win, and on the next day the Stars took over first place when Crowley hit two homers to pace a 6-4 win. The club proceeded to take the Solon series, seven games to two, and were one game ahead of the Angels when the two teams began the crucial series of the year on September 6.

The setting could not have been more dramatic. A doubleheader was scheduled that evening, and the opening game would find the great Frank Shellenback matched against the Angel ace, Buck Newsom. A crowd announced as 24,695 and said to be the largest in PCL history at that time, jammed Wrigley Field an hour before game time. Dan Crowley remembers it well. "Before the game I talked to Shellenback about the big crowd and said they were all here to see him and Newsom. 'What do you mean, Dan?' said Frank, 'They're here to see you. You saved the season. If it hadn't been for your hitting, there wouldn't have been 2000 people here.'"

The game proved to be one of the most memorable in PCL history. Both pitchers were at their best, and there was no score until the last half of the seventh inning. Then with a heavy fog settling in, Cleo Carlyle, usually the most reliable of outfielders, misjudged a fly ball and then committed an error on a ground ball, allowing the only two runs of the game to score. The two teams were now tied for the lead.

Since it was not possible to play the second game, another doubleheader was scheduled for the next day. Hollywood moved back into first place with an 11-8 win behind the fine relief pitching of young George Buchanan, a recent USC graduate. But the fog caused the second game to be called and a third doubleheader was scheduled for Friday. This time the Angels were ready. They took the Stars in both games 3-1 and 4-0 to take over the lead. The two teams split on Saturday, September 9 and then on Sunday the Angels won two, 9-1 as Shellenback was blasted early and then 4-2 in the second game. Los Angeles was now firmly in first place by three games.

That series, which attracted over 70,000 fans, finished the Sheiks. They remained close for a week but then lost an important doubleheader at Mission on September 17 to fall four games back. The club played rather poorly after that and finally fell to third place on the season's last day, a full seven games behind the champion Angels.

It was a bitter pill for Lane and Vitt. The Sheiks were good enough to win in 1933, but injuries and a thin pitching staff killed their chances. The club was well stocked with hitters. Seven regulars were over .300, led by Taitt and Bassler at .336, and Vince DiMaggio hit .348 in his 74 games with Hollywood. Jacobs hit a modest .284 but his 36 home runs were second only to Gene Lillard of the Angels, who had 43. Strange and Haney sparkled on the left side of the infield, giving the club its finest defense since 1930, and the thirty-five year old Haney, supposedly washed up, hit .324 and stole 63 bases, a league high.

For the only time in its history Hollywood had four twenty game winners. Archie Campbell led the way at 22-15. The righthander appeared in 51 games, including seventeen relief appearances. By September Archie was worn out by this heavy load and was not nearly as effective as he had been earlier in the year. Sheehan was 21-13 while Shellenback was 21-12. Clancy was most effective against San Francisco, winning five games from the Seals without a loss. Shellenback was not quite as potent as in prior years, and was hit hard on several occasions. Like the rest of the staff, he suffered from overwork.

Vance Page was the fourth twenty game winner, finishing at 20-15. This was his best year as a Sheik, and he was especially effective in July and August. The only other hurler of any consequence that season was Buzz Wetzel. He had been considered washed up in 1932 but Vitt coaxed 14 wins out of the veteran who was used largely in relief. The rest of the staff was ineffective. Schultze and Buchanan could muster no more than two wins each. A surprise was Johnny Miljus, who left the Long Beach police force in late August to rejoin the club and win three games down the stretch. But the club needed more than that.

The Stars were getting old. Bassler was thirty-eight; Durst thirty-seven; Sheehan and Wetzel each thirty-nine; Shellenback and Haney each thirty-five. The days of greatness were becoming only a memory. But where was Lane going to find replacements?

1933 STANDINGS

	W	L	PCT.
Los Angeles	114	73	.609
Portland	105	77	.577
HOLLYWOOD	107	80	.572
Sacramento	96	85	.530
Oakland	93	92	.502
San Francisco	81	106	.433
Mission	79	108	.422
Seattle	65	119	.353

(From the collection of Dick Dobbins)

Smead Jolley

1934 – THE BEGINNING OF THE END

THE 1934 SEASON SAW THE STARS CONTINUE TO decline. The club finished in fifth place during the first half of the season then rallied in the second half to finish second. But overall, the Stars finished only nine games above .500 and were a rather drab team through most of the season until they spurted in September to move into the runner up spot.

The PCL belonged to the Los Angeles Angels that year. The 1934 Seraphs were the greatest team in league history and perhaps the finest minor league team of all time. They won both halves of the league season by overwhelming margins and defeated a group of All-Stars from the other clubs in a year end series. The Angels won 137 games, the most in one season in PCL history. Except for a brief two week period during the beginning of the second half season, no other team was remotely in contention for the championship.

The Stars were thought to be a legitimate contender when spring training opened. The club had moved its base to Riverside that spring, and Vitt attempted to get the players in shape through a series of exercises climbing the hills around that city. There were a number of new faces in camp. Alan Strange had been sent to the Browns in exchange for three players – pitcher Wally Hebert, infielder Jim Levey and outfielder Smead Jolley.

Jolley was by far the biggest name of this trio. Thirty-two years old, the lumbering slugger was fresh from four years in the American League with Chicago and Boston. His fielding kept him from major league stardom, for as a hitter, he was extraordinary. A left handed pull hitter, at 6'3" and weighing 202 pounds, Jolley had enough strength to hit the ball out of the park in any direction. He had some awesome years with San Francisco before going to the majors – .397 in 1927, then .404 in 1928 with 45 home runs. Both Vitt and Lane thought he would help the Stars. Right field wasn't too difficult to patrol in Wrigley Field, they felt, and Jolley's bat would add some more power to an otherwise light hitting lineup.

Levey took over at shortstop alongside of Fred Haney while Ray Jacobs returned at first. There was a major gap at second when Otis Brannan did not report. The quiet veteran who had performed so well in the past suffered a nervous breakdown over the winter. He had returned his signed contract for 1934 earlier but on March 20 wired Lane "My services will be of no use to you. Please place me on the voluntary retired list." Several attempts to contact Brannan after that were unsuccessful, and he never played at Hollywood again.

Joe Berkowitz was given the second base job after his fine season in a utility role in 1933. Berkowitz did reasonably well with the bat, hitting .279 in 112 games but didn't cover the ground that Brannan did and was more erratic. He missed most of the month of June with an infected hand and was replaced in August by a sixteen-year-old fielding wizard out of Jefferson High in Los Angeles, Bobby Doerr. Doerr would, of course, go on to a long career with the Boston Red Sox. He was probably the finest second baseman in the American League during the late 40's.

The outfield consisted of Jolley in right with Vince DiMaggio taking over in left field on a regular basis. Cleo Carlyle was back in center, but his days in Hollywood were numbered. He had incurred Lane's wrath on the last day of 1933 when he didn't appear for the final game. Lane docked him a day's pay, later had words with Carlyle, and correspondence between the two was decidedly frigid during the off-season. Ced Durst was still around for outfield relief and would see duty at first base as well.

The pitching staff did not look good in the spring. Archie Campbell was offered a pay cut in spite of his twenty-two wins in 1933, and the veteran held out all spring. He finally joined the club the day before the season began. The lack of training appeared to hurt him, for he was never as effective in 1934 as he had been the previous year. Sheehan and Shellenback were back, but Frank reported to camp with a severe case of neuritis and he was unable to get much work. Vance Page reported with an ailing arm and was not nearly as sharp as he had been the previous year. After a few ineffective outings Page was sold to Indianapolis in May.

New faces on the staff were Jim Densmore, on option from the Yankee chain, Jack Hile, a rookie free agent out of the Long Beach semi-pro leagues and left hander Joe Sullivan. Sullivan was on option from Detroit after a fine year in Beaumont the year before. Other pitchers signed as free agents were Jack Quinn and Gordon Maltzberger. Quinn was the oldest Hollywood player ever — forty-nine that spring. He was a spitball pitcher like Shellenback, but saw action in only six games. Maltzberger had been released by Los Angeles after a short trial in 1932 and appeared only briefly with Hollywood in 1934, posting an 0-1 record. He would be a far more important figure when he returned to the Stars in 1948.

Bassler was wearing out behind the plate but would still catch in parts of 123 games. His back up was Willard Hershberger, a product of Fullerton High School, on option from the Yankees. Hershberger was fast and very agile.

Vitt used him at second base from time to time while Berkowitz was out.

The season started out on a sour note when Lane suffered a heart attack on his way to Oakland for the opening game. The seventy-four year old owner missed the opener for the first time. He was virtually incapacitated for several months and did not get back to his regular duties until August. When his trusted aid, secretary Spider Baum, suffered an appendicitis attack in June, the club was left without real leadership for a time. That seemed to affect the players as the play was very spotty.

The club started off badly when it was soundly trounced by the Angels in the first series and hovered around fifth or sixth place through June. At that time the owners, alarmed by the Los Angeles runaway together with falling attendance, called for a split season. When the first half ended on July 2, the Stars were fifth. They began well in the second half and led after one week but the Angel machine blew by them and the club dropped back to fourth. The Stars then rallied to win nineteen of their last twenty-eight games, finishing in second place, twelve games behind the Angels.

Joe Sullivan contributed most to the club's finish. A solid pitcher through most of the season, Sullivan closed fast by winning nine of his last eleven decisions to finish at 25-11. His ERA was a sparkling 2.88. That was far and away the best on the Hollywood staff. It was the finest season of Sullivan's career. He was recalled by Detroit at season's end, but he never lived up to the promise of his great year in 1934.

The attack was led as expected by Smead Jolley and Ray Jacobs. Jolley hit a resounding .360, third best in the league and led the Stars with 133 RBI's. The Ogre from the Ozarks, as Smead was called in the papers, was a real liability in the field, however. Several games were lost as a direct result of his errors, and he covered very little ground in right field. Carlyle had to overplay hitters to prevent balls from going through to the fence.

Jacobs had a very slow start and was hitting a mere .237 when August began. He finished strong to close at .284 and led the club with 24 home runs. Ced Durst hit .299 while seeing reserve duty in center field and at first base, and young Vince DiMaggio hit a solid .288 with 17 home runs. Carlyle had his worst year, hitting only .272 before he was shipped to Newark in August.

In his last year as a regular, Johnny Bassler stroked .351 while Willard Hershberger and Fred Haney joined him in the .300 club at .307 and .306 respectively. Fred was a veritable greyhound that year, stealing a league leading 71 bases while establishing an all-time club record. It was Haney's swan song as a player. At season's end he signed a contract to manage Toledo of the American Association in 1935. But Hollywood had not seen the last of him.

Outside of Sullivan, Hollywood pitching was very ordinary in 1934. Clancy Sheehan posted a 16-14 record in his last season with the club. He signed as a coach with Cincinnati for 1935. Shellenback was hindered all year by his early illness and finished 14-12. Both he and Sheehan were helpless against the champion Angels; each lost five decisions to the Seraphs with Clancy's 12-7 win on July 13 the only victory between them. Jim Densmore was 14-11, both starting and relieving, but he had an unimpressive 4.84 ERA. Archie Campbell was 12-13 and was not nearly the pitcher he had been in 1933.

Shortly after the season closed, Oscar Vitt resigned as manager. He had done so at the request of Bill Lane, he said. The Stars lost money again in 1934, and Lane was suffering financially. He wanted a playing manager in 1935 to save money. Although this announcement seemed plausible on the surface, relations between the two men had not been good for several years. Vitt suspected that Lane had wanted to get rid of him for some time, and poverty was a convenient excuse. Vitt had also been critical of some of Lane's player transactions. A week after Vitt quit, the Newark Bears returned Carlyle to Hollywood and Lane immediately sold him to Los Angeles. "I'd never make that deal," said Vitt. The incident said much about the relationship between the two.

Vitt signed as manager for his hometown Oakland Acorns in 1935 and had his greatest success while at Newark in 1936-37. He became manager of the Cleveland Indians in 1938 and piloted the Tribe to a second place finish in 1940. However, Vitt is best remembered for the personal difficulties he had with that Cleveland team known as the Cry-Baby Indians. It tainted an otherwise successful managerial career. He was extremely popular in Hollywood, and the fans were sorry to see him go. His clubs were always hustling and although they never had much speed, they always seemed to run the bases well. Vitt played hunches a lot and used his bench very well. Oscar would be missed in 1935.

Hollywood affairs were at their lowest ebb since the club had moved to Los Angeles. The players were aging, and there was little money for replacements. The success of the Angels had taken the city by storm, and interest in the Stars was almost non-existent. 1935 did not offer too much hope for improvement.

1934 STANDINGS

1st HALF

	W	L	PCT.
Los Angeles	66	18	.786
Mission	48	37	.565
Sacramento	44	41	.518
San Francisco	40	45	.471
HOLLYWOOD	39	45	.464
Oakland	39	46	.459
Seattle	30	52	.366
Portland	30	52	.366

2nd HALF

	W	L	PCT.
Los Angeles	71	32	.689
HOLLYWOOD	58	43	.574
Mission	53	48	.525
San Francisco	53	50	.515
Seattle	51	50	.505
Oakland	51	52	.495
Portland	36	65	.356
Sacramento	35	68	.340

1935 – GOODBYE WRIGLEY FIELD

IT IS NOT KNOWN WHETHER BILL LANE KNEW that 1935 would be the last season his club would represent Hollywood when the players assembled for spring training at Fullerton that year. But that was the way it would be.

The new manager was Frank Shellenback. He was already the highest paid player on the team so Lane was able to secure his services at a nominal raise. He thought that Frank could impart some of his pitching knowledge to the younger pitchers on the staff. That was not an entirely misplaced hope, for Shellenback would later serve a long career as a pitching coach in the major leagues, primarily with the New York Giants.

At the 1934 winter meeting the PCL directors made an effort to reduce expenses once again. The player limit was reduced to 21 players and the season was reduced by two weeks. Instead of the traditional seven game week long series, the clubs would play two series each week of three and four games in length. This would stimulate attendance, the directors thought.

The Stars had only seventeen players under contract when training opened, but Lane hoped to secure help on option from the major leagues. The roster was a mish-mash of old and young. In addition to Bobby Doerr, who had proved to be a real jewel, the Stars brought two other local youngsters into camp – shortstop George Myatt and first baseman George McDonald. Both were local teenage base-ball stars. McDonald was signed during the 1934 season after he had starred on the Leonard Wood American Legion team with Doerr. Myatt, an El Segundo boy, had made his professional debut with San Antonio in 1933 but had played semi-pro ball since then.

Other than these two youngsters the team was about the same as the 1934 aggregation. Levey was moved to third as Haney's replacement while Ced Durst took over Carlyle's spot in center field. Myatt took over Levey's shortstop position, and although showing much promise the youngster was very erratic during the spring training games. Shellen-back admitted the club needed a lot of help. He was counting on Vince DiMaggio for more offensive help. The club didn't pack much punch outside of Smead Jolley and Ray Jacobs.

The pitching was unimpressive. Shellenback could not be counted on to shoulder the load as he had previously, but he proved to be the best Hollywood had. Other starters were Archie Campbell and three newcomers – Ed Wells, acquired from the Browns, Grant Bowler, on option from Toledo, and Guy Cantrell, from St. Joseph in the Western League. Wells started out impressively, winning his first four decisions, but then slumped to a dismal 9-20 record. Bowler and Cantrell were absolute failures. They had both been winning pitchers in the International League and American Association, and Shellenback had hoped for similar results at Hollywood. Bowler was 0-5 and Cantrell 2-5 during the first month of the season before Lane returned them to their previous clubs.

Catching was in the hands of Gene Desautels, obtained on option from Detroit. A 1930 graduate of Holy Cross, Desautels had signed with the Tigers after completing his collegiate career and spent parts of three seasons in Detroit. But he was sent to Toledo in 1934 when the Tigers acquired Mickey Cochrane, and there was no longer a place for him in that organization. Lane was happy to get Desautels, especially so after Johnny Bassler collapsed during a workout one week before the season started. The doctors diagnosed the ailment as a stomach hemorrhage and said there would be no baseball for Bassler in 1935. Johnny did sneak into five games late in the season but for all practical purposes his playing career was over.

It was sad that Bassler had to end this way, for he was one of the finest catchers in PCL history. He appeared in 866 Hollywood games and finished with a fine .331 average. One will have to search for a long time to find a catcher who posted a better record. A fine catcher with a rifle for an arm, Bassler deserves credit for the success and development of the many fine pitchers who graced the Hollywood roster. He would be missed especially by Shellenback, who relied heavily on his judgement behind the plate.

The Stars opened at Wrigley Field for the first time ever, losing to the Angels 10-8. The club hit well during the first month with Jolley and Doerr leading the way, but pitching proved to be a problem. Hollywood was fourth most of May as Oakland led in the early going. Eventually, the Angels recaptured the lead and surged so far ahead that the owners clamored for a split season again. Attendance was down everywhere, and several clubs were in dire financial straits. On June 18 it was agreed that the season would end on June 30. The schedule also reverted to the traditional seven game series. The split week approach only added to travel costs and did not improve the crowds.

The Angels were the first half champions with the Stars a solid fourth, 9½ games behind. Lane had now strengthened the pitching with the signing of several free agents. Pitchers Berlyn Horne and Herman Pillette were signed in early June after they had been released by Mission and Seattle respectively. Both were veteran PCL mainstays. Pillette was one of the all time great minor league pitchers, winning a total of 264 games in his career. He was thirty-nine when he joined the Stars but would remain in the league for another ten years! Horne had performed well for the Angels in earlier years. Both moved right in as regular starters and were the most effective Hollywood hurlers over the last two-thirds of the year.

Lane also signed third baseman Eddie Mulligan after his release by Oakland in early June. Mulligan had played for six PCL teams previously and was a sparkling fielder, although not much of a hitter. Eddie filled in for Jim Levey at third through most of the second half of the season.

The Stars seemed stronger when the second half began, but then the club slumped badly, falling into last place by late July. The defense was pretty weak by this time. Levey was not a good third baseman while both Myatt and Doerr were very erratic because of their youth. The outfield was a shambles. Only Vince DiMaggio was able to hold his own. Although Durst was still as surehanded as ever, he was not able to cover the ground he had in previous years.

The balance of the year saw the Stars battle Sacramento to stay out of the cellar, but by September it was clear that Hollywood was the worst team in the league. The lineup was rather pitiful by that time. Jacobs was out with tonsilitis and was replaced by George McDonald, while Doerr and Myatt were in severe slumps after hitting sensationally earlier in the year. The club merely went through the motions, ending up a bad last, seven games behind Sacramento.

The season closed in an aura of gloom with attendance at an all time low. On the season's final day, a crowd of under 2000 saw the Missions blast the Stars 14-7 in what was to be the club's last game as Hollywood representatives. With two out in the ninth and no one on base, the famous comedian, Joe E. Brown, took the mound for the Reds to pitch to songwriter Harry Ruby of the Stars. Brown called in all the outfielders to surround him on the mound and then proceeded to strike out Ruby to end the season. A bizarre twist to a dismal season! It could only happen in Hollywood.

The Stars drew less than 90,000 paid in 1935, a tremendous drop from previous years. Lane wouldn't disclose his losses, but everyone knew they were substantial. But it is doubtful that he would have proposed a move at that time had not Angel President Dave Fleming informed the Stars that rent on Wrigley Field would be increased to $10,000. This was an increase of 100%, and Lane was outraged. There was no way he could make money at that price, he said. But Fleming was adamant. Pay the rent or get out.

It was the straw that broke the camel's back. In this instance Bill Lane was the camel, and he had reached the limit of his resources. Three years of losses had eroded his financial capabilities. He had an aging team which needed replacements and he was in competition against a franchise which seemed to have limitless funds and access to players. What choice did the Stars really have?

Lane had looked into opportunities to move his team to Phoenix or the San Francisco Bay Area, but nothing had really been to his satisfaction. Now he was looking in earnest, and the city of San Diego caught his eye. The border town was a small city in 1935, compared to the metropolis it is today, and had never been considered a prospect for a PCL franchise. But the city officials promised to make a park available for Lane, and in early January, 1936 their offer was tentatively accepted. Although there was some disagreement among the PCL directors, what could they really say? Lane was losing money in Los Angeles and couldn't survive there, especially with an increased rent. And Dave Fleming refused to consider a reduction.

So it was on February 1, 1936 that the transfer of the Hollyood baseball club to San Diego was approved. It was a sad day for Los Angeles. The Sheiks had provided many thrills during their tenure at Wrigley Field. There was a nucleus of Hollywood fans who could never follow the Angels. Their insistent clamor for a team of their own would one day produce results, as we shall see.

1935 STANDINGS

1st HALF

	W	L	PCT.
Los Angeles	46	25	.648
San Francisco	41	30	.577
Oakland	41	30	.577
HOLLYWOOD	36	34	.514
Portland	31	39	.443
Seattle	30	40	.429
Sacramento	30	42	.417
Mission	28	43	.394

2nd HALF

	W	L	PCT.
San Francisco	62	40	.608
Mission	59	44	.573
Portland	56	47	.544
Los Angeles	52	51	.505
Oakland	50	53	.485
Seattle	50	53	.485
Sacramento	45	58	.437
HOLLYWOOD	37	65	.363

INTERLUDE AND WHAT MIGHT HAVE BEEN

IT WAS A CALCULATED RISK THAT BILL LANE took when he moved his club to San Diego in 1936. That city was not then the dynamic metropolis that we know today but was a rather sleepy border city of some 200,000 citizens whose primary interest was the Navy. San Diego had no previous background in organized baseball and no ballpark of any consequence.

Yet, Lane's gamble paid off. What would be known as Lane Field was constructed overnight, and the San Diego fans poured through the turnstiles in droves. Over 203,000 paid to watch the brand new Padres finish in a second place tie with Oakland, only 1½ games behind the champion Portland Beavers. It was an auspicious beginning for the franchise, which remained a thriving member of the PCL until the National League came to San Diego in 1969.

One final note before we take leave of the original Hollywood Stars. In 1936 Lane signed a young outfielder out of San Diego's Hoover High School. He had previously tried out with the Los Angeles Angels on an unofficial basis but didn't feel comfortable there and signed with the Padres instead. After two years in San Diego, Lane sold the contract of this young man to the Boston Red Sox. He joined the American League club in 1939 to begin an illustrious career which would lead him to baseball's Hall of Fame.

The reader may pause here and speculate as to what kind of records the great Ted Williams might have set in a Hollywood uniform, playing in friendly Wrigley Field.

The Los Angeles baseball fans were poorer than they knew.

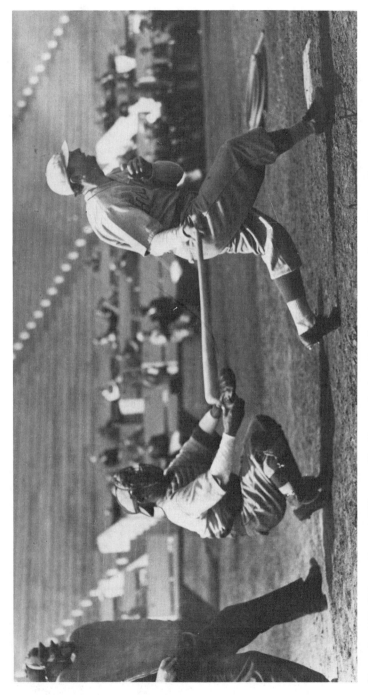

Frenchy Uhalt in action at Gilmore Stadium, during the Stars' one week residence there.

1938 – HOLLYWOOD REDUX

THE MISSION CLUB HAD FALLEN ON BAD TIMES in 1937. It had never done particularly well since the old Vernon club was sold to San Francisco interests and moved to the Bay Area in 1926. Although the team was strong in the late 20's and featured some fine players such as sluggers Ike Boone and Ox Eckhardt, the ball club had never caught on with San Francisco fans and seemed to lack its own identity. Perhaps it was the plethora of nicknames; at various times the club was known as the Monks, Bears, Bells and Reds. Usually it was just referred to as "the Missions."

The Depression coincided with a decline in Mission fortunes, and by 1937 a bad team on the field was producing little revenue at the box office. The franchise was now owned by Herbert Fleischaker of the well-known philanthropic San Francisco family. Fleischaker's primary business interest was a San Francisco brewery which was also losing money, and he could no longer afford the cost of the baseball club.

The PCL directors were well aware of the Mission plight and since a local buyer was nowhere to be found, the idea of moving the club to Los Angeles began to take shape. The key to the move was securing an agreement from the Angels which would allow the Mission team to play in

Wrigley Field. This permission was not forthcoming. President Dave Fleming was firm in his opposition. The club could come south, he said, but it wouldn't play in Wrigley Field. The Angels remembered the disagreements they had with Bill Lane and did not want a repetition of those problems.

A compromise was reached in October, 1937, whereby the club would be allowed to play at Wrigley Field for the 1938 season only. After that it must find its own home. With this agreement in hand the PCL directors voted unanimously to approve the transfer of the team to Southern California at the annual league meeting in November. And so it was that the Mission club of San Francisco was no more. In its place was a brand new entity – the Hollywood Stars.

Fleischaker had hoped to eventually sell the ballclub to Los Angeles interests, but in the meantime he would retain control. His first move was a rather unusual one. He replaced long time president Joe Bearwald with Don Francisco, a Los Angeles advertising man. Francisco had never been associated with baseball and his knowledge of its affairs was slight. He did not last through the 1938 season, resigning his post in July to accept the presidency of the Lord and Thomas advertising agency.

The next step was much more popular. Fleischaker appointed the veteran baseball man, Wade "Red" Killefer as manager on November 22 to replace the incumbent, Willie Kamm. Killefer was a great favorite in Los Angeles baseball circles. He had first appeared in the PCL as playing manager of the Angels in 1917 and had successfully managed the Seraphs through the 1923 season, winning one championship during his tenure there. He left Los Angeles to assume an ownership role at Seattle, remaining there until 1929, when he joined the Mission club in an executive capacity. Since 1933 he had piloted Indianapolis in the American Association.

Fleischaker appointed Killefer to be business manager as well, a wise move since there was no one else with baseball experience in the front office. During that winter there was much activity as Killefer shuffled the roster to bring what talent he could to Hollywood.

The American Association was a natural spot to look for players, and Killefer acquired a number of athletes who would become familiar to Hollywood fans over the next few years. From Milwaukee he acquired catcher Bill Brenzel and outfielder Bernie "Frenchy" Uhalt, then picked up third baseman Joe Coscarart and outfielder Bill Norman from St. Paul. Later he picked up pitcher Jim Crandall and infielder Joe Hoover from his old Indianapolis club.

Uhalt and Brenzel were especially valuable additions. Frenchy had begun his professional career with Oakland in 1928 and except for a brief trial with the White Sox in 1934 and a spring training visit with the Yankees in 1936 would spend his entire twenty-one year career in the minor leagues. A Bakersfield native, Frenchy had spent four years as the regular Oakland center fielder before his Chicago trial. Then it was back to Oakland before spending 1936-37 at Milwaukee. A speedy ball hawk, Frenchy was a good hitter, but he had little power and that more than anything kept him out of the major leagues. He batted lead off much of the time and was a threat to steal whenever he got on base. His best year was 1933 with the Oaks when he hit .350 and stole 62 bases.

Brenzel was an Oakland resident who had briefly appeared in the major leagues with Cleveland and Pittsburgh and had spent the last two seasons at Milwaukee with Uhalt. Never much of a hitter, Brenzel was widely respected as a good handler of pitchers and had a fine throwing arm. Coscarart was one of the baseball playing Basques from Escondido; his brothers Pete and Steve had previously played in the PCL. Joe was a good fielder and a pretty good hitter. He took over third base on the first day of spring training and held the job all season. Norman was a right handed power hitter who was counted upon for whatever punch the club might show in 1938.

Killefer had inherited a rather undistinguished group of

players from the Mission franchise. First baseman Roy Mort had been the regular Mission first baseman in 1937 and while he hit .307 and was a fairly good fielder, he had only one home run. Infielder Don Johnson looked good at second base, but he was unable to handle PCL pitching at that stage of his career and was in and out of the lineup. Catcher Chick Outen was an excellent hitter, but he had a very poor throwing arm, and enemy baserunners had a field day when he was in the lineup.

Most of the pitchers had seen better days. The best was Johnny Babich, a twenty-five year old Serb who had a 12-8 record in 1937. He was joined by Wayne Osborne, Otho Nitcholas, Leroy Herrmann, Walter Beck and Stu Bolen. Osborne would become a Hollywood mainstay over the next few years, although never a big winner. Nitcholas had enjoyed several good years but was bothered by a chronic back problem. Herrmann and Beck were major league rejects who were big losers for the Missions in 1937. Bolen had been a fine pitcher for Baltimore during the late 20's.

The most promising of the lot were youngsters Lou Tost and Rinaldo "Rugger" Ardizoia. Tost was a left hander who could start or relieve. In 1937 he had posted a 9-8 record for Mission. Ardizoia was a native of Italy but had lived in San Francisco since childhood and was signed by Mission after high school graduation in 1937. He appeared in a few Mission games in 1937 and would be farmed out to Bellingham in the Western International League in 1938. These two were the most promising players Hollywood had, and they would go high on the player market after proper seasoning.

The club opened the season on April 2 against the Angels, decked in sparkling red, white and blue uniforms. What pleased the fans more than anything was the recognition of that old nickname, the Stars. The emblem was predominant on the new suits. The "H" on the cap was enclosed by a star as was the number on the back. This was in sharp contrast to the Hollywood uniforms of Lane's teams, which were outfitted in a rather drab fashion.

The opening lineup saw Mort, Johnson and Coscarart in the infield with shortstop Tom Carey, a fiery youngster obtained on option from the St. Louis Browns. In the outfield were Norman, Uhalt and Fern Bell, obtained from the Yankees' Newark farm club on a conditional basis. Bell was a hot hitter in April and May but was returned to New York when the Stars felt they couldn't afford the purchase price.

The Stars played good ball through May 15 when a seven game losing streak saw them plunge to sixth place. They remained there until the last week of June when they fell into seventh.

The playing roster was a veritable revolving door during this period as Killefer tried many combinations. Smead Jolley made a brief appearance in May before it was determined that he was even more of an outfield hazard than ever. After his release, Smead signed with Oakland and led the league in hitting with a .350 average. The Oaks did not benefit much from his presence, however, finishing a dismal last with only 65 wins.

Gordon Slade made a brief appearance at second base before he too was released while outfielder Ced Durst was signed after his release by San Diego. Durst proved to be very useful, hitting .314 in 107 games.

The pitching was very mediocre. Herrmann and Beck were especially ineffective, and they were released on June 1 to open the way for steady work by Wayne Osborne and Lou Tost.

The club lacked hitting power. Norman was hitting well through mid-June when he broke a bone in his foot, an injury which kept him on the sidelines for the rest of the year. Killefer was able to replace him by purchasing outfielder George Puccinelli from the Baltimore Orioles. Pooch was one of the great players in minor league history. He hit a resounding .391 at Rochester in 1932 and in 1935 led the International League in home runs, runs batted in and average while at Baltimore. His 53 homers are among that circuit's all time best. Why he never made the grade in the major leagues remains a mystery to this day. He performed well in his only real chance, hitting .278 in 135 games with the Athletics in 1936. But it was back to Baltimore after that.

In his first ten games with the Stars Puccinelli hit five home runs and finished with 22 round trippers to lead the club. His presence sparked the team in July and August as the team played at a .500 pace, but the Stars lost eleven straight in a September trip to Portland and Seattle and ended up in seventh place. They finished 1½ games behind the Portland Beavers with whom they battled all year for sixth place.

Frenchy Uhalt was the most valuable Star in 1938. He hit .332 to finish second in batting behind Smead Jolley and stole 32 bases to lead the PCL. Uhalt would never do as well again. Tom Carey hit .297 and was an absolute sparkplug in the field. Carey was a very outspoken individual and would criticize teammates who he thought were not giving their best. He and first baseman Roy Mort came to blows in the clubhouse after a discouraging loss to San Francisco in June.

Puccinelli hit .305 to join Durst and Uhalt as the club's only .300 hitters. Of the pitchers Babich had by far the best year. He won his first five games and in spite of a midseason slump finished 19-17 with a fine ERA of 3.27. He had four shutouts and won four of five decisions from the champion Angels. Tost finished 11-16 but didn't get much support. Nitcholas was effective on occasion, especially during the second game of doubleheaders. Bolen and Osborne were hit hard at times although both had their moments.

As the season closed, the search for a playing site was on in earnest. Dave Fleming reiterated his earlier stand that positively Hollywood could not play in Wrigley Field in 1939. The Stars to play somewhere – but where?

1938 STANDINGS

	W	L	PCT.
Los Angeles	105	73	.590
Seattle	100	75	.571
Sacramento	95	82	.537
San Francisco	93	85	.522
San Diego	92	85	.520
Portland	79	96	.451
HOLLYWOOD	79	99	.444
Oakland	65	113	.365

Sacramento won the President's Cup in playoffs.

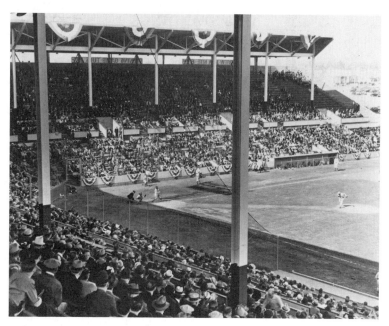

Opening day at Gilmore Field, May 2, 1939.

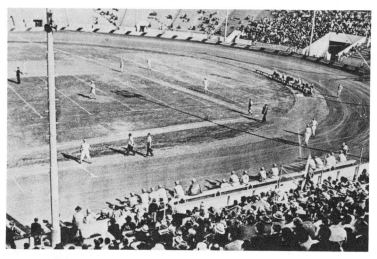

An action shot at Gilmore Stadium. Note the benches for the players, in lieu of dugouts.

1939 — A NEW PARK TO PLAY IN

THE WINTER OF 1938-39 WAS MOST EVENTFUL for the Hollywood Stars. Owner Herbert Fleischaker finally sold his ball club to Los Angeles interests, as he had been hoping to do since moving the franchise from San Francisco. And for the first time in history a Hollywood club would have its own place to play when arrangements were made with the A.F. Gilmore Construction company to build a ballpark in the Fairfax-Beverly district.

The two events happened within a month of each other. Fleischaker was a close friend of Earl Gilmore, who owned a large amount of property adjacent to the Pan Pacific Auditorium. Gilmore Stadium, an oval shaped park designed for football and auto racing, had been constructed several years previously. Now Gilmore Field would be built just to the east of the stadium. The property was located in what was then the western outskirts of Los Angeles. Nearby was the famous Farmers Market which had begun as a depot where farmers sold their produce in the early 30's and had developed into a tourist attraction.

The Gilmore company promised that the ballpark would be ready for occupancy in two months. As it turned out, construction took a little over five months, and workmen were still applying the finishing touches when the Stars played their first game there on May 2.

The park was quite unlike Wrigley Field. It was a completely wooden structure with a seating capacity of 12,987. There were 2,254 enclosed box seats, 8,000 grandstand seats and the rest in the bleachers. The seats were designed with a twelve inch rise between tiers so that no one would have his view obscured by the fan in front of him. The playing field was completely symmetrical. It measured 335 feet down both the left and right field lines with center field 407 feet away. The fences went out fairly rapidly from the lines and the power alleys were a respectable 383 feet in both left and right. Prevailing breezes from right field made it a difficult park for left handed hitters.

Friendly Gilmore Field was a warm and comfortable place. Its fences were covered with advertising signs. Over the years Adohr Farms, the Brown Derby Restaurant, Signal Oil, Western Airlines and 7-Up signs were prominently displayed. In the early 40's a Zesto sign offered any Star player $10 for home runs hit over the frozen custard cup that adorned its ad.

The playing field was especially close to the spectators. The distance from home plate to the screen was a mere 34 feet, compared to a standard 60 feet in most parks. From first and third base it was only 24 feet to the grandstand. Ground rules at Gilmore provided for only one base on an errant throw because of this proximity. The overall result was to provide an intimacy between fan and player unlike anywhere else in the PCL and added to Gilmore's special charm.

The long awaited sale of the ball club was finally consummated on December 8, 1938 when Fleischaker sold the team to a group headed by Bob Cobb, the President of the Brown Derby restaurants. The selling price was said to be approximately $50,000. In his first statement to the press, Cobb announced that Victor Ford Collins, who had replaced Don Francisco as president, would remain as would Wade Killefer. Cobb would serve as vice president. For the next nineteen years Bob Cobb would be the dominant figure in the affairs of the Stars.

Bob Cobb's story is one of rags to riches—or almost riches. He was brought up in Montana and came to Los Angeles in 1919 where his first job was that of messenger at the old Helman Bank at Sixth and Main. Shortly thereafter, he went to work as a checker at the Roma Cafe where he learned the restaurant business. In 1926 he was hired by Herb Somborn who had the idea of developing a chain of restaurants. That idea was carried to fruition when he opened the first Brown Derby in 1927 on Wilshire Boulevard. That was followed by another on North Vine near Hollywood Boulevard and still another in Beverly Hills.

Somborn died in 1934 leaving 25% of the stock to Cobb who quickly made his name known in Los Angeles. He was married to actress Gail Patrick by this time and was friendly with many movie people. Cobb had always been a baseball fan, and when the Stars became available he was most interested.

Cobb did not have the funds to own the entire club. What he wanted to do was to sell small blocks of stock to Hollywood luminaries, no more than 5000 shares each. This would provide the club with operating capital and at the same time enable Cobb to retain control.

When the stockholders list was announced in January 1939, some of the brightest stars of filmdom were included—among them Gary Cooper, George Raft, Robert Taylor, Cecil B. DeMille, Barbara Stanwyck, Bing Crosby and William Powell. The list of stars gave the club a Hollywood identity that it would always have and created an aura of glamour that was completely unlike anything the PCL had previously known.

In February Cobb announced that Oscar Reichow had been hired as business manager of the club. Reichow had recently resigned from a similar position with the Angels. He had originally been a Chicago sportswriter but came West in 1921 to work with the Angels. He was the secretary and general manager of the Los Angeles club and was best known as the first full time radio announcer of Angel games. Problems had developed between Reichow and Dave Fleming during the 1938 season, and Oscar was eased out of any real responsibility with the club. His hiring further enhanced the Hollywood organization. Reichow would serve the Stars until his death during the 1950 season.

The many changes during the off season created an atmosphere of enthusiasm when the Stars assembled at Santa Monica for spring training. The club had developed a working agreement with Bellingham of the Western International League in 1938 and this spring the first crop was harvested – pitchers Rugger Ardizoia and Bill Fleming, outfielders Jim Tyack and George Mandish, and catcher Cliff Dapper. All of these youngsters impressed during the training period and they would play important roles with the Stars that year.

Other new players that spring were not as fresh. Second baseman Chalmers "Bill" Cissell had been acquired from Jersey City during the winter. He had spent nine years in the major leagues after his purchase by the White Sox from Portland in 1927. Cissell had not lived up to expectations, partly because of his own habits, but at thirty-five he was still a good ball player, both in the field and at the bat. Cissell led the 1939 Stars in runs batted in with 83 and was the club's most valuable player that year.

Outfielder Spencer Harris was purchased from San Diego in January. A stocky left handed hitter who specialized in hitting line drives between first and second base, Harris was one of the all time great minor league players. In a career that spanned twenty-eight years Harris had a lifetime .318 average. His greatest years were spent at Minneapolis where he played eight years during the 30's. Spencer was thirty-eight when he joined the Stars, but he was still a fine hitter. In 138 games as the Stars' right fielder Harris hit .339 to lead Hollywood in that department.

The greatest of all, however, was the immortal Babe Herman. He was purchased from Jersey City during the winter meetings in an attempt to strengthen the club's batting attack. The Babe was thirty-five years old, and as a long time Southern California resident, he was glad to be coming home. Not so glad, however, as to accept the first contract offered him. He refused to budge all spring, finally coming to terms on March 31, the day before the season opened.

What can be said about Babe Herman that hasn't already been written? A hitter with possibly the greatest swing ever, Herman compiled a .324 average in twelve National League seasons. His .393 average in 1930 is still the all time Dodger standard, but he also enjoyed marks of .381 and .340 with Brooklyn. Originally a first baseman, the Babe was converted into an outfielder in 1928 and to be char- itable, he was not very good. But through hard work and hours of practice he became a very capable right fielder.

The Babe was a shrewd man with a dollar and usually commanded a good salary as a major leaguer. His 1939 contract called for $10,000, a pretty good sum for the minor leagues in those days. He eventually acquired stock in the Hollywood club but had it registered in the name of his sister to avoid any problems. When Herman went back to Brooklyn in 1945, he sold the stock to George Young, at a nice profit.

The Babe loved batting practice and could stay in the cage for hours. But he didn't always need the work. In 1939 after missing all of spring training, he was inserted in the Stars' opening day lineup at Los Angeles and hit the first pitch he saw that year into the Wrigley Field bleachers.

As these words are written, Babe has missed out on the Baseball Hall of Fame once again. What an injustice! But as he says, "Someday I'll be there."

The Stars opened at Los Angeles in 1939 and then were scheduled for their first home series against Portland the second week in April. But the new Gilmore Field would not be ready for a month, and the Stars were forced to play at Gilmore Stadium. An oval shaped arena designed for football and midget auto racing, Gilmore Stadium was in no way equipped to stage a baseball game. There were no dugouts; players sat on benches on the racing track. Right field was only 270 feet from home plate. Drives that cleared the fence in that direction were good for only two bases. The track around the field was banked for the autos, making it difficult for the outfielders. In the seven game series there were fifteen home runs hit by the Beavers and Stars. Never again would baseball be played at the Stadium.

The long awaited home opener at Gilmore Field finally took place on May 2, and a gala event it was indeed. Gail Patrick threw out the first ball to catcher Joe E. Brown while Jane Withers batted. Other celebrities at the opener were Jack Benny, Al Jolson, Bing Crosby, Martha Raye and Rudy Vallee. The house was packed; well over 12,000 were present. Cobb had placed a large paper *mache* star behind each position in the field and had the players behind. On a given signal the players leaped through the stars and on to the playing field. Only in Hollywood! Then the Stars proceeded to lose to the Seattle Rainiers 8-5.

The 1939 Stars were improved over the previous year, finishing in sixth place. The club played .500 ball through the first six weeks of the season as Herman and Puccinelli provided more sock than the 1938 team had displayed. but a decline set in during the last two weeks of May and the club sagged to sixth place. The Stars dropped into the cellar in July for a month, then rallied in August to end up one game behind the fifth place Padres.

The infield was a problem all season long. Herman opened at first base and he did all that was expected of him until July 1, when a pitch thrown by the Angels' Ray Prim broke his wrist. The Babe had 13 home runs at that point, including a towering 420 foot shot over the right field wall at Seals Stadium, one of the longest balls ever hit in San Francisco. Cobb purchased Len Gabrielson from Baltimore as a replacement. The long time PCL first sacker was adequate, but he posted only one home run in his 86 games.

Shortstop and third base were also troublesome. Joe

Hoover, a youngster from Pomona, opened the season at shortstop and played there most of the year. A utility man in 1937, Hoover showed a great deal of promise. But he was very inconsistent in the field, averaging almost an error every two games. Hoover could cover more ground than most shortstops, but he cost the club a number of games through his erratic play. Killefer sat him down periodically and played Jockey Morehouse, Tim Marble and Rod Dedeaux. Of the three Morehouse was the most effective and batted a solid .302 while he was in there.

The opening day third baseman was Harl Maggart, down from the Boston Bees, and he played there during the first month with occasional appearances by rookie Marble. Then on May 24 the Stars acquired Bob Kahle from the Bees and sent Maggart to Oklahoma City. It was one of the best transactions that Hollywood ever made. Kahle took over the post and remained there through 1942.

Bob Kahle had been an outstanding high school athlete and turned down a basketball scholarship to Indiana University to sign with the Indianapolis Indians in 1934. After a .304 season under Killefer there in 1937 Kahle was drafted by the Boston Bees. He would probably have made the grade in 1938 but suffered an arm injury which virtually incapacitated him. The arm seemed no better in the spring of 1939 and the Bees gave up on him, sending him first to Newark and then to Hollywood. Bob didn't have a very good season in 1939, hitting only .247, but towards the end of the season his arm had recovered and his hitting began to improve.

The pitching staff was sparked by young Rugger Ardizoia, who won his first eight games and finished with a fine 14-9 record, although only nineteen. The handsome San Franciscan had a fine fast ball and a fiery temper which frequently caused him to lose his composure on the mound. But he was an outstanding prospect and would fetch big money in the player market.

Bill Fleming, another Bellingham alumnus, was almost as good. He finished 12-16 and led the club with four shutouts including two 1-0 decisions over the Padres in a June series. Fleming was frequently victimized by lack of support and lost a number of close games.

Other new young faces were Johnny Bittner, a fugitive from the Yankee chain, and Bob Muncrief, on option from the Browns. They both had their moments; Bittner finished 13-14 and Muncrief 11-11. Wayne Osborne was the Twinks' workhorse at 16-17.

The club might have jumped into the first division had Lou Tost lived up to his 1938 performance. The left hander had been sold to the Browns on a conditional basis, but was returned to Hollywood in April. He lost his first seven decisions and finished with a disappointing 5-10 record.

In August Wade Killefer was informed that he would not be retained as manager in 1940. He had already been eased out of his business manager position when Oscar Reichow joined the club, and now it appeared that Cobb wanted his own man in charge. There were also rumors afoot that Hollywood would be affiliated with Detroit in 1940, and the Stars wanted to leave the position open so that the Tigers could aid in the selection.

The 1939 Stars were an interesting club, although not of first division caliber. With a mixture of veterans and youngsters they provided good entertainment. Over 265,000 fans paid their way into Friendly Gilmore Field in 1939, and Cobb was very satisfied. Hopes were high for 1940.

1939 STANDINGS

	W	L	PCT.
Seattle	101	73	.580
San Francisco	97	78	.554
Los Angeles	97	79	.551
Sacramento	88	88	.500
San Diego	83	93	.472
HOLLYWOOD	82	94	.466
Oakland	78	98	.443
Portland	75	98	.434

Sacramento won the President's Cup in playoffs.

The 1940 Stars

Front Row – Roy House, Bill Skelley, George Mandish, Frank Morehouse, Bob Kahle.

Second Row – Frenchy Uhalt, Babe Herman, Rugger Ardizoia, Bill Sweeney, Johnny Bittner, Charlie Moncrief, Rupert Thompson, Bill Matheson.

Third Row – Fred Gay, Bill Cissell, Vince Monzo, Hi Bithorn, Paul Smith, Don Wolin, Bill Fleming, Wayne Osborne, Joe Hoover, Lou Tost, Jim Hill.

1940 – HIGH HOPES AND DISAPPOINTMENTS

THE SEASON OF 1940 WAS VERY DISAPPOINTING for Hollywood. The club expected to be a contender for the championship but finished sixth. After a good start that saw the Stars in the first division through the first two months of the season, the Stars slumped in early June and never emerged from the second division for the rest of the year.

In retrospect it does not seem reasonable to have expected the Twinks to do better than they did. The defense had been rather poor in 1939 and did not really improve in 1940. The offense lacked punch with only 46 home runs hit all year. The combination placed a heavy burden on the pitchers who responded well but were soon weighted down by the other inconsistencies.

The biggest blow to Hollywood hopes was the failure of the working agreement with Detroit to materialize. Cobb thought he had the terms and conditions well resolved at the winter meetings of 1939. But then in January 1940 the Tiger minor league system was decimated when Commissioner Landis declared 91 Detroit farm hands to be free agents as a result of various irregularities in the handling of the player contracts. The arrangement with Hollywood was quickly terminated. There would be no help from the Tigers that year.

The failure of the working agreement was a bitter blow to Bob Cobb. He wanted so desperately to field a winning club in Hollywood. But by 1940 the days of the successful independent minor league owner were numbered. Chain store baseball was becoming more common, even in the PCL where Los Angeles and Sacramento were owned by major league clubs. Emil Sick had developed a strong franchise in Seattle, but he was a far wealthier man than Bob Cobb and was willing to spend for talent. San Diego had a limited agreement with the Red Sox which kept the Padres competitive. Oakland, San Francisco, Portland and Hollywood were left to struggle as well as they could. For the next several years the Stars would be just shy of a pennant contending club.

The Stars had no manager after Killefer had been released at the end of 1939, and it was generally thought the Tigers would provide one. Now the club had to hire its own. The appointment of Bill Sweeney proved to be popular. Big Bill had been acquired from Portland where he had been the playing manager in 1936, driving that Beaver club to a pennant. He was near the end of his fine career as a slugging first baseman, but Reichow especially thought Sweeney could add some sock to the lineup. He was a natural choice for the manager's job. Well liked by players and fans alike, he had a reputation for getting the most out of players. Unfortunately, he did not have the benefit of an abundance of talent while he was the Hollywood skipper.

The Stars strengthened their pitching during the off season when they sold their fine young pitcher, Rugger Ardizoia, to the Yankees for 1941 delivery. In addition to cash New York transferred three pitchers to Hollywood – Ivy Paul Andrews, Hi Bithorn and Fred Gay. Andrews, a major league veteran on the way down, did not last long at Gilmore, but Bithorn and Gay both made fine contributions to the Stars, although not in 1940.

Outfielder Rupert Thompson was purchased from the Browns to strengthen the outfield. Tommy had enjoyed a fine season at San Diego in 1937 before going to the major leagues for two years and much was expected of him. However, he was a dismal failure at Hollywood, hitting an anemic .210 with only 5 home runs. Sweeney played Thompson in 151 games but frequently benched him as he tried Bill Matheson and George Mandish in the left field spot. Eventually, veteran Jack Rothrock, signed in July after his release by the Angels, settled in the position. The club seemed at its best when that former member of the Gas House Gang Cardinals was in the lineup.

The infield, which had been woefully unsettled during 1939, seemed destined for more of the same during April and May as Sweeney experimented with youngsters Bill Skelley, Don Wolin and Sig Gryska at shortstop. Finally in mid-May he restored Joe Hoover to the lineup. It was one of the best moves Sweeney made that year. Hoover had been a disaster at shortstop in 1939, but he was a completely different player this year. He covered as much ground as any shortstop in the league, and his arm, which had been a positive menace to box seat patrons, was almost flawless. Hoover hit .250 in 1940, a considerable drop from the year before, but he was much more valuable to the club.

Bob Kahle reigned supreme at third and showed his real talents by hitting .312 to lead the Stars. A line drive hitter, Bob drove in 83 runs to lead the club in that respect also. He was selected as the Hollywood Most Valuable Player that year. Bob was sold to the Philadelphia Athletics at the close of the season.

Young Cliff Dapper had been a catching prize in 1939, hitting .316 in 88 games and handling the catcher's position with all the aplomb of a veteran. He was the starting catcher ahead of Bill Brenzel when the season opened but broke his thumb during the first week of the season and missed six weeks of action. When he returned he seemed to have lost his batting eye, and his inexperience behind the plate began to show. Brenzel was also injured during this period and the club signed Vince Monzo to help out, after he had been released by Portland. Dapper slumped to

.249 in 79 games while Brenzel hit a strong .294. The two shared the catching with Monzo filling as needed.

Babe Herman had a fine year after starting off very slowly, hitting .307 and leading the club with 9 home runs. The Stars suffered from a total lack of power that year, hitting only 46 home runs. It was the lowest total ever achieved by a Hollywood team.

Pitching was the strong suit of the 1940 Stars. The club boasted of five pitchers who won 10 or more games and the won-loss records could have easily been better with more support in the field and at bat. Bill Fleming was the leader of the staff with a 17-12 record. His sparkling ERA of 2.77 was one of the league's best, and he lost several one run games which could have easily gone the other way. Fleming was sold to the Red Sox in August.

Ardizoia was not as effective as he had been in 1939. The hard throwing right hander finished 14-20 with a 4.09 ERA. Once again he led the Stars in strikeouts and walks. He was helpless against the Padres, who decisioned him in five straight close games.

Wayne Osborne was the club's big winner with 18 victories. He won his first five decisions but then dropped back to finish 18-17. Johnny Bittner pitched several nice games to finish 10-9. He won four one run victories from the hated Angels.

Bithorn was 10-17. The Puerto Rican right hander had a world of stuff but like most the staff that year, pitched in hard luck. Freddie Gay, used both as a starter and reliever, was 6-6 while Lou Tost was 4-6, primarily in relief roles.

The pitchers showed a lot of promise and with a reasonable hitting attack would have produced many more victories. Cobb and Reichow were determined to do something about the offense for 1941.

1940 STANDINGS

	W	L	PCT.
Seattle	112	66	.629
Los Angeles	102	75	.576
Oakland	94	84	.528
San Diego	92	85	.520
Sacramento	90	88	.506
HOLLYWOOD	84	94	.472
San Francisco	81	97	.455
Portland	56	122	.315

Seattle won the President's Cup in the playoffs.

Bill Sweeney and a group of his Stars with actress Gail Patrick, Mrs. Bob Cobb in private life. Note the dark blue Hollywood uniforms worn by the Stars during the 1941 season.

1941 – A FIRST DIVISION CLUB

THE STARS FINALLY BROKE INTO THE FIRST division in 1941, finishing in fourth place. It was not a very impressive club, finishing six games below .500 and 20 games behind the first place Seattle Rainiers. Nevertheless, this was the best aggregation to represent Hollywood since Bill Lane's 1934 team. Both Vic Collins and Bob Cobb were immensely pleased with the Stars' performance, especially so since the arch rival Angels finished well behind Hollywood in seventh place.

An improved offense led to the first division finish. The club finished second in batting with a .280 team average and scored more runs than anyone else in the league. Babe Herman hit .346 as a part time first baseman and pinch hitter, while Bob Kahle hit .319 and Johnny Barrett .313 to lead the regulars. Except for Joe Hoover at .235 everyone in the starting lineup hit .280 or better.

Barrett was one of several new players imported by Hollywood that spring. He and pitcher Frank Dasso had been assigned to the Stars by the Red Sox as part of the Fleming deal. A fleet footed left handed hitter, Barrett stole 24 bases that summer while holding down the right field position most of the time. Dasso was a hard throwing sidearmer who had control problems. He was somewhat ineffective until June when new coach Johnny Bassler

113

changed his delivery to an overhand motion. Dasso was much better after that and won 15 games.

Other new players that spring were infielder Ham Schulte, outfielders Johnny Dickshot and Harry Rosenberg, and pitcher Roy Joiner. Schulte had been procured from the Phillies where he had been that club's second baseman in 1940, and he assumed the same role with the Stars. A fine competitor, Schulte hit .280 in 1941 and was voted the club's Most Valuable Player. Dickshot and Joiner came from Jersey City via the New York Giants. A Lithuanian from Waukegan, Illinois, Dickshot was the Hollywood left fielder. Rosenberg had been obtained from Portland in a trade for the disappointing Rupert Thompson. Rosenberg was expected to add more hitting strength, and while he hit a satisfactory .286, he had only one home run in 120 games.

Third base was open throughout spring training, but Bob Kahle was returned by Philadelphia the day before the season opened to fill the gap. Kahle's return was peculiar, to say the least. He had enjoyed a fine spring and had seemingly won the A's third base job when it was announced that he was being returned to Hollywood. The purchase price was said to be more than the Athletics could afford. Whether this was true or not is open to question. Kahle would have been eligible for the draft in 1940, but he was "sold" to Philadelphia just prior to that annual event. When he was returned to Hollywood, the club had effectively circumvented the intent of the draft and could subsequently sell him at a higher price. Kahle enjoyed another fine season with the Stars but would never again receive a chance to play in the majors.

The club started out well but suffered through a ten game losing streak, falling into sixth place in mid June. The Stars then rallied back to over .500 in July and remained at that level through early September. They remained a solid fourth through this period and had hopes of finishing higher but an eight game losing streak at San Francisco pricked that bubble. The club then resumed its .500 pace until losing its last six games. In spite of that slump the Stars finished comfortably ahead of San Francisco and Oakland, who tied for fifth place.

The 1941 PCL pennant race was dominated by Seattle, Sacramento and San Diego with the other clubs well behind their level. Hollywood was easily the best of the rest and proved it in September by taking four games from Sacramento when the Solons needed every victory and then knocking off the Padres in two games to eliminate that club. The Stars were a tough club at Gilmore Field in 1941 with a record of 49-36 in those friendly confines but they were a bad road team. Sacramento was a graveyard for Hollywood hopes as the Stars lost all ten games played at Cardinal Field.

Hollywood participated in the championship playoffs for the first time in 1941, but unfortunately the club was required to go against the first place Seattle Rainiers, a much better ball club. The Stars made a contest out of the series through four games but then superior pitching by Ed Cole and Kewpie Barrett resulted in two Seattle victories by identical 2-0 scores.

There was much to be satisfied with in 1941. The infield was very solid with the exception of first base. It always seemed in those days that the Stars had one troublesome position, and in 1941 it was first base. Herman and Sweeney split time there in the early season, but in these late stages of their careers, neither was very agile. An infielder had to be right on target with his throw to be sure that it would be caught. Both the Babe and the Irishman were injured in early June, and young Bill Gray, an ex-UCLA star, was recalled from Santa Barbara in the California League. Gray had played during the dog days of August and September, 1940 and was not impressive, but he was much improved this year both in the field and at bat. In 90 games Gray hit .283.

Cliff Dapper was the first string catcher and rebounded back to his 1939 form. Still a youngster at twenty-one, Dapper hit .277 in 125 games and led the PCL with 91 assists. Coach Johnny Bassler worked long hours with him and improved both his catching techniques as well as his hitting. Dapper may well have been the best catcher in the league that year. The Washington High graduate was selected by Brooklyn in the 1941 major league draft and would probably have enjoyed a fine major league career had World War II not intervened. Returning to Brooklyn after years of service, he found his path to major league success blocked by Gil Hodges and Bruce Edwards and spent most of his remaining career in the minor leagues.

The pitching was led by Hi Bithorn and Lou Tost. Bithorn had not been successful in 1940, partly because of a nagging arm problem. But with the miseries gone in 1941 he showed a fine fast ball and was the Stars' best pitcher. He finished 17-15 with a 3.59 ERA and enjoyed a stretch during July and August when he won seven consecutive starts. Bithorn was drafted by the Cubs at the close of 1941 and spent two excellent years in Chicago before the military called. His life was cut short under mysterious circumstances in Mexico in 1952. He was only thirty-four years old at the time of his death.

Tost was the club's workhorse in 1941 with 243 innings pitched, both as a starter and reliever. His record was 13-10, and he was sold to the Boston Braves for 1942 delivery. Freddie Gay pitched well at times and was the Stars' ERA leader at 3.31. Johnny Bittner and Wayne Osborne were steady at 12-14 and 12-12, respectively, while Pappy Joiner had a miserable 2-12 record. Dasso was the club's most spectacular pitcher, but his lack of control cost him several games he could have won. Frank threw a one-hitter at Oakland in August, winning 1-0 when he walked with the bases loaded to drive in the only run.

By 1941 the Stars had become an integral part of the the Hollywood scene. The club had fine sense of public relations. The appearance of movie celebrities at friendly Gilmore Field was widely noted, and Bob Cobb made every effort to identify the ball club with the movie industry. But there were other factors. The concessions were outstanding. The Stars had hired Danny Goodman from the Yankee farm at Newark to run this aspect of the business, and he did a fine job. The refreshments were first rate, and the score cards were of major league quality. Radio was given an important role. Mike Frankovich and Joe Bolton handled the broadcasts, and in 1940 the Stars experimented with a new phenomenon – television.

The Stars appeared to be on the upgrade as 1941 closed. But then on December 7 the Japanese struck at Pearl Harbor, and the United States was plunged into war. No one knew whether there would be any baseball at all in 1942.

1941 STANDINGS

	W	L	PCT.
Seattle	104	70	.598
Sacramento	102	75	.576
San Diego	101	76	.571
HOLLYWOOD	85	91	.483
San Francisco	81	95	.460
Oakland	81	95	.460
Los Angeles	72	98	.424
Portland	71	97	.423

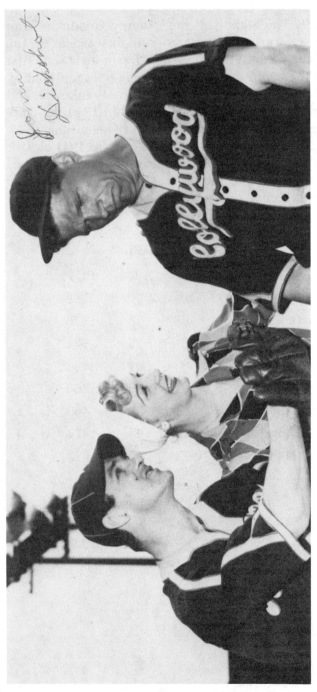

Johnny Dickshot looks very unhappy as actress Martha Scott and an unidentified studio man pose in a publicity shot.

The 1942 Stars

Front Row – Bill Brenzel, Bill Atwood, Eddie Erautt, Fred Gay, "Ham" Schulte, Del Young.
Second Row – Babe Herman, Joe Hoover, Frank Kalin, Oscar Vitt, Bill Garbe, Charlie Root, Frenchy Uhalt.
Third Row – Trainer Doc Meikle, Wayne Osborne, Johnny Dickshot, Manny Perez, Ed Weiland, Bob Kahle, Pappy Joiner, Jack Devincenzi.

1942 – VITT RETURNS

THE 1942 SEASON DID NOT BEGIN ON A VERY positive note. There was grave doubt during December and January that another baseball season would be allowed to begin. But on January 14, 1942 President Roosevelt gave his approval for the continuation of Organized Baseball in his famous "green light" letter to Judge Landis.

Of course, baseball would have to adjust its procedures to the war effort, and there would be no favoritism shown to the players. But the President thought that the continuation of baseball would be important for the nation's morale.

The coastal regions were under the jurisdiction of the armed services command, leaving the PCL in a very precarious position. All during December and the early months of 1942 the threat of Japanese invasion was considered a very real possibility. But as the danger subsided, it was decided by the PCL directors that spring training should begin as usual. Army approval for the 1942 season was officially given on March 24 by Lieutenant General John Dewitt of the 4th Army Command. The only stipulation was that night crowds would not be allowed to exceed the 1941 average – which in Hollywood's case meant no more than 3,423 spectators. Later in the year the Army rescinded its permission for night ball, effective August 20.

The edict continued in effect for the 1943 season.

Training operated as usual for the PCL clubs once the uncertainty had been removed. During that first wartime season the Stars were not adversely affected by the draft. First baseman Bill Gray, who joined the Army in February, was the first Twink called to the colors. As the war deepened, more and more players would be called into the service. But in 1942 manpower was not a problem.

The Stars had a new field boss in 1942. The popular Bill Sweeney was released by Cobb at the close of the 1941 season. The usual puffery was given by Hollywood management about a change of managers being beneficial to all. But nobody believed it. Sweeney didn't have the ballplayers to be any more successful than he was, but he was well liked by his players and the Hollywood fans. The dismissal proved to be a tactical mistake for Cobb. Sweeney signed as a coach for the Angels in 1942, then took over as Los Angeles manager in 1943. All he did was win two PCL championships in his first two years as Seraph manager. Sweeney made sure the Stars remembered him; the Angels took 42 of the 60 games played between the teams in those years.

The new Hollywood manager was Oscar Vitt. Vitt was extremely successful during his long tenure as boss of the Stars during the Bill Lane days, and it was hoped that Oscar would be able to duplicate his earlier results. But it didn't turn out that way. Vitt had seen his major league managerial career shortened when he became involved in the famous "Cry Baby" Indians controversy in 1940. A group of the Cleveland players had demanded that Vitt be fired, that the club couldn't win with Oscar at the helm. Cleveland President Alva Bradley refused to do so but the story became public knowledge, and the Cleveland players were ridiculed for the rest of the season. The Indians finished in second place after squandering an early lead, and Vitt was let go at the end of the season. He managed Portland in 1941 without success and was eager to vindicate himself in Hollywood in 1942.

The Stars were not impressive in spring training, and no one except Vitt thought that Hollywood would do well. New players included catcher Bill Atwood from the Phillies and outfielder Frank Kalin from St. Paul. Kalin had a fine season, hitting .304 while Atwood handled the catching chores along with Bill Brenzel.

The pitching looked very weak in the spring. Johnny Bittner was the most impressive but it was feared that he would soon be called into the Army so Vitt couldn't count on him. Johnny remained until July before enlisting in the Navy. He was enjoyed his best season with the Stars and was 13-9 with a fine ERA of 2.48 when he left for the service. The Stars got a lucky break when they signed the ancient Charlie Root. The forty-two year old Hollister resident had spent sixteen successful years with the Chicago Cubs, who had released him in December. Root is primarily remembered for his role in the famous home run called by Babe Ruth in the 1932 World Series. This is unfortunate. Root was one of the best pitchers in the National League during his day. He won 201 games for the Cubs and was the bulwark of their pitching staff during years when they were a prime pennant contender. At this stage of his career Root couldn't perform as he had in the past. Nevertheless, the veteran started fast, winning seven of his first eight decisions and managed to pitch 215 innings.

Otherwise, the club was virtually the same as the 1941 version. Dickshot was moved to right field while Kalin took over in left. Young Bill Garbe took over first base and although a pretty good fielder, he didn't impress at the plate, hitting .265 with only 2 home runs. Later, Charlie Sylvester spent some time there while the ageless Babe Herman saw action in 35 games. By this time the Babe's primary role was that of pinch hitter, and he was one of the league's best.

The Stars played at the .500 level in April but experienced a bad May to fall into seventh by the end of the month. They stayed there for the remainder of the season, only occasionally mounting a threat to the sixth place Oaks. Eventually the club came to rest with only 75 wins and a .421 percentage. It was the worst Hollywood club up to that time.

The infield, which had sparkled in 1941, fell apart in 1942. Second baseman Ham Schulte had a terrible year, both at bat and in the field. He wasn't turning the double play as he did in 1941, and his batting average dropped to .247. The Stars shipped him to Oakland in August, and utility infielder Del Young played the position for the rest of the year.

Joe Hoover had a fine season at the plate, hitting .327, but he suffered a relapse in the field. Joe made a number of spectacular plays but committed frequent errors on easy chances. Bob Kahle suffered a torn cartilege in his side which sidelined him for a time, and he suffered an off year, hitting only .262.

The outfield was not up to expectations as Dickshot seemed out of position in right field and misplayed a number of balls. Uhalt had slowed down in center field and didn't cover the ground he once did.

The pitching staff performed much better than expected. In addition to Root and Bittner young Manny Perez pitched quite well as did the veteran Pappy Joiner. Perez had been brought up from Santa Barbara, and he showed that the PCL hitters didn't frighten him. In 41 appearances the Bakersfield native won 14 games and posted six shutouts to go with a fine 3.33 ERA. Joiner pitched well through July but then slumped to 12-18. Freddy Gay was the club's hard luck pitcher. He finished 8-19 but was the victim of some exceptionally shabby defensive support and was also the loser of six shutouts. Walter "Whitey" Hilcher was 5-9 after being obtained from Portland in a mid season trade for Wayne Osborne.

The surprise of the season was the veteran Bill Thomas. This rather enigmatic man won 383 games in his career, all of which was spent in the minor leagues. He had been in the PCL since 1937 with Seattle, Portland and San Diego.

He had a creditable 17-15 record with the Padres in 1941, but when he got off to a terrible start in 1942, San Diego released him in June. The Stars signed him on June 18 for relief work, but when Whitey Hilcher failed as a starter, Vitt used Thomas in his place. A sidearmer with a good curve ball, Thomas relied on his control to be effective. He won six straight during August and finished 9-5 with a 1.70 ERA, the lowest ever by a Hollywood regular starter. Only Red Munger's 1.85 in 1955 came close to Thomas' mark. It was a remarkable record, considering Thomas was 0-9 when he joined the Stars.

The season ended in gloomy fashion as the club merely went through the motions in September, losing fifteen of its last twenty games. Oscar Vitt was not the same manager he had been in his previous tour of duty in Hollywood. He sniped at the players, was critical of them in the press and seemed much less organized than previously. Perhaps the experience at Cleveland soured him. It was a foregone conclusion at season's end that he would not be back.

1942 STANDINGS

	W	L	PCT.
Sacramento	105	73	.596
Los Angeles	104	74	.584
Seattle	96	82	.531
San Diego	91	87	.511
San Francisco	88	90	.494
Oakland	85	92	.480
HOLLYWOOD	75	103	.421
Portland	67	110	.379

Seattle won the President's Cup in playoffs.

(Courtesy of Mr. Kahle)

Bob Kahle

1943 — CHARLIE ROOT GETS A CHANCE

THE WAR BEGAN TO HAVE A MUCH GREATER impact on the Stars in 1943. During the winter many of the Hollywood stalwarts were called to the colors — Bob Kahle, Freddie Gay, Manny Perez, Bill Atwood, Bill Garbe — all would be gone for the duration. Veteran Bill Brenzel took a job in a shipyard, and it appeared that he would also be unavailable. When spring training began the Stars had only fifteen players under contract.

Although Vitt had been released at the close of 1942, Cobb took a long time to appoint Oscar's successor. Finally on March 2 Charlie Root was named as manager. The move seemed to be dictated by economy, for the club had to pay Vitt for the 1943 season. Root had never managed before, and although he was liked by the players and writers, many thought that the Stars were taking a chance.

Root certainly didn't have much to work with at the beginning. He had Johnny Dickshot back as the only returning regular. During the winter Frenchy Uhalt and Del Young had been traded to San Francisco for outfielder Brooks Holder. Holder had been with the Seals for seven years and was a pretty good outfielder, although just a fair hitter. Uhalt had slowed down somewhat in 1942, and Holder, who was four years younger, took over in center field. Long time PCL regular Marv Gudat was acquired

126

from Oakland, and he opened in right field. Gudat had enjoyed many fine years with the Angels, but he was now thirty-eight years old and was well past his prime. After Gudat's release in June, young Roy Younker up from the Western International League took over the position.

The infield opened with thirty-five year old Jimmy Adair at shortstop providing the only experience. The rest were kids. At first base was Butch Moran. Art Lilly was at second and Harry Clements at third. Moran was not exactly a youngster at twenty-eight, but his experience was class B or lower. Lilly was a recent USC graduate where he had captained the baseball team. Clements was up from class C ball.

The pitching was thin – only manager Root, Bill Thomas and Pappy Joiner were experienced. Younker and Jim Hill shared the catching while Bill Brenzel was away, but eventually Bill came back into the fold. Babe Herman was still available, his batting eye as keen as ever, even though he was pushing forty. Kenny Richardson and Tod Davis were available as substitutes. Richardson had been around and had been a rookie standout with the Angels back in 1936. Davis was a promising youngster out of El Monte High, who didn't hit much but was a fine fielder.

Hollywood wasn't much of a club on paper and the experts picked the Stars for seventh or lower. But the team played surprisingly well and finished in a tie for fifth place.

There was no pennant race in the PCL in 1943. The Angels spreadeagled the field and finished an amazing 21 games ahead of San Francisco. Los Angeles took an early lead and was never threatened.

The PCL acknowledged the effect of war demands by reducing the league schedule. The season opened on April 17, the latest date in history and lasted only twenty-two weeks. Night baseball was banned, a continuation of the policy established in August 1942.

The Stars played poorly during April and much of May. They then made two fortunate acquisitions by signing free agents Bill Knickerbocker and Cy Blanton. Knickerbocker had been released by the Yankees after a ten year American League career, but he still had a lot of good baseball left in him. He took over at second base, sending Art Lilly to the bench. The club played well while he was in the lineup and might have finished higher had Knickerbocker not suffered a broken foot at Portland on July 31. Kenny Richardson replaced him for the rest of the year.

Blanton had enjoyed several good years at Pittsburgh during the 30's, but he was one of those players who totally ignored training rules, and by 1943 this behavior pattern resulted in his release by the Phillies. The Stars signed him on May 9 and after losing his first three decision, Blanton won his first starting assignment over Oakland, 5-3 on June 10. He pitched several nice games after that, finishing 9-9 with a sparkling 2.70 ERA.

The club played at close to .500 ball through most of the balance of the season and made several moves to reach the first division but to no avail. The Stars played well against all of the clubs except Los Angeles and San Francisco. The Angels were especially devastating at Gilmore, winning nine of the eleven games played there. About the only noteworthy event in the series from the Stars' viewpoint was Pappy Joiner's 4-2 victory on May 20. It ended a twenty game Los Angeles winning streak, the longest in PCL annals.

The offensive star of the 1943 Stars was Johnny Dickshot. He had enjoyed good years in 1941 and 1942 but always had a tendency to take too many pitches with the result that he was often behind on the count. Not so in 1943. The Waukegan strongman came out swinging aggressively from the start, and for a long time the pitchers despaired of ever getting him out. He hit safely in the club's first 33 games and drove in many important runs. He hit over .400 until well into June and although he slumped a bit during August and September, Dickshot hit .352 for the year to finish second in the batting race to the Angels' Andy Pafko. Dickshot's fine year earned him another big league chance with the White Sox in 1944.

The other .300 hitting regular that year was third baseman Harry Clements who closed at .306. His performance was a distinct surprise. Clements was a fine fielder, leading the PCL third baseman in total chances and fielding. Butch Moran had a satisfactory year, hitting .284 and demonstrating the hustling qualities that made him one of Gilmore Field's all time fan favorites.

The pitching wasn't bad in 1943, especially after the addition of Cy Blanton. Manager Root showed some of his old cunning as he paced the club with a 15-5 record. In a season of little offense Charlie's ERA of 3.09 was only middling, but he was a fine dependable pitcher for the Stars that year. He pitched two 1-0 victories over Sacramento and won three games from the champion Angels.

Two young pitchers stood out that year. Nineteen year old Eddie Erautt had seen limited action in 1942 but in 1943 he became a regular starter. Although his 5-9 record was not impressive, he threw several low hit games before being drafted on July 3. In the last half of the season Ron Smith was the club's strong man out of the bullpen and had one stretch where he won seven straight decisions. Given a starting opportunity in August he did well in that role, too. Smith finished 12-9 and was the club's most effective pitcher in August and September.

Young Tod Davis did well after getting a chance to play regularly. After Jimmy Adair was released in early August, Davis stepped in for the balance of the year and was spectacular in the field. He boosted his hitting over thirty points during this period.

The 1943 Stars were obviously not of championship caliber but they played as well as they could and hustled throughout. In his first year as manager Charlie Root deserved much credit for taking the club as far as he did.

1943 STANDINGS

	W	L	PCT.
Los Angeles	110	45	.710
San Francisco	89	66	.574
Seattle	85	70	.548
Portland	79	76	.510
HOLLYWOOD	73	82	.471
Oakland	73	82	.471
San Diego	70	85	.455
Sacramento	41	114	.265

San Francisco won the President's Cup in playoffs.

(From the collection of Dick Dobbins)

Frank Kelleher

1944 – WARTIME BASEBALL

1944 SAW ONE OF THE CLOSEST PENNANT RACES
in PCL history and for the first time since the rebirth of
the franchise, the Stars were in the thick of the chase.
Although the club slumped over the last six weeks of the
year to finish in sixth place, it was a legitimate contender
before losing an important series to Los Angeles in mid
August. This was the best Hollywood team of the Cobb era
so far.

The Twinks were not as adversely affected by the war as
other PCL clubs. They opened the season with a pretty set
lineup. The only worrisome spot was at third base where
Harry Clements had received notice to take his Navy
physical. The pitching staff had been strengthened with
the addition of several free agents who had returned from
military service – Joe Mishasek, Alex Weldon and Johnny
Intlekofer. Mishasek had been declared a free agent from
Utica at the end of 1942 by Judge Landis just before going
into the Army. He received a medical discharge late in
1943, worked out with the Stars in the spring and earned a
contract. Weldon also had received a medical discharge.
He had seen limited duty with the Stars in 1942 before
enlisting. Intlekofer, at thirty-one the oldest of the trio, had
bounced around the minor leagues since leaving Notre
Dame in 1931 to sign with the White Sox. Johnny was to

prove valuable to the Stars as a spot starter. He excelled at winning those short seven inning games of the Sunday doubleheaders that were so common in those days.

The Stars opened at home behind Earl Escalante and won their first three games over Seattle. A Hollywood team had never opened that well. The club played at or slightly above the .500 mark through April and early May. The Twinks had an absolute hex over Oakland, and this served them well during the early going. They took fourteen of the first fifteen games from the Oaks and were in fourth place when May ended.

The race was exceptionally close. Portland and San Francisco took turns in first place, but the rest of the clubs were bunched tightly just behind the leaders. Only Sacramento seemed out of the race.

There was little offense in the league during early 1944, and the press complained about the quality of the baseballs. Fly balls seemed to die in the outfield even when well hit, and there were few home runs hit anywhere. The Stars did not connect for a four bagger at Gilmore until three weeks had passed, and the experience was repeated in other cities. Eventually the PCL admitted that the balls were of 1942 vintage and had been in storage, obviously affecting their performance. New baseballs were quickly discovered, and the hitting improved immediately.

The Stars made two important player transactions with Cincinnati during this period. In May they acquired outfielder Frank Kelleher from Syracuse on option from the Reds and then, on June 14, purchased third baseman Buck Fausett. Both were to play important roles in the Hollywood baseball scene during the next few years.

Of the two, Kelleher was by far the more important. He had been signed by the Yankees off the St. Mary's college campus in 1936 and had languished in their farm system for most of his career. He hit a resounding .348 with Akron in 1936 and as a result was promoted to Newark where he spent the next three years as a part time player. This may have hindered his development. The Yankees were loaded with minor league talent in those years, and Kelleher was never able to find a place to play, spending some time at third base as well as the outfield. He came into his own with the Bears in 1941, hitting 37 home runs to lead the International League and help Newark to the pennant. After a fast start in 1942, Kelleher was sold to the Reds.

This was Kelleher's chance to make the major leagues, but he failed to impress, hitting an anemic .182 in 38 games. Frank was sent to Syracuse in 1943 where he had a miserable year. When he was assigned to the Chiefs again in 1944, Kelleher balked. It would be a California team or nothing, he said. The Reds gave in and sent him to Hollywood on option.

A big rangy fellow, Kelleher had a nice easy swing that belied the power he packed. He joined the Stars on May 23 and made his presence felt immediately, driving in the winning run in the ninth inning of a 5-4 victory over Portland. Frank hit .500 in that first Gilmore series, and the faithful had a new hero. He would be one of the most popular players ever to don a Hollywood uniform.

Fausett had also been around and in recent years had turned to managing. In 1943 he had been the playing manager at Little Rock, where he managed the Travelers into second place in the Southern Association while hitting .362. That was impressive enough for the Reds to give him a trial, but he saw little action before the Stars bought him on June 14.

These two players strengthened the club immensely. The Stars now had a solid middle of the batting order with Butch Moran and Kenny Richardson having fine years. The pitching was surprisingly good. Ron Smith was a hard worker, both starting and relieving. Young Clint Hufford, out of Alhambra High School, sparkled in several appearances. Mishasek and Intlekofer did well while Escalante was inconsistent. The years appeared to be catching up to manager Charlie Root, who was restricting himself to infrequent appearances. Newt Kimball was purchased from the Phillies in June to strengthen the staff. He had been working in a defense plant in Santa Monica. The big right hander had been an Angel prospect in 1935 and had seen limited service in the majors with the Cubs, Dodgers and Phils before joining the Stars.

Only 5½ games behind and in third place at the beginning of August, the Stars surged into second place on August 12. The Angels, however, were the league's hot team. The Seraphs had played badly through most of the first half season but were now at their best and were moving far ahead. They were six games in front when the two clubs opened a series at Wrigley Field on August 22.

A 7-3 victory by Newt Kimball in relief of Cy Blanton in the first game of the series raised the Hollywood hopes, but that was to be the high point of the season for the Stars. The Angels turned on them with a vengeance, winning the next six games to drop the Stars eleven games behind in third place. That started a tailspin from which the Twinks were unable to recover. By Labor Day they were below .500 in fifth place. Then the Angels made sure that the Stars wouldn't threaten again, taking five of eight at Gilmore, in a series climaxed by Ray Prim's sixth win of the year over the Stars without a loss. A week later the season closed with Hollywood in sixth place. The Stars finished only four games out of second as Los Angeles breezed to its second straight championship behind Bill Sweeney.

Kelleher had a marvelous season and was the club's Most Valuable Player. This was probably the finest season of his career. He came within .00032 of a point of leading the PCL in batting, losing out to Oakland's Les Scarsella by that minute margin. Frank was the league leader in both home runs and runs batted in. His 29 circuit clouts were the most by a Gilmore Field based Hollywood player at that time as were his 121 runs batted in. For several weeks he was well ahead in the batting race but slumped along with the rest of the team in September to finish one hit behind the Oaks first baseman.

Butch Moran had a fine year, hitting .315 and driving in

many important runs. His pay was only about $350 a month in 1944 and when Butch thought he deserved a new contract in mid-season, business manager Oscar Reichow greeted him with a resounding "No!" So Butch did the only thing he could in those days before free agency – he went on a sit down strike. The club suspended him, and the chastized Moran was back after one day's absence. The incident didn't affect Moran's play as he always gave his best.

Shortstop Tod Davis showed remarkable improvement over his first year with the Stars and played in all of the club's 169 games. His play in the field was positively brilliant at times, and he improved his hitting to .248 with 77 runs batted in. Tod was called into the Navy shortly after the season ended.

The Stars batted .267 as a team, second only to the champion Angels, and scored a lot of runs. But the pitchers gave up more runs than any other PCL club, and that consigned the club to the second division once again. Charlie Root could have used one more solid starting pitcher. Ron Smith and Joe Mishasek were the club's most effective workers, at 15-11 and 16-10 respectively, while Earl Escalante pitched well at times but was bothered by wildness and posted a 10-15 record. Johnny Intlekofer had the club's best record, 11-6 with a fine 2.92 ERA. He pitched three shutouts, all of the seven inning variety.

Hollywood might have fared better had Cy Blanton joined the club at the beginning of the season instead of mid-July. His record was only 5-5, but he pitched several nice games. Charlie Root was not the great pitcher of past years, winning only three games.

The fans took to the 1944 Stars in fine fashion and turned out some 324,000 strong. This was the best Gilmore attendance yet. Better times appeared to be on the way.

1944 STANDINGS

	W	L	PCT.
Los Angeles	99	70	.586
Portland	87	82	.515
San Francisco	86	83	.509
Oakland	86	83	.509
Seattle	84	85	.497
HOLLYWOOD	83	86	.491
Sacramento	76	93	.450
San Diego	75	94	.444

San Francisco won the President's Cup in playoffs.

1945 – A STELLAR CELLAR

ALTHOUGH THE WAR WAS DRAWING TO A VIC-
torious close in 1945, baseball in general and the Stars in
particular suffered through a rather dismal season. The
War Department stepped up its demands on ballplayers,
reclassifying many former rejects as 1-A. Draft calls were
significantly higher than in the previous years, and most
clubs had to scramble for players. The resulting disorder
meant that many line ups contained players who would
not be playing in more peaceful times.

The Stars suffered their worst season ever, finishing in
last place for the only time in Hollywood history. The
Twinks fell into the basement on April 8 and did not
emerge for the balance of the season. The team finished
eighth in batting and fielding and scored fewer runs than
any other club in the league. Players came and went with
depressing regularity as new manager Buck Fausett tried
desperately to put a competitive team on the field.

In an unpopular move following the 1944 season Bob
Cobb sacked Charlie Root as manager. It appeared that he
was upset with the apparent collapse of the club during the
last six weeks of the season. Root quickly signed to manage
Columbus in the American Association.

The choice of Fausett was undoubtedly one of economy,
for Buck was counted upon to hold down the third base

138

position as well. At the beginning of spring training it looked as if he would be the only infield returnee from 1944. Tod Davis had joined the Navy while Butch Moran had received notice to take his Army physical. Kenny Richardson was a doubtful prospect as a result of an off-season auto accident. Fortunately for Hollywood Moran flunked his physical, and Richardson recovered faster than expected. The two were about the only offensive bright spots of the year.

Hollywood felt the sting of the draft more sharply in 1945 as Frank Kelleher, Clint Hufford, Earl Escalante and Ray Olsen were called into the service. Another familiar face was missing that year. Babe Herman decided to call it quits, electing to stay on his turkey ranch in the San Fernando Valley rather than suffer the rigors of another spring training. The Babe was approaching forty-two and felt it was time to stay home with his growing family.

Herman enjoyed some very productive years at Hollywood and his statistics are remarkable, considering that he was well into the sunset of his career and was hitting against an inferior base ball for three of his six years. His average in a Hollywood uniform was .325 and included season marks of .354 and .346. Twice, in 1941 and 1944, he was the nominal league leader. As a pinch hitter he was unsurpassed. During one eight game series in 1944 against the Angels the Babe drove in the winning run in three of the four Hollywood victories. Hollywood fans would miss him.

The Babe didn't stay in retirement very long. In early July the Brooklyn Dodgers, needing some hitting punch, purchased his contract from the Stars, and Herman joined Brooklyn on July 3. He managed a .265 average as a pinch hitter in spite of missing the entire training period.

The Stars' biggest weakness in 1945 was at shortstop. No fewer than seven players tried to fill the position. The club opened the season with the improbably named Jack Dempsey Smith, and he was followed at one time or another by Mike Chozen, Ralph Watson, Vern Reynolds,

John Cavalli, Hugh Willingham and Al Gonzales. Willingham was perhaps the best known. At thirty-six he had seen many years of service in the minor leagues and appeared briefly with the Phillies in 1931. But he averaged more than an error every two games, and the others were as bad.

The outfield was weak with only young Eddie Stewart showing any batting prowess. But he was called into the Navy in June after hitting .323 in 63 games. Brooks Holder was plagued by arm trouble and hit only .256. Veteran Les Powers took time out from his duties as Loyola University baseball coach to hit .287 as a part time outfielder.

The pitching was dreadful through most of the year. Only Joe Mishasek, Ron Smith and Newt Kimball posted respectable records. Mishasek won his first three games, struggled through a mid-season slump when he lost seven straight, then finished strong to close at 17-16. Smith was a hard worker, but wildness and a poor defense held him to 15-20. Kimball was the most effective pitcher and was one of the best pitchers in the league. He won 19 and missed out on a twenty game season when he lost to Oakland 4-2 on the last day of the season. Kimball threw four shutouts and would have had a much more impressive record had Portland and Seattle been more kind. Newt lost ten of eleven decisions to those clubs.

The Angels were almost as bad as the Stars in 1945, finishing in seventh place, only three games ahead of Hollywood. The season series between the two clubs was hotly contested all year, and the fans turned out in surprising numbers when the rivals got together. The fourteen games at Gilmore drew almost 76,000 fans, virtually one fourth of the entire season's attendance. Hollywood won the season series for the first time since 1941 with the high point being an 18-0 shutout pitched by Steve Le Gault in August.

What little hitting there was in 1945 was supplied by Moran, Richardson and Fausett. Butch had his best season in Hollywood, hitting .302 and setting a club record for doubles with 56. Richardson hit .301 and led the club with

14 homers. This led to his purchase by the Phillies at the close of the season. Fausett hit .315 and was the leader on the field as well as in the dugout.

As a promotional stunt, Fausett and manager Pepper Martin of the Padres opposed each other on the mound on August 25. Buck didn't do badly, either. He went the distance in losing 6-4 while giving up twelve hits. Pepper lasted only five innings but received credit for the win.

A total of forty players graced the Hollywood roster during that war weary season of 1945. Most are only memories now—John Rager, Hal Schimling, Neal Montank, John Grohavec among others. Spencer Harris appeared in a few games at the close of the season, while Lin Storti appeared briefly at second base. The veteran minor league star committed three errors in his first game and was soon on his way.

They all served in one way or another, those 1945 Hollywood Stars. The fans were coming out of wartime hibernation—362,000 passed through the Gilmore turnstiles. What they wanted to see was a competitive team. That would not be long in coming.

1945 STANDINGS

	W	L	PCT.
Portland	112	68	.622
Seattle	105	78	.574
Sacramento	95	85	.528
San Francisco	96	87	.525
Oakland	90	93	.492
San Diego	82	101	.448
Los Angeles	76	107	.413
HOLLYWOOD	73	110	.399

San Francisco won the Governor's Cup in playoffs.

(From the collection of Dick Dobbins)

Butch Moran

142

(From the collection of Dick Dobbins)

Tony Lupien

143

1946 – DYKES AT THE HELM

1946 PROVED TO BE A BANNER YEAR FOR THE Stars. For the first time since 1934 a Hollywood team won more than half its games. The Stars finished in third place, edging the Angels by one game in the standings. The fans were enchanted by this team and turned out 513,000 strong. That was the highest attendance for one season by a Hollywood team up to that time. The long gloomy period of the war seemed to have ended.

The club had more ballplayers at spring training than ever before as many returning servicemen were back for their old jobs. Frank Kalin, Bob Kahle, Fred Gay, Manny Perez and Johnny Bittner were prominent in camp. In addition the club had beefed itself up during the winter by acquiring Johnny Dickshot from the White Sox, infielder Woody Williams and catcher Al Unser from the Reds and first baseman Tony Lupien from the Phillies. Buck Fausett wondered what he was going to do with all his players.

The key to the season, however, was a new working agreement with Pittsburgh. For years Collins and Cobb had attempted to develop a relationship with the major leagues but had been unsuccessful in their quest. Under the new arrangement the Pirates agreed to send the Stars eight players in exchange for the right to purchase any two off the Hollywood roster at the end of the season. Hollis

Thurston also joined the Stars as a coach and scout.

The agreement was a harbinger of good things. The Stars had always been a team which had several good players but with one or two major weaknesses. Consequently, the club usually finished well back in the pack. Now the Pirates could plug any gap that occurred, and the club was notably improved.

The first delivery from Pittsburgh consisted of shortstop Huck Geary and pitcher Hank Gornicki, neither of whom was of much help. Later on the Pirates sent outfielders Culley Rikard and Tommy O'Brien and pitcher Art Cuccurullo on option, and pitcher Xavier Rescigno outright. These four players helped to form a good nucleus for the club, and the Stars looked extremely sharp in the spring.

1946 was the season that major league fever first struck the West. PCL president Pants Rowland petitioned the major leagues to recognize the league as a third major league just prior to the opening of training camp. Actually, all he was really after was freedom from the major league draft and the right to option players to the other Triple A leagues while still retaining title to them. After a few days of deliberation, the moguls denied the request. They did agree to take it under advisement at some time in the future. But as we now know, nothing was ever done in this regard. The idea was simply too revolutionary for the conservative baseball men to handle.

The Pacific Coast writers and fans were naturally very interested in the matter, and all summer long articles appeared in the papers, speculating on what could be done to bring major league baseball to the Coast. The general consensus was that the PCL should be given independent status for a five year period while it brought its ballparks to major league standards and improved the overall financial strength of the league. At the end of the period the PCL would become an equal partner with the American and National Leagues. It was doubtful that all of the present PCL cities would remain. Sacramento was too small to support a major league team and there was some question about Portland. Denver, Houston and Dallas were mentioned as possible replacements.

The concept was interesting but unrealistic. Major league baseball was a closed circle, and there was no way that the moguls were going to allow a group of Western upstarts to enter their exclusive club. Not until the Eastern owners became aware of the immense profits that could be made would they be interested in bringing major league baseball to the West. And as we know today, a different method was chosen – the shifting of established franchises.

Sports writers picked the Stars for second place in 1946. But the club started out slowly and was in fourth place after a month's play. The lineup was in a constant state of flux as Fausett tried to sort out his players. The opening day lineup saw Lupien, Williams, John Cavalli and Kahle in the infield with Dickshot, Rikard and Butch Moran as outfielders. By the end of April Kahle had been traded to Seattle for pitcher Paul Gregory, and Dickshot had been released to Milwaukee. The Kahle trade was very suspect. Bob was hitting over .300 when he left and hit a solid .287 for the year. He was a better fielder than Fausett and was six years younger. Could the manager's judgement have been somewhat biased?

Cavalli was not hitting, and he was replaced at shortstop when the Pirates sent Alf Anderson on April 27. The thirty-two year old Georgian had a brief trial with the Pirates before the war and had a good field – no hit reputation. But he was just what the Stars needed. Anderson played as well as any shortstop in the PCL that year and hit a solid .264.

Second base appeared to be in good hands with Woody Williams, but he broke his ankle at Seattle during the last week in April, leaving a gaping hole. Fortunately, the Stars were able to pick up Glen "Gabby" Stewart from Oakland. He was installed at second and was an immediate success. Stewart batted .280 in a Hollywood uniform while working well as Anderson's double play partner.

The pennant race was soon dominated by the San Francisco Seals and Oakland Oaks, who pulled far ahead of the rest of the league in a two team race. The Stars were mostly fourth and fifth, and this caused consternation in the Hollywood front office. Both Victor Ford Collins and Bob Cobb thought the team was better than that. Gradually, they began to hold Fausett responsible for the club's failure to do better, and soon daily rumors of Fausett's firing began to appear in the Los Angeles newspapers.

The club received additional strength in June when Frank Kelleher and Ed Stewart returned from the service, the Pirates sent pitcher Aldon Wilkie and the Phillies returned Kenny Richardson after his brief trial. Pitcher Frank Dasso was purchased from Cincinnati on June 10, giving Hollywood a great deal of pitching depth.

Hollywood moved into fourth place and remained there through July. A frequent spectator at Gilmore during this period was Jimmy Dykes, the recently deposed Chicago White Sox manager. He was well known in Southern California as a result of the many years spent by the Sox at their Pasadena spring training base, and the sportswriters were certain that he would become the new Stars manager.

Matters finally came to a head when Buck Fausett announced his resignation on August 4. He was needed in Albuquerque, he said, where Buck had a part interest in the ball club. The Hollywood management professed great surprise. "This announcement is a great shock to management," said Oscar Reichow. "We have no immediate plans. Nothing can be done until Vic Collins returns to the city." Buck had thought he would last until the end of the season, but on August 8 the club asked him to leave. The new manager was (surprise!) Jimmy Dykes.

Dykes is one of the legendary names of baseball. The long time third baseman of the Philadelphia Athletics during the 20's and early 30's, Dykes had turned to managing with the White Sox in 1934. The Sox were a poor bedraggled club in those days, but Jimmy turned in a masterful job as manager, finishing in the first division several times with very mediocre teams. He was let go by Chicago in May, 1946 after the Sox had been off to a rather miserable start. The Hollywood post was an interim position for Dykes, who was looking for a return to the major leagues.

The hiring of Dykes proved to be a real shot in the arm for the Stars. They won their first five games under Jimmy and were a solid fourth when August ended. They shot into third place by taking 12 of 13 games from Sacramento and Oakland, and though the Stars staggered a bit thereafter, they clinched third place with a 4-1 win over Seattle the day before the season ended, behind young Al Yaylian out of Fairfax High in Los Angeles.

The Stars were in the playoffs for the first time since 1941 and once again they did not fare so well, losing four straight games to the champion Seals. San Francisco pitching effectively stifled the Hollywood bats as the Stars scored only twelve runs in the series.

Offensive performance was at a premium in the PCL during 1946. There was a general lack of hitting and very little power. Only 478 home runs were hit during the entire season. The Stars led the league in hitting with a .261 mark and also were on top in home runs with 92. There was a great deal of controversy throughout the season over the quality of the baseballs used, and finally the PCL officials admitted that the 1946 ball was composed of inferior wartime materials. A better specimen was promised for the 1947 season.

Several Stars enjoyed fine years in spite of the poor quality of the baseball. Culley Rikard led the club with a .325 mark and was in contention for the batting crown until almost the last day, losing out to Harvey Storey of Portland who hit .326. Rikard was one of those unfortunate players who left his best years in the service. He was thirty-one in 1946 and although he spent a fruitful 1947 season in Pittsburgh hitting .287, he was back in the minors in 1948; too old, everyone said. Not true in 1946. Rikard played most of the time in center field where he showed he could handle virtually everything hit his way, hit with consistency and power and was an all around fine ballplayer.

Frank Kalin was right behind Rikard at .311 and was one of the two players selected by Pittsburgh at the close of the season. Tony Lupien was a fine first baseman and hit a solid .295. His 77 runs batted in paced the Stars in that department, and he also stole 43 bases, the best since Fred Haney was running the Hollywood bases.

Although Lupien had a fine year with the Stars, he was not altogether pleased to be in the PCL. Tony had been acquired from the Phillies prior to the beginning of spring training. As a returning serviceman he was entitled to a fair trial with Philadelphia for whom he had performed so well in 1944. His original inclination was to fight the demotion in the courts but, realizing that it could take years before the issue was resolved, accepted the sale to Hollywood.

The Hollywood home run leader in 1946 was Frank Kelleher, who socked 18 circuit clouts after joining the club in June. Frank hit .286 in 91 games with the club and played left field for most of the last two months of the season. Butch Moran, who had enjoyed a very hot start, saw little action after Dykes took over and was sold to Indianapolis at season's end.

The pitching staff was deep and strong as was necessary during this punchless year. Eddie Erautt was the ace of the staff. He was the first Hollywood twenty game winner since Joe Sullivan in 1934, finishing at 20-14. Erautt had a blistering fast ball which he used to good advantage, striking out 234 batters. That is the all-time Hollywood record and is a remarkable total for the era in which he pitched. He threw eight shutouts, another all-time Hollywood record, and had a fine 2.76 ERA. His won loss record could have been better, for he was the victim of five shutouts himself and lost six one run decisions. Erautt was sold to Cincinnati at the close of the season.

Other fine years were enjoyed by Frank Dasso at 12-5, Xavier Rescigno at 11-9 and Aldon Wilkie at 9-7. Dasso threw a one hitter on June 16 at San Diego in his first start with the club. Frank had a world of stuff that year, the best on the staff, according to Eddie Erautt. But he was never able to harness his skills and become a consistent winner in the major leagues.

Although the trade for Bob Kahle was unpopular, Paul Gregory did good work in relief as did Ron Smith. The club could have used one more consistent starter. Rescigno pitched well until July when he was sidelined with a sore arm. He was never effectively replaced, and his absence was costly.

The 1946 season was the most profitable that the PCL had experienced. All clubs drew very well with San Francisco setting an attendance record of 670,653 for the high minors that was not broken until 1982. Oakland, Los Angeles and Hollywood were not far behind. The league drew 3,718,716 as a whole, the highest up to that time. One important series between the Oaks and Seals at San Francisco in July drew 111,622, also a record. The two Los Angeles clubs exceeded one million paid with the Stars outdrawing the Angels by 12,000 fans.

The 1946 Stars were a fine club. They really did not come together until the last two months of the season what with all the personnel changes during the year. During that period, however, they were as good as any club in the league. Dykes was widely acclaimed for bringing the club to its full potential. Everyone was hopeful for more success in 1947.

1946 STANDINGS

	W	L	PCT.
San Francisco	115	68	.628
Oakland	111	72	.607
HOLLYWOOD	95	88	.519
Los Angeles	94	89	.514
Sacramento	94	92	.505
San Diego	78	108	.419
Seattle	74	109	.404
Portland	74	109	.404

San Francisco won the Governor's Cup in playoffs.

Gus Zernial

1947 – BACK IN THE SECOND DIVISION

AFTER THEIR FINE PLAY IN 1946, THE STARS were unable to show improvement the following year and fell back to sixth place. The club was never in contention for the championship, occupying the cellar for most of April and May and only once reaching as high as fifth place. The Hollywood performance was quite disappointing to Collins and Cobb, who had expected much better results.

Perhaps the biggest contributing factor to the club's slide was the loss of the working agreement with Pittsburgh. The Pirates were sold during the off-season to a group headed by Frank McKinney, a successful Indianapolis businessman. McKinney also owned the Indianapolis franchise in the American Association, and he informed Collins shortly after the Pittsburgh transaction was completed that the Indians would be the Pirates' top farm club in 1947.

The Stars were left in need of a major league connection, but they were able to secure a limited agreement with the White Sox during the winter meetings. Jimmy Dykes still had good relations with Chicago, and it was widely assumed that he had much to do with the arrangement.

The White Sox were not able to provide the Stars with much help. Although Chicago promised a number of players, only infielder Fred Vaughn and pitcher Al Hollingsworth were White Sox property on the spring training roster. Oscar Reichow scurried around for players to fill the tremendous void left by the recall of the Pirate farmhands and came up with a number of veterans – pitchers Joe Krakauskas and George Caster, infielders Don Ross and Carl Cox, and outfielder Al Libke. Later on the White Sox sent outfielders Jim Delsing and Andy Skurski, who joined the club just as the season opened.

This was Dykes' first full season as manager of the Stars. He had enjoyed good press relations in Chicago, and the same was true in Hollywood. The reporters found him easy to talk to and very honest in his evaluation of the club's prospects. The players enjoyed playing for him. Dykes ran the club with a firm hand but was not a martinet. He tried to instill a sense of discipline which was not always easy to do.

The Stars were not impressive during the spring. Pitching was the greatest weakness, and there was some question about the infield. Krakauskas, Xavier Rescigno, Frank Dasso and Ron Smith were the starters with George Caster and Clint Hufford available for spot duty. The season wasn't a month old before this rotation was shattered. Rescigno and Smith had arm problems while Dasso was ineffective after winning his first start, 3-1 at Sacramento. Caster was well past his prime and was shelled in most of his appearances. Hufford was in and out of the rotation after returning from service duty.

The infield was not up to the standard of the previous year. Although Tony Lupien was back and on the verge of his finest year, the other three positions were suspect. Woody Williams opened at second base after missing most of 1946, but he didn't hit and was soon shuttled to Indianapolis. His replacement was Fred Vaughn, who was a much better hitter but just average in the field. The opening day shortstop was Tod Davis, back from service. He was not nearly the ballplayer he had been in his earlier Hollywood stint. Davis was much more erratic and showed a great propensity for striking out. Carl Cox soon replaced him but was not better in the field although a stronger hitter. At third was Don Ross, a Pasadena resident, who had seen major league service with Detroit and Cleveland.

Although the Stars began badly, they soon demonstrated an ability to hit. This was the strongest offensive team to represent Hollywood since 1933. They broke out with a rash of base hits and had a power packed lineup from top to bottom. Lupien was enjoying an exceptional year with Frank Kelleher, Jim Delsing and Al Libke not far behind. But the pitchers were having difficulty maintaining the lead, and the Stars were involved in many high scoring games, in which they were frequently left on the short end.

As if the club needed more offensive help, the club strengthened itself on April 23 when outfielder Gus Zernial was acquired from Cleveland. "Ozark Ike," as he was called, was a remarkable find. He had been drafted by Hollywood from class B Burlington at the close of the 1946 season, but the Indians had also claimed him and as a major league team, had priority. When Gus couldn't make the Indian roster, he was optioned to Baltimore, but the alert Dykes pointed out that Hollywood had first claim on Zernial in the minors, and he was awarded to the Stars.

Zernial was twenty three years old and had enjoyed a fine year in the Carolina League in 1946 after three years of service. A big strong right handed hitter, Zernial would never win any plaudits for his fielding but he was a fine hitter. Gus joined the club on April 30 and had three hits in a 10-9 loss to San Diego. The next day he had three hits again as the Stars clobbered the Padres 16-4. Gus hit .487 in his first ten games with the club and for the balance of the year rotated between left and right field with Kelleher and Libke. He hit .344 in 120 games and was considered the rookie of the year in the PCL.

The Stars improved their pitching in May, acquiring Rugger Ardizoia from the Yankees, Ed Albosta from the White Sox and Pinky Woods from Pittsburgh. The club finally gave up on Frank Dasso, sending the fireballer to Sacramento for pitcher Hugh Orphan, a submarine ball pitcher. Dasso had probably the best stuff on the club but could never put it all together.

With the strengthened pitching the Stars began to play better and finally emerged from the cellar on June 4. They stayed in sixth through most of July and August and moved into a fifth place tie with Seattle on Labor Day but they settled back into sixth when the Rainiers took a doubleheader at Gilmore on September 17.

In spite of Hollywood's mediocre performance, the club was very entertaining and a box seat to a Stars' game was the toughest ticket in town to acquire. The Stars were tough at Gilmore, playing at a .543 pace, but they were an easy mark on the road. The club was especially ineffective at Oakland, winning only three of the fifteen games played at the Emeryville park.

Offensively, the club had no peer in 1947. Hollywood led the league with a .285 mark and crashing 113 home runs. The PCL as a whole was more offensive minded that year, but the Stars could out hit anybody. Dykes could put a team on the field that boasted six .300 hitters at any given time, and shortstop Carl Cox was over .300 for most of the year before dropping to .293. Zernial's .344 in 120 games was the high mark, but Lupien's .341 in 186 games was more impressive. Tony also belted 21 home runs to tie Frank Kelleher for the team lead, and his 110 runs batted in and 40 stolen bases were also the best on the club. The outfield was an all-.300 hitting aggregation as Kelleher, Jim Delsing and Al Libke all hit .310 or better.

Defensively, the Stars were another story. Although they finished fifth in team fielding, this was deceptive. Hollywood was last in double plays, while Vaughn and Cox were last among regulars at their positions. The outfielders were slow, and no one except Delsing, a fine center fielder, could cover much ground. Many balls that should have been caught would get through for hits. Libke had an exceptional arm, but the others were average.

The pitching staff was not helped by this situation and as a result, compiled very ordinary records. Pinky Woods, who was to be a very important part of future Hollywood successes, won his first five decisions and finished 13-10. Four pitchers won eleven games each – Ed Albosta 11-6; Rugger Ardizoia 11-10; Xavier Rescigno 11-9; and Joe Krakauskas 11-17. Albosta wasn't a regular starter until July but was the club's best pitcher during the last two months. Ardizoia, returning to the club where he had pitched so well as a youngster in 1939-40, pitched effectively but was often betrayed by the defense. Krakauskas, the big Canadian left hander, lost seven one run games as he pitched in tough luck most of the time. Mr. X was plagued by arm trouble most of the season. The club suffered with a poor bullpen. Veteran Paul Gregory, so impressive in 1946, was 0-7 with a horrendous 6.18 ERA.

As a result, the Stars were involved in numerous slugfests with the pitchers struggling to hold the enemy at bay. In two memorable games with Oakland on July 2-3 the Stars lost the first, 15-12, as the two teams established a league record of forty hits in one game. That standard lasted one day as Hollywood came back the next night to win, 16-7, in a game that saw 41 hits. And Gilmore was supposed to be a pitchers park!

The fans loved it and filed through the Gilmore turnstiles at a pace almost equal to the record setting 1946 season. A total of 500,607 paid to watch the Stars, a remarkable attendance for a second division club in a small ballpark.

At season's end the White Sox took their first pick from the Hollywood orchard, purchasing Tony Lupien and young prospect Gordon Goldsberry. This was a break for Tony, who richly deserved another chance in the majors. He was the Stars Most Valuable Player in 1947 and was a crowd favorite – one of the most popular Stars ever.

Although the Twinks put on a good show in 1947, they needed much to become contenders in 1948. It was hoped that the White Sox would provide that help.

1947 STANDINGS

	W	L	PCT.
Los Angeles	106	81	.567
San Francisco	105	82	.561
Portland	97	89	.522
Oakland	96	90	.516
Seattle	91	95	.489
HOLLYWOOD	88	98	.473
Sacramento	83	103	.446
San Diego	79	107	.425

Los Angeles won the Governor's Cup in playoffs.

Al Hollingsworth. The Stars had great hopes for this veteran pitcher, but he won only one game in a Hollywood uniform.

(From the collection of Dick Dobbins)

Pinky Woods

1948 – SOMEWHERE BETWEEN FIFTH AND SEVENTH PLACE

THE STARS OF 1948 WERE NO BETTER THAN those of 1947. In fact, a fan who had left Los Angeles in the middle of the 1947 season and did not return until the middle of the next year would have felt right at home. The cast of characters was virtually the same, the team played the same – good hit, no field and the finish was just what might have been expected. Once again the club finished in that favorite resting spot of Hollywood clubs down through the years – sixth place.

The Stars were affiliated with the White Sox again in 1948, and Jimmy Dykes was once again at the helm. The writers detected a change in Dykes' attitude that spring. The novelty of managing a minor league club had begun to wear thin for Jimmy, and he made no attempt to hide his desire to get back to the major leagues, preferably in his home town of Philadelphia. The old Dykes enthusiasm wasn't there that spring, and the club suffered from it.

As spring training ended, the club filled out its roster with White Sox optionees, most notably Gus Zernial and Jim Delsing, who were back for a final year of seasoning. The Stars had their usual holes in the infield, however. At first base was Dick Adams, obtained from the Athletics. But he didn't hit, and the job passed briefly to rookie

Gordon Goldsberry and Al Libke before Hollywood acquired veteran Rip Russell from Sacramento for outfielder Al "Fuzz" White. Although the trade solved a vexing problem, the Stars gave up a good ballplayer in White, a consistent .300 hitter for the next six years in the league.

Second base looked to be a major gap but was filled just as the season opened when Lou Stringer was purchased from the New York Giants. He had been a fine prospect for the Angels before the war and after a few so-so years with the Cubs had been returned to Los Angeles in 1947. There he had shown his former brilliance and was purchased by the Giants. But there was no room for him in New York, and Hollywood was glad to have him.

Don Ross was back at third base while shortstop was handled at times by Carl Cox, Ray Boone, Tod Davis and Gene Handley. No one played particularly well, and they all showed a marked inability to turn the double play. The Stars finished last in the PCL in that important department.

Frank Kelleher was back in the outfield along with Delsing and Zernial while Lou Kahn, a youngster with a fine arm and a pretty good bat, handled most of the early catching duties. Eventually, he shared the job with Jim Gladd, a Long Beach boy acquired on option from the Giants.

The pitching staff was thin at the beginning of the season. Pinky Woods and Rugger Ardizoia were returning starters while thirty nine year old Vern Kennedy, obtained from San Diego for Xavier Rescigno, was a third member of the rotation. The rest was up for grabs. At one time or another Dykes tried Edgar Smith, Joe Krakauskas, Pete Gebrian, Clarence "Hooks" Iott, Bill Butland and Ed Albosta but was never able to settle on a set rotation. Arm trouble plagued this staff as Ardizoia, Albosta, Krakauskas and Gordon Maltzberger were out for various periods with ailments.

Maltzberger was the most important addition to this staff, and his name looms large in Hollywood history. Originally signed by the Angels after graduating from

Colton High in 1932, Maltzy had briefly appeared with Hollywood in 1934 and had made the rounds of the minor leagues until 1943 when he came up with the White Sox. He spent the war years in Chicago as a relief pitcher and was turned over to Hollywood during the winter of 1947.

Maltzberger was ideally suited for relief pitching because of his sinking fast ball which led to many ground ball outs. He was also utterly nerveless; no tight situation really bothered him, and he was able to throw strikes when it counted. Maltzy was in the bull pen when the season opened but went on the shelf in June with bone chips in his elbow. When he returned in August, Dykes used him as a starter and Maltzberger responded with an 11-2 route going performance against San Francisco. He was a starter the rest of that season and together with Pinky Woods would form the nucleus of the fine Hollywood pitching staff during the next several years.

Zernial joined the club as the season opened and made his presence felt immediately with two towering home runs in a 17-2 win over Seattle. Big Gus wouldn't be stopped this year. He appeared in all but two of the Stars' games, swatting 40 home runs with 156 RBI's while hitting .322. He had plenty of mates on base to drive in. Stringer, Delsing and Kelleher all hit .333 while Gene Handley, playing all around the infield, hit .321 in a utility role. The Stars batted over .300 through July when they hit a prolonged batting slump to finish at .285.

Hollywood played at slightly below .500 through July, but a miserable August when the Stars were 10-26 plunged them into seventh place. That was too much for Dykes and he resigned on August 28. He had been the subject of much criticism during the weeks just prior to his leaving, primarily for his handling of the pitchers. But Jimmy really didn't have enough good players to build a winner at Hollywood.

Lou Stringer was named to replace Dykes, and this was a great surprise to all. Lou had never managed anywhere before, although he seemed capable of doing so. The Stars were defeated by Portland 7-2 in Stringer's debut but played at a .500 pace while Lou was the boss. On September 20 Stringer's tenure came to an abrupt end when he was sold to the Boston Red Sox. Coach Mule Haas ran the club during the last week of the season. This was the only year that the Stars had three managers.

As the season drew to a close the fans began to stay away from Gilmore in droves. Sunday crowds dipped as low as 2,539 on September 5. That was unheard of in the immediate post-war years. The club's position in the standing contributed, of course, but there was a new villain — television. The first Hollywood game was televised in late 1947, and by the middle of 1948 the Stars were televising all of their weekend games. That had to have an impact. Hollywood attendance declined to 416,725 in 1948, a drop of almost 20%. In future years the effect of television would be more severe. But no one really foresaw that in 1948.

The Stars were the butt of many jokes that year as their continued poor play inspired many snide remarks from the movie colony. Perhaps the most cutting came from Groucho Marx who said "there's only one solution for Hollywood this year. Ship the whole team to Little Rock, tear down the grandstand and drill for oil." Diehard Star fans cringed when they heard that. They had been waiting patiently for years for a champion, a ball club they could be proud of. But there was one disappointment after another. 1948 was just another in the long string of failures. If Hollywood fans had been told at the end of that dismal season that they were on the verge of their club's greatest years, they would have immediately questioned the speaker's sanity.

But that was exactly where they were.

1948 STANDINGS

	W	L	PCT.
Oakland	114	74	.606
San Francisco	112	76	.596
Los Angeles	102	86	.543
Seattle	93	95	.494
Portland	89	99	.473
HOLLYWOOD	84	104	.447
San Diego	83	105	.441
Sacramento	75	113	.399

Oakland won the Governor's Cup in playoffs.

Gordon Maltzberger

The 1949 Champions. This picture was taken at Wrigley Field late in the year.

First Row — Ed Oliver, Johnny O'Neil, Bob Wakefield, George Fallon, Gene Handley, Gordon Maltzberger, Art Schallock, George Genovese.

Second Row — Frank Kelleher, Herb Gorman, Al Unser, Willie Ramsdell, Coach John Fitzpatrick, Manager Fred Haney, Walt Olsen, Tom Seats, Trainer Frank Jacobs.

Third Row — Pinky Woods, Jean Pierre Roy, Jim Baxes, Al Leap, Jo Jo White, Mike Sandlock, Glen Moulder, Jack Salveson, Chuck Stevens, Murray Franklin, Irv Noren.

1949 – A PENNANT AT LAST

TWO EVENTS OCCURRED DURING THE WINTER of 1948 which were to transform the Hollywood Stars from an also-ran into a championship team. They were the hiring of Fred Haney as manager and the development of a working agreement with the Brooklyn Dodgers.

Haney came first. He was no stranger, of course. Fred had been broadcasting the Stars games since 1946 and was dearly beloved by Hollywood fans. Cobb had been trying to hire him since Buck Fausett had left, but Haney had professed disinterest. He had done enough managing, he said, and enjoyed the broadcasting booth. Haney had managed Toledo in 1935 after leaving the Stars and moved up to the Browns after four years with the Mud Hens. The Browns were a miserable franchise in those years, and Haney lasted until June, 1941 before he was fired. After another year at Toledo in 1942 Fred thought that was enough, and he returned to his Los Angeles home where he soon took up the broadcasting profession. At first he did both Angel and Stars games; but when the Wrigleys wanted Bob Kelley as the full time announcer, Fred shifted his total allegiance to the Stars.

Haney was the most popular announcer the Stars ever had. His fine commentary converted many Angelenos to the Stars as well as demonstrating his vast knowledge of the game. When Cobb made a substantial offer at the close of 1948, Haney couldn't turn it down.The managerial bug had bitten him deeper than he thought.

The agreement with the Dodgers was somewhat of an accident. The White Sox having terminated their agreement at the end of 1948, Cobb and Vic Collins were looking for another tieup when Haney was informed by Brooklyn scout Wid Matthews that the Dodgers were in need of another Triple A farm club in 1949. Brooklyn had cornered so many young talented players in the post war period that there were not enough places to play them. Would Hollywood be interested in a limited agreement?

The Stars would indeed, and Collins made a tentative agreement with the Dodgers during the 1948 winter meetings. He and Cobb then went to New York a few weeks later to complete the arrangement. But Bob was a bit reluctant. He was suspicious of Branch Rickey and his practices and feared that the Stars would be taken advantage of. That reluctance melted away when Cobb met the great Mahatma for the first time. He became a complete Rickey disciple, so much so that when Rickey left Brooklyn after the 1950 season Cobb immediately terminated the Dodger agreement.

Branch Rickey's story would take up several volumes, and relating the details of his career does not serve a real purpose here. Suffice it to say that Mr. Rickey had a profound effect on Organized Baseball and is certainly one of the titanic figures of the sport. In 1949 he was at the zenith of his career. He had rebuilt the Dodger franchise to the point where its role as a pennant contender would be assured for decades. He had opened up a new source of talent when he signed Jackie Robinson to a contract, making him the first black to enter the ranks of Organized Baseball in this century. Rickey's success would filter down to the Stars. For the remaining years of their existence, they would be of championship caliber and they became the glamour team of the PCL.

There was a wholesale change in personnel as the 1949

training season began. There were only eight holdovers from 1948. Several Dodger farmhands were in the San Fernando training camp—pitchers Glen Moulder, Walt Knothe and Art Schallock, outfielder Dave Pluss and infielders Bob Bundy and Jim Baxes. The latter, a twenty year old from San Francisco, was especially impressive. He was quick as a cat around third base and Haney said, "I've never seen a finer arm on an infielder." Baxes had power, too and although he frequently struck out, he impressed observers with his hitting ability. Jim clinched the third base position with a long home run off Jess Flores of San Diego in one of the last exhibition games. He made the jump from Class B Newport News with ease and was in 184 Hollywood games that year.

The Stars infield was shaping up as its best in years. One of the first moves Haney made upon taking over was to install Gene Handley at second base. Handley had played all over the infield in 1948 and had done well. But he needed to settle down to one position, and Haney's move was the right one. Handley was the best second baseman in the league that year, and he turned the double play as well as any Star in history. He hit a solid .294 to go along with his fine fielding.

The first base question had been resolved late in the 1948 season when the Stars purchased Chuck Stevens from the St. Louis Browns. Chuck had spent his entire career in the Browns system and finally made the major leagues in 1946 after three years of military service. But the Browns were very disorganized and shuttled players in and out as they struggled to find a winner. Chuck was thirty, a vulnerable age for a ballplayer, and when St. Louis attempted to send him to San Antonio, Stevens refused to report. Hollywood acquired his contract in August, 1948 and he played regularly during the last month of the season, hitting .321.

Stevens was the finest fielding first baseman in the PCL. He saved many an errant throw with his fine stretches and ranged far beyond the bag to cut off ground balls heading to right field. As a hitter, Chuck was much maligned. He did not fit the stereotype of a first baseman, for he was a line drive hitter who rarely hit more than ten home runs a year. But he was a solid hitter with good speed, one whose hits were often legged into doubles and triples. He was exceptionally good in clutch situations and seemed to come up with the game winning hit with amazing frequency. Stevens was one of the many fine ball players who came out of Long Beach Poly High in the 30's and 40's.

Shortstop had been a chronic problem for Hollywood teams over the years, but it was solved when the Stars traded Rugger Ardizoia to Seattle for Johnny O'Neil. The little Kentucky native had never been much of a hitter, but he could hound that ball. He had played five years in the PCL and was given much credit for helping Portland to the 1945 championship.

This infield—Stevens, Handley, O'Neil and Baxes—was virtually air tight and ranks as the best in Hollywood history. The reserves were good, too. George Genovese, up from Denver, filled in well at second and shortstop as did George Fallon, obtained from St. Paul in May.

Frank Kelleher was the only returning outfielder but just as spring training was about to close, Haney journeyed to the Brooklyn base in Vero Beach and came back with more Dodger surplus—outfielders Herb Gorman and Irv Noren and catcher Mike Sandlock. Gorman and Noren were quickly given regular positions in right and center while Sandlock handled the catching along with veteran Al Unser.

The pitching was much strengthened over 1948. Schallock and Moulder were very impressive during training while veteran Jack Salveson, obtained from Oakland, beefed up the bull pen. Gordon Maltzberger and Pinky Woods were returning from 1948, and both looked good during training.

The Stars were an unknown commodity as the season opened. The consensus of the sportswriters was that Seattle would win the championship in 1949 with Hollywood in fourth. Haney was cautiously optimistic. "We will be a hustling club," he said "although we won't have the power of '48. If we can play .500 ball for the first month, we'll be all right."

The club opened in San Diego, winning three of five there. Noren arrived in time for the third game and was installed in center field, from whence he never left that year. One week later Haney made another of his outstanding moves. He installed Stevens as the leadoff hitter with O'Neil dropping to eighth and Noren batting third. That became the basic 1949 lineup, and it was a good one. With Noren, Kelleher and Baxes hitting back to back behind Stevens and Handley, the Stars scored a lot of runs. It was soon apparent that this club was going places with a tighter defense and good pitching.

The Stars moved into first place on April 14 and after jousting with Seattle for the position for two weeks, moved in front to stay on May 2. By mid May the club had moved five games ahead, and an eight game winning streak extended the lead to eight games on June 3. Schallock, Maltzberger and Woods were winning regularly, and the Stars received an additional bonus when Brooklyn sent Willard Ramsdell on option at the major league cutdown date.

Ramsdell was a thirty one year old righthander who relied almost exclusively on the knuckleball. Although he had a tendency to throw home run balls, he was a very effective pitcher. He was fortunate to have in Mike Sandlock a catcher who was adept at handling the knuckler. Willie the Knuck won three games during his first week as a Star and added depth to an already solid staff.

The Stars moved out to a ten game lead in late June and by that time the entire city of Los Angeles was captivated with the team. Celebrities were always very much in evidence at Hollywood games, but this year they were more visible than ever. Clark Gable was at Gilmore virtually every evening while Jack Benny, George Raft,

George Burns and Robert Taylor hardly missed a game. And a handsome actor named Ronald Reagan was also a Gilmore regular. When he broke his ankle later in the summer and spent a week in the hospital, he insisted on a television set in his room to watch his favorites play.

The Stars were ten games ahead on July 10, and it seemed as if the pennant race was over. Then Hollywood slumped. Little by little the great lead evaporated until on August 21 the Stars lost a doubleheader at Oakland to reduce their lead to three games. The defending champion Oaks were surging now and further cut the lead to two games on August 25. The Stars were hurting. Schallock and Moulder were experiencing arm miseries, while Gorman and Kelleher were out of action with injuries. The club recalled Andy Skurski from Fort Worth, signed forty year old Jo Jo White and brought up Bob Wakefield from Pueblo to add some hitting strength. But the club was sagging badly.

A doubleheader win over Sacramento behind Ramsdell, who pitched a 2-1 one hitter and Jean Pierre Roy seemed to turn the tide. The club rebounded and played outstanding ball in September. The Oaks stayed close but suffered a fatal blow when they lost a doubleheader to the last place Angels on September 18. The Stars lead was four games with only seven to go. On September 22 the pennant was clinched when Ramsdell defeated Seattle 7-4. Reserve infielder Murray Franklin hit a three run homer in the eighth inning to win it. The clubhouse was bedlam that night. At last, the Hollywood Stars were champions of the PCL.

The playoffs for the Governor's Club were anti-climactic after the exciting pennant chase, but the Stars responded to the challenge. They easily handled the third place Solons four games to one and then after losing the first two games to San Diego took four straight from the Padres. Ramsdell was the winner in the final game of that series, 8-4, as Kelleher's two run homer clinched that game. The win meant $550 per man – a fair sum in 1949.

The club and league Most Valuable Player was center fielder Irv Noren. The award was nothing new to Noren who was MVP in the Texas League the year before. Noren had been a star athlete at Pasadena City College in 1942-43 where he built a reputation as a fine basketball player, one of the best of the era. The agility required of the court game was demonstrated time and time again in 1949 as Noren covered center field like a blanket. He had 30 assists that year, a feat not achieved by a PCL outfielder since Vince DiMaggio had 31 for the 1936 Padres. Noren hit .330 to finish second in the PCL batting race, and he showed surprising power with 29 home runs, an impressive total for a left handed hitter at Gilmore.

Noren was typical of so many Brooklyn prospects in those days. In spite of his obvious ability there was no room for him at Ebbets Field. Duke Snider, who was two years younger, had taken over the Dodger center field position and Carl Furillo was in right. Left field could have been Noren's spot, but he never got the chance. Irv was sold to Washington during the winter and later spent most of his major league career with the Yankees.

Many Stars enjoyed fine years as befitting a championship team. Herb Gorman was the club's only other .300 hitter at .310, but Chuck Stevens and Gene Handley were close at .297 and .294. Frank Kelleher tied Noren for the club home run lead with 29, while young Jim Baxes had 24 to go along with a .287 average. Jim was the epitome of a Branch Rickey ballplayer, receiving a paltry $300 a month while performing well just one step below the major leagues.

The pitching staff was a thing of beauty and was the key to the success of this team. It had five solid starting pitchers and one strong man in relief in Jack Salveson. Willie Ramsdell was the PCL ERA leader with a sparkling 2.60 to go along with his 18-12 record. He was the victim of poor offensive support during July and August, losing several low hit games that could have just as easily been won. Maltzberger was not far behind Ramsdell at 3.34 and he enjoyed his finest year in the PCL at 18-10. His sinker ball was made to order for the fine Hollywood infield. Maltzy gave the boys a lot of the credit for his great year.

Pinky Woods was the club's leader in victories as he finished 23-12. The 6' 5" righthander had enjoyed only fair success in 1947-48 but this year came into his own. Woods had signed with the Red Sox in 1941 after a brilliant collegiate career at Holy Cross and made it to Boston in 1943. He was a hard throwing overhand fastball pitcher, but he lost the big toe on his left foot after a spiking injury and was unable to throw as hard. By 1947 he was a sidearm pitcher who wasn't nearly as fast. He underwent a transition period during the next two years before blossoming in 1949. Pinky was quite a pitcher that year, leading the PCL in appearances while tying Guy Fletcher of Seattle and Hal Saltzman of Portland for most wins.

Little Art Schallock finished 12-9 while Glen Moulder was 14-10. Both missed several starts while suffering from injury. Salveson was 11-7, mostly in relief, but he frequently was called upon in spot starting assignments and did well.

Fred Haney was recognized for his important role in molding the Stars into a pennant winner when he was chosen Minor League Manager of the Year by the Sporting News. It was a fine honor for Haney, who was finally given the respect he had long deserved. Although the Stars had a good nucleus of players for the first time, it is not certain if they would have triumphed with any other hand at the helm.

Hollywood attendance improved to 502,445 after the slump in 1948. It would probably have been more were it not for the continued impact of television. The Stars were televising most of their games in 1949, and many fans preferred to stay home to watch the game. Gilmore Field itself may have contributed to the situation, and there were many complaints about the park. Fans complained that parking at Gilmore Island was becoming impossible. The city had reduced the number of streetcars and buses, forcing more people to drive. The park's limited capacity also came in for criticism. Most of the good box seats were sold as season tickets, and fans were unwilling to fight the traffic for bad seats. Housekeeping at Gilmore had deteriorated, and that was not conducive to good attendance.

The 1949 championship was the first for Hollywood since 1930. As the years have passed, the two teams have frequently been compared. They were quite different. The 1930 version won on power along with two fine pitchers. The 1949 club was not as powerful, but its inner defense was better and its pitching staff was deeper. The 1949 club had more team speed, but the 1930 club really didn't need it. The PCL was probably stronger in 1930 than in 1949. Haney was a better manager than Vitt, but Oscar did a fine job with the 1930 club. Remember that the 1930 club did not really begin to shine until Jess Hill and Dave Barbee joined the Stars in June. It wasn't the same team previously. The comparison is fascinating. Each club has its spokesman.

With one pennant under their belts, the Hollywood moguls looked forward to more success in 1950.

1949 STANDINGS

	W	L	PCT.
HOLLYWOOD	109	79	.583
Oakland	104	83	.556
Sacramento	102	85	.545
San Diego	96	92	.511
Seattle	95	93	.505
Portland	85	102	.455
San Francisco	84	103	.449
Los Angeles	74	113	.396

Hollywood won the Governor's Cup in playoffs.

(From the collection of Dick Dobbins)

Fred Haney

Jack Salveson

Cliff Dapper

Irv Noren

Ed Sauer, Glen Moulder and Andy Skurski model the Stars'
shorts in 1950.

(Courtesy of Mr. Stevens)

Safe at home! Chuck Stevens scores a Twink run against Oakland in 1950. Catcher Don Padgett of the Oaks and Umpire Ed Runge look on. This was one of the first games in which the Stars wore shorts.

1950 – LOOK AT THOSE LEGS

THE 1950 SEASON WAS A DISAPPOINTMENT TO Hollywood fans, who had envisioned a string of PCL championships. The Stars finished a poor third after leading the pack for most of the first half of the season.

It was a troublesome season for the PCL. Attendance had declined in 1949, and the league directors in an effort to bolster revenues increased the schedule to 200 games for the first time in twenty years. The change failed to help. PCL attendance was down 15% from the 1949 figures in spite of the longer schedule, and talk of becoming a third major league was stilled for the moment. Many reasons were given for the reduced patronage, but the main culprit seemed to be television. Nowhere was this more of a factor than in Los Angeles. Both the Stars and Angels televised the majority of their home games, and each club suffered for it. Over 160,000 fewer spectators went through the Southland turnstiles in 1950.

A secondary cause seemed to be the wide spread radio broadcasting of major league games into PCL cities. The Mutual *Game of the Day* was transmitted coast to coast for the first time that year, and it had the effect of making PCL fans more major league conscious. They were becoming less interested in the local teams. The reduced interest in the PCL race combined with the rapid growth of television

181

kept the fans away from the ballparks. It was the beginning of the end for the league as an independent entity.

The Stars looked stronger in the spring than at the close of the 1949 season. The club was virtually intact; Noren, Ramsdell and Baxes were the only missing regulars while reserve George Genovese had been drafted by Washington. But Haney thought his club had improved with several new acquisitions—pitchers Ben Wade, Lee Anthony and Ken Lehman, outfielders Cliff Aberson and Ed Sauer, catcher Cliff Dapper and shortstop Buddy Hicks. Wade and Anthony came to Hollywood by way of Los Angeles when the Cubs acquired Paul Minner and Preston Ward from the vast Dodger surplus. They were big strong right handers who could throw a ball through a brick wall, and Haney eased them into his starting rotation when the season began. Aberson had been the most promising power hitter in the Cub system at one time but had suffered a poor season as an Angel in 1949. The Stars acquired him in hopes of improving their power, but Aberson was a flop in a Hollywood uniform. He hit a meager .158 before he was sent to Mobile in April.

Sauer was another ex-Angel, and he proved to be a valuable addition to the club. Blessed with one of the strongest arms in the league, Sauer played all the outfield positions and hit a solid .260. Dapper was returning to Hollywood after an absence of nine years. He had managed the Atlanta Crackers in 1949.

Buddy Hicks was sent from St. Paul just before the season opened and was thought to be the last link in another championship team. Although Haney was satisfied with Johnny O'Neil, the club was stronger with Hicks. Buddy was faster than O'Neil and had as good an arm. He led off for the Stars during most of the season.

Towards the end of spring training Haney made a remark that came back to haunt him. When asked how the Stars would finish in 1950., Fred said "I don't know where we'll finish, but one thing is for certain. We'll finish ahead of the Angels, or my name isn't Fred Haney." The Angels were coming off their worst season in history and weren't much better in 1950. But manager Bill Kelly evidently inspired the Seraphs with Haney's remarks, and the Angels were extremely troublesome as a result. They took the season series from the Stars, 18-10, in spite of their lowly seventh place standing. Veteran lefty Bob Muncrief, a Hollywood stalwart a decade earlier, decisioned the Stars seven times that year. Perhaps Haney should have avoided his spring time comments.

Hollywood opened the season in new pinstriped uniforms against Portland on March 28 before a slim crowd of 5,770. Then on April 1 the Stars set a fashion standard when they appeared in shorts! It was a Saturday afternoon game, and the fans as well as all of baseball were agog, to put it mildly. The players wore rayon T-shirts, pin striped flannel shorts and long socks which reached the knees. "This is no joke," said Haney. "We think these suits will give us more speed." That was true, according to Chuck Stevens. "I was a step and a half faster going to first," he says. The Stars won that first game in shorts, 5-3, and the next day a crowd of 9,264 showed up for the doubleheader, which the Stars split. They were to win eight of their first nine games in shorts.

The idea had its origins in a Braven Dyer column in the *Times* when he wondered why baseball was so slow to change its fashions. Haney had been thinking of shorts for some time after watching a touring British soccer team in action. Branch Rickey was certainly impressed. He ordered a set for the Dodger Fort Worth farm and predicted that before the year was out all Southern teams would be so outfitted.

Unfortunately, the idea never took hold. The Stars wore the shorts primarily on the weekends and holidays for the next three years, but they were never joined by other PCL teams. The major leagues never adopted the garb at all, calling the shorts "bush". Perhaps the masculine image of the players was at stake. At any rate, the shorts became a pleasant memory, but they did act as a forerunner to the lighter, more colorful uniforms in use today.

The Stars roared out of the starting gate in 1950, winning nineteen of their first twenty five games, and led the league through most of April and May. The pitching staff seemed especially strong. Both Wade and Anthony won their first four decisions while veteran Jack Salveson was quite effective in a starting role this season. Young Kenny Lehman was impressive, too. The offense was led by Chuck Stevens, who was off to his finest start. Through mid-May Chuck was the league's leading hitter and paced the Stars in RBI's.

The Stars received reinforcements in May when Jim Baxes was returned by St. Paul, and outfielders Bill Antonello and Clint Conatser were obtained from the Brooklyn farm system. The team was strengthened by these moves, and the fans were certain of another pennant.

There were problems with this team, however. The Stars had a preponderance of right handed hitters which meant that they saw virtually no lefties all season. Haney looked all over for a left handed power hitter to back up Kelleher and Baxes but could find none available. The club missed Irv Noren badly. Although Antonello and Conatser were fine outfielders, neither hit well enough. The Stars were last, or next to last, in batting all through the early part of the season, placing a great burden on the pitching staff.

Things began to go sour for the Stars in June. Pinky Woods and Ken Lehman went out of action in early June, and neither won a game for two months. Wade also missed several starts with a sore elbow. This threw a great burden on Jack Salveson, who responded to the challenge. He was the only consistent starter during June and early July. Maltzberger and Pete Mondorff, a Dodger farmhand up from Mobile, pitched well in spots. But Lee Anthony faded after his early strong start, and Glen Moulder slumped from his fine work of 1949. In desperation the Stars signed Kewpie Barrett after his release by San Diego in June and purchased Herb Karpel from Seattle. Barrett, one of the all-time pitching greats of the PCL, won several games, but was hit hard at times. He was well past his prime at forty three. Karpel, a former Yankee farmhand, pitched well but lost a number of close games.

The Stars clung to first place during the first weeks of July, but Oakland was surging and had advanced to second place when the two clubs squared off in a critical series at Emeryville on July 12. The Stars owned a two game lead, but were hobbling. Lehman, Woods, Stevens, Handley, and Mike Sandlock all missed that series. The Oaks won the first six games of the series before Salveson salvaged a 2-1 victory in the second game of the Sunday doubleheader. The Stars left town three games behind the Acorns. They were never a factor in the race thereafter.

The Stars continued their slump and eventually settled in third place. San Diego and Oakland waged a terrific battle for the championship with the Oaks eventually triumphant by four games.

As if the Stars hadn't suffered enough injuries, Salveson hurt his elbow on August 24 and missed the last seven weeks of the season. The veteran was enjoying his finest PCL season at 15-4 and undoubtedly would have won twenty had he finished the year. A one-time fireballing right hander, the thirty-six year old Salveson now relied on cunning and control. He was one of the fastest workers in league history, rarely requiring more than one hour and forty five minutes to get his work done.

Chuck Stevens was another who saw his finest season ruined by injury and illness. Chuck was hitting .399 in mid May and had enjoyed a streak of ten straight hits at Oakland when he suffered an allergic reaction to a pencillin shot. When he came back after missing a week, he was not the same hitter and was further hobbled with a severe ankle injury in July. Chuck gamely limped through the rest of the season but slumped badly to finish at .288.

Frank Kelleher bore up under the club's misfortunes. He had started the season poorly and through May was hitting a weak .240 with only five home runs. But he snapped out of his slump in June when he crashed eight homers in ten games at Sacramento and San Francisco. The veteran provided much of the club's power over the last half of the season. He finished with 40 home runs to tie Gus Zernial for the best Gilmore Field record and raised his average to .270.

Jim Baxes was the club's only other power, finishing with 31 home runs but he fell off badly from his 1949 performance, dropping to .243. Jim was rusty when he arrived from St. Paul in May. He had held out, missing much of spring training, and then was forced to move to second base with the Saints, a position he didn't like. The result of Baxes' off-year in 1950 was to send him on the rounds of the Brooklyn farm system for the next few years – Montreal, Fort Worth, Mobile and other points in between. This probably prevented him from reaching the potential he had shown in 1949.

As the season drew to a close, Hollywood crowds fell off to virtually nothing. Only 1,942 fans paid to see the last Sunday doubleheader of the season on October 1. Overall, the Stars attendance fell to 422,389. It was apparent that the 200 game schedule was a mistake, and PCL directors promised to adjust it in 1951.

At the close of the 1950 season Branch Rickey announced that he was selling his stock in the Brooklyn club. A group led by Walter O'Malley had forced the Mahatma out in a power struggle which would eventually have a profound impact on Los Angeles. Shortly thereafter, Rickey signed a five year contract as General Manager of the Pittsburgh Pirates.

Bob Cobb, who was by this time a complete disciple of Mr. Rickey, announced that where Branch went, there would go Bob Cobb. He terminated the Brooklyn agreement and entered into a relationship with the Pirates. The 1951 Stars would have a new flavor.

1950 STANDINGS

	W	L	PCT.
Oakland	118	82	.590
San Diego	114	86	.570
HOLLYWOOD	104	96	.520
Portland	101	99	.505
San Francisco	100	100	.500
Seattle	96	104	.480
Los Angeles	86	114	.430
Sacramento	81	119	.405

(Courtesy of Mr. Stevens)

Chuck Stevens

1951 – UNDER THE PIRATE FLAG

THE STARS MOVED UP A NOTCH IN 1951, FINISHING a strong second to Rogers Hornsby's Seattle Rainiers. This was a much better club than the 1950 edition and unlike the previous year, the Twinks finished strong. The stage was set for the finest period in Hollywood baseball history.

The PCL directors had embarked upon a pattern of changing the schedule every year. After the disappointing results of the 200 game schedule in 1950, the number of games was reduced to 168 in 1951. The season would close on September 13, thereby avoiding some of the competition with football season. The traditional seven game series would be eliminated. The fans grew tired of the same team in town for a full week, the directors thought. A split week of three and four game series would be played in order to stimulate attendance.

The Hollywood training camp was one in a state of flux that year. As a result of the termination of the working agreement with Brooklyn and the new arrangement with Pittsburgh, everyone was uncertain what to expect. Most of the Dodger farmhands who had been so successful during the previous two years were now gone. Only Ben Wade, Art Schallock and George Schmees were back, although Herb Gorman was returned before spring training was very far along. But the Pirates were not deep in playing talent and would provide little help. The Stars would be forced to make do with what they had.

Fortunately, the Stars had made some excellent moves. The veteran Lou Stringer was acquired from the Red Sox to take over the third base position vacated by Jim Baxes. Lou was not pleased with his initial salary offer by the Stars and held out through much of the training session, but he soon came into the fold and was a valuable member of the Stars that year.

George Genovese returned after a year at Chattanooga, and he was installed at shortstop in place of Buddy Hicks. The rest of the club was the same – Stevens and Handley rounded out the infield with Murray Franklin in reserve. The outfielders were Kelleher, Sauer and Gorman with Clint Conatser as a substitute. Sandlock and Dapper were the catchers. Wade, Maltzberger, Salveson, Woods and Schallock were the starting pitchers.

The most interesting experiment in training that year was the conversion of outfielder Johnny Lindell to pitching. Long John had been acquired in July, 1950 from Columbus in a trade for Glen Moulder. Lindell had an unusual career. He had begun as a hard throwing right handed pitcher in the Yankee chain and had made the big club in 1942 after a fine 23-4 year at Newark in 1941. But his arm went bad and he was converted to an outfielder to take advantage of his fine hitting ability. Lindell stayed with the Yankees until the 1950 season, when he was deemed expendable and was sold to the St. Louis Cardinals. He seemed to be washed up and was released to Columbus.

Lindell joined the Stars in August and played part-time in right field, hitting only .247. He was obviously well past his prime as an everyday player, but Haney thought he might be effective as a pitcher. Lindell had developed a knuckleball, pitching on the sidelines in recent years. Although he had not pitched for eight years, Haney used him in two games late in the year and was pleased by what he saw. The conversion of the ex-Yankee began in earnest during the spring. When the season started, Lindell was one of the starters. He succeeded beyond anyone's wildest expectations.

The spring of 1951 was cold and wet, and the Gilmore faithful stayed away from the ballpark in droves. The Stars had restricted TV to a mere two games weekly, but that did not result in improved attendance. The opening day crowd of 1,804 was the smallest ever for a Gilmore Field debut and one had to go back to the days of the Depression to find a more sparsely attended opener.

Unlike the previous year, the Stars started out poorly in 1951 and were deep in the second division through much of May. They finally moved over .500 on May 27 and thereafter played very well. The PCL race was very close during this period but as June drew to a close, the Stars and Seattle began to pull away from the others.

Haney used his players well this year. With Lindell's development as an effective starter, Maltzberger was sent back to the bull pen. The club was suddenly deep in pitching as Ben Wade and Art Schallock showed a remarkable recovery from their 1950 arm ailments. Little Vic Lombardi was impressive at times while Salveson was as crafty as ever. The club acquired Roy Welmaker from San Diego, and he joined Schallock and Lombardi to give the Stars the strongest left handed pitching in the league. The only disapointment was Pinky Woods, who was bothered by a sore arm much of the year.

The Stars were four games behind the Rainiers when they invaded Sicks' Stadium for an important series July 19. Lombardi was blasted 9-3 in the opener and after Woods won the next night, Hollywood proceeded to lose three straight to Rogers Hornsby's team. That widened the Seattle lead to six games. Over the next thirty days the two clubs kept pace with each other setting the stage for another confrontation, this time at Gilmore beginning August 23.

Once again the Stars did not fare well. After Maltzberger won the opener in relief of Lindell, 7-5, to cut the lead to five games, the Rainiers rallied behind Bob Hall to defeat Salveson 5-1. In that game right fielder George Schmees, who had been carrying the club offensively, injured his right shoulder and missed the rest of the series. The club could only muster two runs in the next two games and split the balance of the series. Seattle left town with a five game lead and only fifteen left to play. The Rainiers clinched the flag on September 5, a week before the season's close.

There were playoffs again in 1951 after a year's respite, and the Stars made it to the finals for the second time. But they succumbed to Seattle, three games to two. The Stars were tied at two games each and led 2-1 through six innings of the finale behind Lindell. But the Rainiers scored four runs in the seventh to take command and put the game away with three in the ninth to win 9-2. There was little interest in the playoffs that year, and Gilmore crowds were below 3,000 in all games.

The Stars were a typical Haney club in 1951 – a club which relied on pitching, good defense and power. The Stars pitchers allowed the fewest runs in the league while the hitters swatted 141 home runs, second only to the Angels. Schmees had a marvelous year. The Dodger farmhand had joined the Stars in August 1950 and did not impress the Brooklyn management, hitting a weak .174 in 41 games. But he was ready when spring training started. An ex-San Jose State star athlete, Schmees hit .328, the only Star above .300. He led the club with 100 RBI's and socked 26 home runs besides. George was fast afoot, too. He led the PCL with 17 triples and was the Stars' leading base stealer. Schmees was drafted by the St. Louis Browns for the 1952 season.

Other Stars enjoyed fine productive years. Frank Kelleher again led the club with 28 home runs, but this year the great slugger showed signs of slowing down at age thirty five. His average dropped to .253 and he compiled 98 strikeouts. Dino Restelli gave the club good center fielding after joining the Stars in June and hit a solid .281 in 76 games. Veteran Lou Stringer played well at third, hitting

.284, but he too was showing the effects of many years in the game. Gene Handley and Chuck Stevens once again provided a virtual wall on the right side of the infield.

The pitching staff was led by Ben Wade at 16-6. He lost for the final time in 1951 when Eddie Barr of Portland hit an eighth inning home run to beat him 1-0, July 17. Wade proceeded to win his last eleven games and earned his chance with Brooklyn in 1952. Ben threw four shutouts, including a 1-0 ten inning gem against Warren Hacker at Wrigley Field on August 30.

Little Art Schallock started fast and was the club's best at 11-5 when he was sold to the Yankees in July. The Stars received catcher Eddie Malone and pitcher Wally Hood in exchange and although both helped, the club missed Schallock over the last half season Salveson enjoyed another fine year at 15-10. The thirty seven year old amazed one and all with the speed with which he dispatched enemy hitters. Salveson didn't try for strikeouts. He wanted the batter to hit the ball, preferably the first pitch.

Lindell was the club's Most Valuable Player in 1951. As a pitcher his record was 12-9 with an impressive 3.03 ERA. Throwing the knuckler on almost every pitch, Lindell was a menace to his catchers as well as opposing hitters. Mike Sandlock was the most successful in handling Lindell's slants, and caught him most of the time. John numbered three shutouts among his victories, including a masterful three hitter against Oakland in May.

When Lindell wasn't pitching, Haney used him as an outfield replacement, at first base in relief of Stevens and as a pinch hitter. John responded with a .292 average that included nine home runs. For much of the season Lindell was over .300 and was especially dangerous in the clutch.

The club might have fared better had outfielder Herb Gorman not missed half the season with a serious knee injury. The promising lefty had a brief lookover by the Cardinals in the spring after two .300 plus years with the Stars and was just beginning to round into midseason form when he was injured in late June. Gorman hit .275 in 80 games, the first time in his career that he was below .300.

Attendance at Gilmore fell to 287,977 in 1951, the lowest so far in the post war period. The dismal spring weather held the crowds down in the spring, and the fans never returned that year except on the weekends. But the 1951 Stars weren't especially exciting to watch. They were a strong team but very methodical. The veteran club didn't have much team speed and relied heavily on the long ball. The hustling young players of the Dodger system were conspicuously absent from this team.

At the end of the season the Stars experienced their first major change in ownership since the club came to Hollywood in 1938. George Young sold all of his shares to Branch Rickey, representing the Pittsburgh organization. It was not a surprising occurrence to insiders. Young had experienced many disagreements with Collins and Cobb during the last several years, especially in regards to breaking off the Brooklyn agreement.

The sale of stock to Rickey was important for the future of the Stars. For the first time ownership was in outside hands. Previously, the club was strictly local. Gradually, policy would come to be made in Pittsburgh rather than Hollywood and the club would lose some of its local flavor as a result.

But none of this was important to the fans, for the Stars were about to resume their championship ways.

1951 STANDINGS

	W	L	PCT.
Seattle	99	68	.593
HOLLYWOOD	93	74	.557
Los Angeles	86	81	.515
Portland	83	85	.494
Oakland	80	88	.476
San Diego	79	88	.473
Sacramento	75	92	.449
San Francisco	74	93	.443

(From the collection of Dick Dobbins)

Carlos Bernier

1952 – BACK IN THE THRONE ROOM

THE PCL LOOKED FORWARD TO THE 1952 season with a great deal of hope. At last the league had been granted special status on the road to becoming a third major league. The officials of Organized Baseball established guidelines for a new Open Classification in the minor leagues. Among the requirements were aggregate population of 10,000,000, annual average attendance over the last five years of 2,250,000, and removal of all salary limitations. The Open Classification had new regulations pertaining to the player draft. A player had to have played five years in the minors before becoming eligible for the draft, and he could waive his right at the time of signing his contract. The PCL had been seeking this freedom since 1919. The Open Classification also had first call on drafted players returned to the minor leagues.

Many PCL observers felt that Open Classification was the first step towards becoming a major league, and interest was stimulated in all league cities. The schedule was increased to 180 games and the familiar week long series was restored after a year's absence.

The Stars were now a Pirate farm club. Pittsburgh had disposed of the Indianapolis franchise during the winter, and Hollywood would have first call on all Pirate surplus. For the next several years there was some question as to what was surplus and what was not. This was the Rickey era at Pittsburgh, and a number of rather strange player moves were made between the Pirates and the Stars. Several players on the big league team could have been better served with experience at Hollywood or New Orleans while the Stars acquired a number of players who seemingly had major league ability. The Hollywood fans didn't complain, for these were the very best years of the franchise.

The 1952 training season was unsettled as the Hollywood roster was in a state of flux. Many of the veterans who had played such prominent roles in the success of the past three years were now gone – Salveson, Franklin and Gorman to San Diego; Maltzberger to St. Jean in the Provincial League as that club's manager; Genovese to Batavia in a similar role. They were replaced by Pittsburgh farmhands – shortstop Dick Cole, outfielders Tom Saffell and Ted Beard, second baseman Monty Basgall, pitchers Jim Walsh, Paul Pettit, and Mel Queen. The old order changeth. Only Stevens, Handley, Kelleher Woods and Sandlock remained from the 1949 champs.

Paul Pettit was the most familiar new name. He had been signed as one of the first bonus babies for a reported $100,000 after graduation from Narbonne High School in 1950. A hard throwing left hander in high school who could hit as well, Pettit suffered an arm problem in 1951 and was of little use at Indianapolis. But he looked good in the spring and said his arm felt fine.

The most interesting player at the Anaheim camp that year was a twenty three year old outfielder drafted from Tampa in the Florida International League, Carlos Bernier. He had been in professional baseball since 1947 but had yet to play above class B. This appeared to have been a mistake. Bernier could chase down virtually every fly ball hit in his direction, possessed a good batting eye and appeared to be the best base runner to wear a Hollywood uniform since Haney himself, eighteen years before.

The Stars began the 1952 campaign slowly as San Diego

was the early pacesetter. Hollywood was never far behind, however, but the lineup was very fluid. Basgall and Cole took early possession of second and shortstop respectively while Lou Stringer opened at third. But the veteran was sold to San Diego when Pittsburgh sent infielder Jack Phillips in May. Phillips had spent several years with the Yankees before joining Pittsburgh in 1950 and could play all the infield positions.

The outfield saw Bernier in left with Tom Saffell, another speedster in center. Saffell, at twenty nine, was no kid. He had shuttled between Indianapolis and Pittsburgh for several years, and there were some who thought he should have been the Pirate centerfielder in 1952. Ed Steele, acquired from the Birmingham Black Barons, played in right field along with Dick Wilson during April, but Beard took over after he was sent outright to the Stars in May. He too possessed fine speed, and the Hollywood outfield was the finest defensively in the league.

The pitching staff was led by Johnny Lindell, Paul Pettit, and Larry Shepard with occasional starts by Pinky Woods, who seemed past his prime. Jim Walsh joined the staff in May and soon took his regular turn as did Mel Queen, who joined the Stars during the first week of May. Haney had been worried about his bullpen with Maltzberger gone, but the club made a good trade on May 17 when Royce Lint, a Pirate optionee, was sent to Portland in exchange for Red Lynn. The redhead had been a fine starting pitcher for the Angels in the mid 40's and looked to be washed up by 1952. Maybe Haney saw something that other managers didn't. The crafty veteran soon became the ace of the Hollywood bullpen, helped mightily by Lee Anthony, back after a season in New Orleans. It must be noted that Lynn didn't come cheap, for Lint was a fine pitcher who compiled a 12-3 record with the fourth place Beavers.

The race was close during the first two months, but Hollywood moved into first place on June 20; and thereafter it was clear that the Stars were the team to beat. Hitting was down considerably in the PCL that year, and a strong pitching staff was essential. Hollywood seemed to have the best of them all. The addition of thirty five year old George "Red" Munger from the Pirates added to the already strong mound corps.

As July opened, the Padres began to fade from the scene, and the Oakland Oaks demonstrated that they were a very formidable team. They took an important series from the Stars, seven games to one, during the first week in July to move past Hollywood into first place. That series was highlighted by a no-hitter thrown against the Twinks by Oak southpaw Roger Bowman. Haney never quite got over that. He delivered a number of scathing comments on Bowman's pitches after the game and seemed to harbor animosities against Roger when he became one of Haney's pitchers at Pittsburgh in 1953.

The two clubs battled for the lead during the next month with neither able to pull away from the pack. The Stars were hurting by early August. Bernier and Saffell were out with injuries, and the pitching was ineffective. An important series opened with the Angels on August 5. Los Angeles was in the midst of a hot streak which saw them reach third place, just 8½ games behind the Oaks. Hollywood was second, 1½ games behind.

It was a memorable series. The Angels won the first three games as the Stars could only muster two runs. Hollywood had lost nine out of ten games and was reeling. The next day, Thursday, 23,497 fans, the largest midweek crowd in Wrigley Field history, saw a thrilling game. The Stars defeated the Angels 6-5 behind Munger, with four scoreless innings in relief by Lynn. That turned the season around. The Stars took the remaining four games of the series including a doubleheader sweep on Sunday, 12-8 and 5-1 that moved them back into first place. A crowd of 17,517 precipitated one of the worst riots in Los Angeles history at that one. Cushions and other debris were thrown on the field, and a fan wrestled umpire Ed Runge to the ground.

The Stars were moving now and they received a timely

reinforcement when Pittsburgh sent left hander Paul La Palme to Hollywood. He joined the club on August 20, and the next night his two hitter at San Diego put the Stars in first place to stay. La Palme's career at Hollywood, while brief, was amazing. He appeared in only nine games but started seven and had six complete games, allowing only eight runs. His ERA of 1.29 is the lowest ever achieved by a Hollywood Star who pitched in fifty innings or more.

The Hollywood pitching was now virtually invincible. Lindell had won his twentieth game August 19 and Queen was at his peak, pitching 26 consecutive scoreless innings during late August. The Hollywood lead had grown to 4½ as August ended. An important series was to begin at Oakland on September 1.

The Stars were ready. Behind their superlative pitching staff Hollywood took three of the four games. Before a hostile Oakland crowd of 9,834 on September 1, the Stars took a doubleheader, 9-1 and 6-5 behind Munger and Shepard in relief of Queen. After Walsh lost, 4-3, the next night Hollywood took the final game, 6-5. The Stars now led by 6½ games with just three weeks to go. Hollywood had won only one game at Oakland in 1952 prior to that series.

The two clubs met once again, this time at Gilmore. The Hollywood lead was still only 4½ games, and Oakland could cut the lead to one half game with a sweep. But the Stars took three of four. Queen and Munger were victorious in the first two games and a doubleheader split virtually eliminated the Oaks from the pennant chase. The Stars were officially crowned champions two nights later at Portland.

There were no playoffs in 1952 and perhaps it was just as well, for the fans had time to savor this fine team. Haney did perhaps his finest managing job. He platooned everywhere he could, and the technique paid off. Although Basgall played in most of the games at second base, the 1951 incumbent, Gene Handley, appeared in 131 games around the infield and was outstanding in relief of the starters.

Veteran Frank Kelleher, now beginning to slide, saw action in 82 games; and although he hit a mere .239 he managed to hit eleven home runs to tie Beard for the club leadership. Haney used three catchers – Mike Sandlock, Eddie Malone and Jim Mangan – and had fine results with all of them.

The club offensive leader was Carlos Bernier who hit .301 with 79 RBI's. He provided an element in the attack which hadn't been seen at Gilmore before by stealing 65 bases to lead the PCL. Carlos was successful in his first 27 attempts before Portland's Aaron Robinson threw him out June 11. Bernier usually battled lead off and often would open a game with a single, steal second and score on a Basgall hit. He unnerved the pitchers greatly. Beard and Saffell were also active base thieves with 24 and 19 each. The Stars stole 142 bases that year, almost twice the number of the second place Seattle Rainiers.

Lindell was the dominant player on this team and was easily the Most Valuable Player of the league. At thirty six big John seemed to have imbibed at the Fountain of Youth. His knuckleball totally baffled the PCL hitters. Lindell won 24 games, the most in the league, led in strikeouts with 190 and compiled a fine 2.52 ERA. He was rarely taken out for poor pitching. He usually stayed close and appeared to get stronger in the late innings. Lindell provided an additional bat in the lineup, and although he slumped to .213 this year, he managed to hit eight home runs. John's bat kept him in games where other pitchers would have been relieved. His major league career was reborn that year when the Pirates purchased his contract for the 1953 season.

Lindell was aided greatly that year by his battery mate, Mike Sandlock. The veteran catcher enjoyed a fine season, hitting .286 and handled Lindell's dancing knuckleball as well as anyone could. Sandlock had 20 passed balls that year but who could have done better? He had a fine arm, averaging almost an assist a game and called a nice game as well. Sandlock earned a return to the majors with this fine showing.

The infield was strong that year as shortstop Dick Cole and second baseman Monty Basgall enjoyed fine seasons. This was probably Cole's best. The tall bespectacled alumnus of Wilson High in Long Beach had first appeared in the PCL in 1943 as a seventeen year old with Sacramento. He had bounced around the Cardinal farm system until joining St. Louis in 1951. But he was traded to Pittsburgh that year, and the Pirates sent him to Hollywood for more seasoning. Never a great hitter, Cole was a speedy shortstop with an excellent arm. Dick hit .286 for the Stars and was on his way back to Pittsburgh.

Lindell was ably supported that year by Mel Queen and Paul Pettit. Queen joined the club in May that year after an indifferent major league career with the Yankees and Pirates. Mel didn't get started right away, but by August he was taking his place as one of the finest pitchers in the league. Queen was basically a fast ball pitcher and had a good one. He tied for the lead with five shutouts to go with his 14-9 record.

Paul Pettit enjoyed a fine season at 15-8 while Pinky Woods and Jim Walsh were also effective at 11-9 and 10-9 respectively. The staff turned in 22 shutouts, easily the most in the PCL.

The Stars played at a .667 pace in Gilmore and were the best road team, too. They annihilated the Padres that year, taking 23 out of the 28 games between the clubs. At one stretch the Stars defeated San Diego twelve straight times.

The only negative about this 1952 team was attendance. Although the Gilmore crowds improved to 311,043 that was a result of a longer schedule. The Stars reduced their television schedule to two games a week after providing almost unlimited coverage in the previous years, and that helped slightly. But the viewing habits had been set. Hollywood fans shunned the week night games and came out in satisfactory numbers only on the weekends. For the rest of the Stars' history this would be the pattern.

The 1952 Stars were very likely the best team in Hollywood history. The outfield defense was superb, and the overall team speed was exceptional. The pitching staff was the best in the league, especially after La Palme and Munger joined the club. Haney used his players well, platooning with great skill. Reserves Eddie Malone, Gene Handley and Frank Kelleher all contributed greatly to the team's success.

At the close of the season, Fred Haney officially resigned as manager of the Stars to accept the job as boss of the Pittsburgh Pirates. There were those thought that Fred was joining a poorer team. Those 1952 Stars were really something.

1952 STANDINGS

	W	L	PCT.
HOLLYWOOD	109	71	.606
Oakland	104	76	.578
Seattle	96	84	.533
Portland	92	88	.511
San Diego	88	92	.489
Los Angeles	87	93	.483
San Francisco	78	102	.433
Sacramento	66	114	.367

(From the collection of Dick Dobbins)

Gene Handley

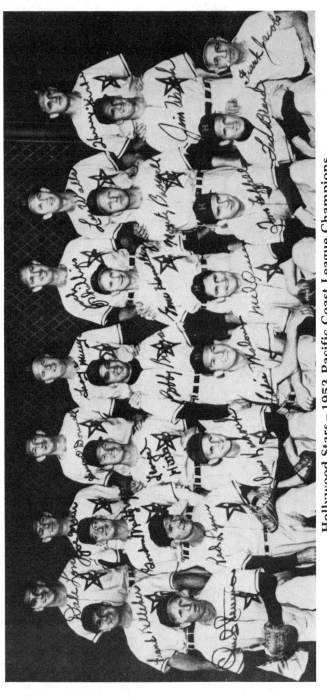

Hollywood Stars—1953 Pacific Coast League Champions

From Left to Right: Bottom Row: (1) Chuck Stevens, (2) Red Lynn, (3) Red Lynn, (4) Eddie Malone, (5) Mel Queen, (6) Tommy Saffell, (7) Ted Beard, (8) Frankie Jacobs, Trainer.
Middle Row: (9) Frank Kelleher, (10) Gordon Maltzberger, Coach, (11) Lloyd Hittle, (12) Bobby Bragan, Manager, (13) Gene Handley, (14) Monty Basgall, (15) Jim Walsh.
Top Row: (16) Dale Long, (17) Joe Muir, (18) George O'Donnell, (19) George Munger, (20) Jack Phillips, (21) Lee Walls, (22) Harry Fisher.

206

1953 – MAYBE THE BEST

FOR THE ONLY TIME IN THEIR HISTORY AT Gilmore Field the Stars repeated as league champions in 1953. After a very contested race during the first half of the season, Hollywood broke into the lead to stay in mid July and won going away. The Stars finished eight games in front of second place Seattle.

Although the club had a glorious year on the field, 1953 was very unsettled for the Stars. This was an eventful year for the whole of the baseball structure. For the first time since 1903 the major league map was changed. The Boston Braves were transferred to Milwaukee just one week before the season opened. The Braves had suffered severe losses during the past several seasons and simply had to move to survive. The transfer to Milwaukee succeeded beyond their wildest dreams. The team drew 1,826,397 fans in Milwaukee in 1953, setting a National League record at that time and dramatically showing what could happen when major league baseball moved into new territory. The Browns had hoped to move to Milwaukee before the Braves got there, but Bill Veeck was thwarted in his attempt to do so by his fellow owners and was forced to operate as a lame duck in St. Louis in 1953. During the season there would be many rumors that the Browns would move to Los Angeles in 1954.

The PCL continued to operate as an Open Classification league in 1953 with the added provision that no team could accept players on option from the major leagues. Under ideal conditions this would have been a wise decision if the PCL were to become a third major league. However, the clubs had been severely hurt by declining attendance during the previous three years, and funds to buy new talent were not available. The quality of play declined somewhat in 1953, and the no option proviso was rescinded in 1954.

The Stars experienced important changes in their front offices during the off season. The sale of George Young's stock brought out disagreements between Vic Collins and Bob Cobb, and in March Collins was appointed Chairman of the Board while Cobb became President and General Manager. The Assistant General Manager and Vice President was Robert C. Clements, a Rickey disciple who came from Pittsburgh. Clements had worked for Branch Rickey in Brooklyn and was extremely loyal to the Mahatma.

A new tone in Hollywood baseball affairs was established by this arrangement. Previously the Stars had been characterized by a strong local flavor. The club represented the Hollywood community and identified itself accordingly. But now Pittsburgh interests began to take precedence. The change would be gradual at first but would accelerate in future years. The fans sensed this transition and responded by staying away from Gilmore Field. Attendance declined to 274,522 in 1953 and continued to do so during the remaining years of the franchise.

The Stars needed a new manager when Haney left for Pittsburgh, and they received a good one in Bobby Bragan, another Rickey protege. Bragan was an average major league player with the Phillies and Dodgers; but he had impressed Mr. Rickey, first with his convictions and approach to life, and then with his obvious intelligence. Bragan began his managerial career at Fort Worth in 1949 and in four years as skipper of the Cats, finished first once and second twice; he was said to be all business on the field and a good man to play for.

Hollywood had a strong nucleus of players with which to defend the championship. Although Johnny Lindell, Mike Sandlock, Paul La Palme, Carlos Bernier and Dick Cole had been promoted to Pittsburgh, the club had impressive talent to replace them. First baseman Dale Long and outfielder Lee Walls, pitchers George O'Donnell and Harry Fisher all looked good and proved to be valuable additions to the club.

Long had gained a bit of fame when Mr. Rickey tried to convert him into the first left handed catcher in modern times. Critics scoffed at this move but failed to recognize that Long was a skillful enough athlete to attempt the conversion. He had been drafted from the Yankee system in 1951 and had enjoyed a good season at New Orleans in 1952, blasting 33 home runs for the Pelicans.

Walls had been a star athlete at Pasadena High School and had done well in his first two years of professional baseball. Only twenty, Walls had all of the prerequisites for baseball success – he could run, hit with power and had a fine throwing arm.

O'Donnell was a tall lean youngster who had a fine sinker ball. He, too, had been at New Orleans in 1952 and moved right into the starting rotation.

The Stars had their usual shakedown period during the first two months of the season, but were never far from the lead. The shortstop position was an early problem. The Stars opened with Johnny O'Neil and Clem Koshorek splitting the duty, but neither was able to hit. O'Neil who had been so important to previous Hollywood teams, seemed to be through; he was sent to Oakland on April 29 in exchange for pitcher Lloyd Hittle. The tiny Koshorek was no better with the bat, although he was adequate in the field, and was released to New Orleans. Jack Phillips moved to shortstop and Gene Handley took over at third base. This solidified the infield for the balance of the year.

The pitching corps was led by Jim Walsh and George O'Donnell during the early going. Mel Queen and George Munger pitched well, although each had arm problems and missed several starts. Harry Fisher, a Canadian right hander, was effective in spots, while left hander Joe Muir helped. The bullpen was manned by Red Lynn and Lloyd Hittle. The trade for Hittle proved to be one of the keys to the season's success. He and Muir were the only left handed pitchers on the staff, and Bragan was able to use Muir as a regular starter, where he was more effective. Then when Joe suddenly retired in June to join the Maryland State Police force, Hittle was used as a spot starter. Bragan played the percentages very heavily and liked to use Hittle against predominately left handed hitting clubs. He frequently brought him in to pitch to one or two left handers in a critical situation.

Much of the offensive spotlight shone on Ted Beard during the early season. He enjoyed the most productive day in Hollywood history April 4, when he crashed four home runs at Lane Field to drive in all the runs as the Stars defeated the Padres 6-5. No other Hollywood player was able to duplicate that feat. Beard wasn't a big man, but he possessed a surprising amount of power. His blows all travelled at least 400 feet over the right center field fence.

Later in the month, Beard tied a PCL record set by Mickey Heath in 1930 when he had twelve straight hits against Oakland and Portland. Bragan was such an advocate of the platoon system that he then benched Beard for the next two games in which the opposing pitchers were left handed. Upon his return to the lineup Beard flied out in his first time at bat to end the streak.

Hollywood fell as far back as six games off the pace in early June but began to turn things around by the end of the month. The Stars jumped into first place on July 4 behind a doubleheader sweep of Sacramento. That day was featured by Red Munger's seven inning no-hitter, the first ever by a Hollywood pitcher. The Stars and Rainiers then took turns in the lead. A key four game series between the clubs began on July 10 with Seattle holding a slim one half game lead.

The Stars were easy winners in the first game, 16-2 behing O'Donnell, but Seattle won the next day to regain first place. Then on Sunday the Stars took both games to go 1½ games in front. The first game was a thriller and was won, 8-7, by Dale Long's inside the park home run in the bottom of the ninth with Tom Saffell on base.

Hollywood continued its winning ways while Seattle stumbled and had a 4½ game lead when the two teams met a week later at Sicks Stadium. The clubs split a four game series as they met for the last time that year. By the end of July the Stars increasd the lead to six games and never looked back. They were in front by as much as 11½ games in August before subsiding in September to the final eight game margin.

The pitching staff was outstanding during the last half of the season as Munger and Queen returned from their ailments. Walsh was especially effective, winning eight straight during July and August, while O'Donnell came on strong after a mid-summer slump. He won his twentieth game on the season's last day. Walsh finished 16-9 while Munger and Queen were 12-10 and 8-7, respectively.

The bullpen was quite valuable. Lynn appeared in 53 games, compiling a 10-4 mark, while Hittle made 23 relief appearances. After Muir left, Bragan activated coach Gordon Maltzberger and the forty year old sinkerballer still had his old cunning. Working in 29 games, most of them for an inning or less, Maltzy had a sparkling 3.10 ERA while winning five games.

After Beard's early exploits, most of the offense was centered on Dale Long. The big first baseman was the PCL's leading home run hitter in 1953 with 35. This was the most ever achieved by a left handed hitter playing at Gilmore, a difficult park for southpaws. Long didn't pull the ball so much that year and hit a number of shots over the right center field fence. His performance resulted in Dale's selection as the PCL's Most Valuable Player.

Once again batting averages were down in the league, but the Stars had consistency throughout their lineup – Beard .286; Saffell .273; Phillips .270; Long .272; Walls .268; Eddie Malone .261. Veteran Frank Kelleher led the team with a .329 mark, playing mostly against left handed pitching. Outfielder Bob Bundy was signed in July after his release by Dallas and gave the Stars some additional punch, hitting .324 in 35 late season games.

Bragan was recognized as a fine manager for the work he did with this team. He ran a game well, used his bench effectively and juggled his pitching staff to the best utilization of each man. Walsh gave Bragan much credit for his improvement over 1952. He changed Jim's delivery from overhand to sidearm, and his fastball had more life to it as a result.

Bragan was a colorful individual and sometimes was very unpredictable. He fought the umpires regularly and was frequently asked to leave the premises early. On one occasion he was so upset at his ejection that he sent out sixteen year old batboy Dick Wisebard to the third base coaches box in protest. Another time he stripped off his uniform on the field after he had been thrown out for protesting a decision too vigorously. Both times he was fined and he was briefly suspended for his strip tease act.

The Stars were participants in a game that year they would rather have forgotten. On April 5 at San Diego, outfielder Herb Gorman of the Padres collapsed on the field and was helped to the clubhouse where he died of an apparent blood clot. The twenty eight year old Gorman had been very popular in his years with the Stars, and his death stunned the players and fans alike.

One of the memorable events of 1953 was the biggest riot seen at a PCL park in years. In a game with the Angels on August 2 at Gilmore Frank Kelleher was hit by a Joe Hatten fast ball and charged the mound. The two scuffled on the ground before the umpires could break it up and when the smoke cleared, Kelleher was ejected. That should have ended the problem right there. But then Ted

Beard, running for Kelleher, raced to third base on a hit and slid hard into Murray Franklin, who had joined the Angels that very day. Franklin came up swinging, and both benches emptied. It was a real fight. Eddie Malone was spiked while Bud Hardin of the Angels suffered a black eye. Many others received cuts and bruises. After restoring order, umpire Cece Carlucci ejected both Beard and Franklin as well as Gene Handley and Fred Richards of the Angels. He then ordered the reserves of both teams to the clubhouse. "I had no choice," Cece recalls. "The crowd was angry and restless. Another incident could have caused a lot of problems. The security forces might not have been able to keep the fans in the stands." He was probably right.

Television continued to plague the Stars in 1953. Although the club had reduced the number of games it televised, a new element was introduced when the televised major league *Game of the Day* was piped into Los Angeles homes every Saturday. The Stars tried to accommodate the fans by moving their Saturday starting time back to 3 o'clock, to allow the fans to come to Gilmore after the major league game was over. But the new time didn't seem to help attendance, and the hard core Hollywood fans complained so much about the later time that the Stars went back to the old one o'clock hour.

Los Angeles fans were now totally addicted to watching their baseball on TV. Perhaps the low point was reached when a fan wrote in that summer complaining that the Gilmore Field billboards created too much glare on his TV screen and would the Stars please paint over them!

As the season wound down to its successful conclusion, the Stars were notified by the Angels that the territorial agreement which expired in 1957 would not be renewed. In other words, the Stars would have to leave Los Angeles. To this day no one knows what P. K. Wrigley had in mind when he gave this news to Bob Cobb. The Hollywood prexy realized that Gilmore had outlived its usefulness by 1953 and that it was time for the club to look for new facilites, preferably in the San Fernando Valley, which was outside the Angel jurisdiction. But he didn't have the capital himself to begin to build a new park. The PCL situation in Los Angeles was shaky anyway; the recurrent rumors of a major league club coming to Los Angeles did not help build one's confidence in the league's viability.

Shortly after the Wrigley announcement, CBS made it known that an option had been taken on the Gilmore Field property to build a new television facility. It had purchased the old Gilmore Stadium property in 1951 as the initial parcel of the installation. A construction date was not made public, but sources indicated that CBS hoped to be in the new facility no later than 1960.

The PCL was in dire straits at the close of the 1953 season. In addition to the Hollywood situation the Bay Area clubs were suffering. Oakland attendance had declined ominously; San Francisco had fared as poorly and owner Paul Fagan had turned the franchise back to the league. The decision to refuse optioned players had been a disaster. All clubs were in need of help. The 1954 season would be critical to the PCL's success.

1953 STANDINGS

	W	L	PCT.
HOLLYWOOD	106	74	.589
Seattle	98	82	.544
Los Angeles	93	87	.517
Portland	92	88	.511
San Francisco	91	89	.506
San Diego	88	92	.489
Oakland	77	103	.428
Sacramento	75	105	.417

Remember the Mother's Cookies Baseball cards? The Stars were prominently displayed in this series during 1952 and 1953. *Clockwise from Top* – Jack Phillips, Lee Walls and Lou Stringer.

Dale Long

(From the collection of Dick Dobbins)

Tom Saffell

From Left to Right, Bottom Row: (1) Frank Jacobs, Trainer, (2) Mel Queen, (3) Larry Dorton, (4) Jack Smith, Bat Boy, (5) Jim Martin, Bat Boy, (6) Dick Smith, (7) Carlos Bernier, (8) Bob Bundy.
Middle Row: (1) Forrest Main, (2) Jack Lohrke, (3) Eddie Malone, (4) Lino Donoso. (5) Bobby Bragan, Manager, (6) Gordon Maltzberger, Coach, (7) Roger Bowman, (8) Tom Saffell, (9) Fred Strobel.
Top Row: (1) Dale Long, (2) George Munger, (3) Jack Phillips, (4) Lee Walls, (5) Frank Kelleher, (6) Jim Walsh, (7) Monty Basgall, (8) Bob Hall.

218

1954 – ONE GAME TOO MANY

THE 1954 STARS MADE A GAME EFFORT TO WIN a third straight pennant, but the season ended in disappointment. Hollywood and San Diego tied for first place at the end of the regular season but the Padres defeated the Stars in a one game playoff, 7-2 for the championship. The Stars had led the PCL through much of the season, and the outcome was a bitter pill for Bobby Bragan and his team to swallow.

The PCL directors decided to resume accepting players on option from the major leagues after a one year hiatus. They also adjusted the length of the schedule once again, reducing it to 168 games and reinstating the playoffs. Overall, the league seemed stronger. The San Francisco franchise had been rescued by a new local group, and the other clubs were in reasonable financial strength.

By 1954 the Stars were a full-fledged Pittsburgh farm. There was little room for the older players and during the season old favorites Chuck Stevens, Gene Handley and Ted Beard were eased out. Pinky Woods had been cut the year before. Only Frank Kelleher was left from the 1949 champions.

Spring training was the usual getting acquainted process. Many new players came and went, but as the season opened the Pirates provided much help – pitchers Roger

Bowman and Bob Hall, infielder Jack Lohrke, catcher Larry Dorton. Carlos Bernier was back after a year at Pittsburgh as was Paul Pettit, this time in the role of an outfielder – first baseman. Paul's arm had gone completely dead, and he was learning to be a hitter. But when the Pirates returned Dale Long, Pettit was sent to Salinas in the California League.

The pitchers were sorely needed, for Bragan had only Red Munger and Mel Queen back from the previous year. Bowman was a hard throwing lefthander who had been signed by the Giants in 1946 out of Colgate University. Roger made good progress through the Giant system until 1950 when he experienced shoulder problems which robbed him of some of his speed. He spent the next two years refining his skills, but the Giants gave up on him in 1953, sending him to Pittsburgh on waivers. It was unfortunate that he landed with the Pirates at that time. Fred Haney had little respect for Bowman's ability and still seemed to resent the no-hitter Roger had thrown against the Stars in 1952. Bowman was used sparingly by the Pirates, compiling an 0-4 record and was sent to Hollywood on an outright basis.

Hall had been battered around while at Pittsburgh in 1953, winning but three of fifteen decisions, but Bragan was glad to get him just the same. The thirty two year old righthander had been a Hollywood nemesis while at Seattle and Sacramento, and the Stars were glad to get him on their side for a change.

The Stars suffered a dismal start, losing ten of their first twelve games and were seventh as April ended. They then experienced a remarkable May, winning twenty six of thirty three games and moved into first place on May 16. By Memorial Day the club had taken a six game lead over Oakland on the heels of a ten game winning streak. San Diego was third, 8½ back. It looked like a sure championship for Hollywood.

As had been the case in 1953, the club took shape in May. Long was back at first base while Jack Phillips was again at third. Monty Basgall was at second base, although he shared time with Jack Lohrke. The shortstop position was originally manned by Ed Wopinek, but Open Classification baseball was a bit too difficult for him and he was sent to Williamsport. Jack Phillips moved to shortstop for a time; then on May 7 the Pirates optioned Dick Smith to Hollywood. The big gap was now filled. Smith had enjoyed a good season in New Orleans during 1953 and was probably the best shortstop prospect in the Pittsburgh system. The Stars won seventeen of their first twenty one games with Smith in the lineup.

At the same time Pittsburgh sent left pitcher Lino Donoso to the club, and the pitching staff was immensely strengthened. A Cuban, Donoso had pitched in the Mexican League in 1953 and was somewhat of an unknown commodity. He soon demonstrated that he could throw hard and had very good control. Bragan was pleased to find that Donoso could both start and relieve without any ill effects.

Munger and Queen were at the top of their game that spring, and Bowman, after a slow start that found him 1-5, began to win with regularity. Hall pitched well although he seemed to lose most of the time. When the Cardinals returned Jim Walsh to the Stars, Hollywood had the best pitching staff in the league. The traditional elements for victory at Gilmore – speed, pitching and defense – were now at hand.

Bernier was a little out of shape when he reported, but his performance didn't indicate it. Carlos reached base eleven of his first fourteen plate appearances. He was an absolute daredevil on the bases, and he and Tom Saffell were far and away the best base runners in the league.

Jack Phillips enjoyed a good start and the versatile infielder was hitting .453 after a month. He was the team's clutch hitter, driving in many important runs. Lee Walls began to develop as a power hitter that spring, although he still had high strikeout totals.

The Stars maintained a sizeable lead through mid June,

but then problems began to develop. Queen, who had won his first eleven decisions and was almost unhittable at times, suffered a recurrence of his shoulder problems and stopped winning. Hall, who had pitched well in spite of a mediocre 4-9 record, was recalled by Pittsburgh and then sold to Seattle. The vaunted pitching staff was suddenly weakened.

The Padres had now developed into a threat. The Stars handled them easily in the clubs' early encounters, winning twelve of the first fourteen games played, but the Padres were beating everyone else and had moved into second place. They had been strengthened with the addition of the great slugger, Luke Easter and pitchers Bill Wight and Al Lyons. San Diego began a winning streak in late June that saw the Padres come within one half game of the lead on July 5. Talk that Hollywood was one of the best clubs in PCL history was suddenly stilled.

The Stars rallied from this crisis and aided by the addition of righthander Ed Wolfe from New Orleans, moved out to a good lead once again. Wolfe won his first four starts in July, Queen bounced back to win twice and the Stars led by five games on July 25. But then the club suffered a bitter blow. Donoso underwent an appendectomy which sidelined him for a month. This was a serious loss. Bragan had used the lefthander both as a starter and in relief and relied on him heavily in key situations. With this loss the only other Hollywood southpaw was Bowman. The Hollywood skipper sent out a plea for help and received George O'Donnell back from Pittsburgh. But even with this aid the Stars were operating with only seven pitchers going into August.

An important series between the Stars and Padres during the first week of August found the Stars in poor physical condition, and the Padres cut the lead to 1½ games. Long had suffered a thumb injury which robbed him of much of his power; he was not the same home run threat he had been in 1953. Basgall was also ailing, forcing Bragan to use Jack Lohrke at second where he was not as effective.

The Stars managed to increase the lead to 4½ games when they met the Padres two weeks later at Gilmore. But San Diego took the first four games of the series before Roger Bowman won the finale in relief, 4-3, leaving Hollywood 1½ games in front. But the club experienced another setback when Carlos Bernier lost his temper over a strike call by umpire Chris Valenti and attacked him, slapping Valenti before he could be restrained. He was immediately suspended for the balance of the year by PCL president Pants Rowland. "Baseball cannot and will not tolerate umpire assault," he said, and Bragan had to agree. Bernier was very repentant after the game and apologized to Valenti, blaming no one but himself. But the damage had been done. The Stars picked up Bobby Del Greco from the Pirate system as a replacement and although he was a fine outfielder, Del Greco did not hit much and was not in Bernier's class as a base runner.

By now it was clear that the Stars would be lucky to win the pennant. They held on to the lead until August 29 when they finally fell a game behind the Padres. But then the Twinks bounced back. Walsh and Donoso pitched two nice games against San Francisco while San Diego was losing twice at Sacramento. A three run homer by George Vico the next night gave the Stars a 7-5 win over the Angels while the Padres continued to lose at Sacramento. When Munger blanked the Angels 7-0 on September 3, the Stars led by three games with only eleven to go.

Alas, Hollywood lost a doubleheader to Los Angeles the very next day while the Padres turned on Sacramento twice. The lead was back to a game as the Stars departed for a season ending trip to Seattle and Portland.

The Stars split four games at Seattle but then stumbled at Portland. Walsh was beaten 6-1 in the first game there as San Diego won at Los Angeles, cutting the lead to a game. While the Stars were idle the next night, San Diego won again at Wrigley Field to creep within one half game of first place. On the final Saturday the Stars were scheduled for a doubleheader with the Beavers and Bragan had his ace,

Roger Bowman, and George Munger set to go. But Bowman was hit hard and Bragan relieved him in the first inning as Portland went on to a 12-1 victory. Munger salvaged the night cap 5-3 as the Padres defeated the Angels again. The two clubs were now tied with a doubleheader remaining on the season's final day.

Bragan chose Lino Donoso to pitch the first game. If the Stars won, it would put the pressure on the Padres. The Cuban responded with a beautiful game, allowing only five hits. But the Hollywood attack was helpless, and Donoso was beaten 1-0. That left everything up to Roger Bowman, who was coming back after his poor showing on Saturday. It was the finest game of his career. The hard throwing southpaw pitched the second no hitter of his career, a perfect game as the Stars breezed to a 7-0 win. It was the 22nd victory of the year for Bowman. No other PCL hurler won as many as 20 that season.

The Padres also split their doubleheader with the Angels, leaving the two clubs tied at the end of the regular season. A one game playoff was scheduled for Monday at San Diego. This put the Stars at a distinct disadvantage, for they had to travel the long distance to face a much healthier Padre club. Bragan's pitching choices were limited. It would have to be Walsh, who had not been effective in recent games after doing yeoman work in July or August, or Munger, pitching with only one days rest. Bragan gambled on the redhead. His opponent would be the well rested Bob Kerrigan, a fine left hander who had a 16-11 record and had pitched well against the Stars in earlier outings.

The gamble failed. Munger was tired and showed it. He served up a home run ball to Bob Elliott in the first inning and a second blast by the veteran third baseman hastened Munger's departure in the fourth inning when the Padres scored four runs. Kerrigan went the distance in an easy 7-2 win. It was San Diego's first regular season championship in history.

The Stars were hopeful of meeting the Padres in the

Governor's Cup finals, but they were worn out and lost in the first round to San Francisco, two games to one. All the games were played at Gilmore Field and were totally anti-climatic. The Hollywood fans turned their backs on the Stars after the pennant fight and a slim turnout of 1,826 attended the three games.

In retrospect Hollywood should have won the 1954 pennant with ease. That the Stars were unable to do so was traceable to the large number of injuries they suffered. Long was victimized by the thumb injury he had suffered in July and went for a month without a home run. Basgall and Phillips were walking wounded at times, while Queen's sore shoulder and Donoso's illness were important losses. Injuries are part of the game, of course, but it seemed as if the Stars had more than their fair share.

The recall of pitcher Bob Hall in June did not seem so important at the time, but it proved to be a critical loss. Not only was his absence felt when the pitching staff was weakened, but the sturdy right hander came back to haunt his former teammates with two important wins while in a Rainier uniform. Hall seemed to have the hex over the Stars throughout his career and 1954 was no exception. Had he remained at Hollywood—one must pause here amidst much speculation as to what might have been.

The disappointing climax notwithstanding, Hollywood fans could look back upon one of the finest years in Gilmore history. The pitching staff was a thing of beauty and certainly ranks as one of the very best in PCL history. The club compiled an ERA of 2.92, by far the lowest in the league, and registered 23 shutouts. Six pitchers had ERA's under three—Munger, Donoso, Bowman, Forrest Main, Wolfe and O'Donnell. Munger and Donoso finished just behind league leader Bill Wight of the Padres. Their records of 17-8 and 19-8, respectively, were indicative of their all-around good work. Bowman was simply outstanding. Both as a starter and reliever, he was the most dependable Hollywood pitcher, and his no-hitter in the season's final game has to rank high among clutch performances. Roger earned another trip to Pittsburgh as a result of his fine year.

Jack Phillips was voted the league's Most Valuable Player in 1954 and deservedly so. The ex-Yankee hit a solid .300 and filled in at first base and shortstop when required. Phillips was a fine clutch hitter, driving in many a game winning run. Hit outstanding play earned him another major league chance with the White Sox, although he was thirty three years old. Jack Lohrke did well as an all around utility man, seeing action in 132 games while hitting .263. The versatility of these two players was vital to the club's success, and Bragan used their talents wisely.

Lee Walls came on fast during the last half of the season and finished at .290, leading the Stars with 93 RBI's. Tom Saffell enjoyed his third successful season with the Stars, hitting .279 and stealing 48 bases to lead to the PCL. Saffell was a very underrated player. He never distinguished himself as a major leaguer, but during his three years as the Hollywood center fielder he hit a solid .275, was a constant threat to steal and roamed the outfield with as much skill as any one in the league. It is no coincidence that Hollywood enjoyed the greatest years in its history while Saffell was the center fielder.

The club would have won the pennant easily had Dale Long repeated his 1953 performance. But the big first baseman, beset by back problems all season long, hit only 23 home runs and drove in a mere 68 runs. Nevertheless, he was an obvious talent and was on his way to Pittsburgh to begin a successful seven year major league career.

At mid season veteran Frank Kelleher announced his retirement at the end of the season. A day was held in his honor during which his familiar number "7" was retired, the only occasion in Hollywood history when this was done. Frank was used primarily as a pinch hitter in 1954, and although his average of .246 was not high, he won five games with clutch blows and was always a threat. Kelleher hit 226 home runs in a Stars' uniform, more than anyone who ever lived. He was probably the most popular

226

Hollywood player ever and is usually the first player mentioned today when the Stars are remembered. He was not particularly fast and was just slightly better than average in the outfield; those two deficiencies kept him from enjoying a long successful major league career. But he was a good hitter and served the Stars well during his ten years at Gilmore.

Once again in 1954 major league talk was rife in Los Angeles. The Browns had moved to Baltimore that year and the Athletics appeared to be nearing the end of their time in Philadelphia. Would Los Angeles get that club? Or would the Senators move West? No one knew the answers.

Almost lost in the major league rumors was the fine play of this 1954 Hollywood team. That was unfortunate. During the middle of the season this club was easily the best in the league and is remembered as one of the finest in PCL history. The failure to win the pennant notwithstanding, the Stars deserved more attention than they received. Never again would they be as good.

1954 STANDINGS

	W	L	PCT.
San Diego	102	67	.604
HOLLYWOOD	101	68	.598
Oakland	85	82	.509
San Francisco	84	84	.500
Seattle	77	85	.475
Los Angeles	73	92	.442
Sacramento	73	94	.437
Portland	71	94	.430

Oakland won the Governor's Cup in the playoffs.

(From the collection of Dick Dobbins)

Bobby Bragan

Roger Bowman

Monty Basgall

From Left to Right, Bottom Row: (1) Al Zarilla, (2) Bob Del Greco, (3) Cholly Naranjo, (4) Carlos Bernier, (5) J. W. Lohrke, (6) Rog Bowman.

Middle Row: (1) Frank Jacobs, Trainer, (2) George Freese, (3) Curt Roberts, (4) Dick Smith, (5) Bobby Bragan, Manager, (6) Bill Hall, (7) Bob Prescott, (8) R. C. Stevens.

Top Row: (1) Bob Garber, (2) Lee Walls, (3) Ben Wade, (4) George Munger, (5) George O'Donnell, (6) George Vico, (7) Joe Trimble.

231

1955 – THE BEST IN LOS ANGELES

THE STARS SLIPPED BACK TO THIRD PLACE IN 1955, finishing four games behind the champion Seattle Rainiers and a game behind San Diego. After a miserable start the Twinks came alive in July and August and briefly moved into the lead on September 2 before losing a critical series to the Angels. The club's finish was its lowest since 1948, and Hollywood suffered the ignominy of sharing third place with the Angels, who caught them two days before the season ended.

Although it was not apparent then, Hollywood had reached the pinnacle of its glory years and now would begin to slide back, both on the field and in popularity. Attendance fell to 248,000, the lowest since the war years. While the Stars continued their insane policy of televising an excessive amount of home games, the fans' attention was drawn to the slugging exploits of Steve Bilko and the Angels amidst much speculation as to the future of major league baseball in Los Angeles.

The Stars had lost their identity as an independent team by 1955. Nowhere was this more obvious than at the Anaheim training base that year. Young players were predominant; only manager Bobby Bragan, Jack Lohrke and George Munger were over thirty. The rest were young Pittsburgh hopefuls who would be using Hollywood as a temporary stop on their way to the major leagues.

There were many fine prospects in camp that year—pitchers Bob Garber and George Witt; catcher Bill Hall; infielders R. C. Stevens, Bill Mazeroski, Jim Baumer and Leo Rodriguez; outfielders George Prescott and Gail Henley were among the most impressive. Paul Pettit was back, this time as an outfielder-first baseman exclusively. Carlos Bernier was returning, totally repentant from his suspension of the year before. "I know I cost us the pennant last year. But I'm a good boy now. No more trouble and we win this year," he predicted.

Bobby Del Greco, who had played part time down the stretch in 1954, had improved his hitting, it seemed, and was Bragan's choice for center field. Just as the season opened the Pirates returned Lee Walls for his final year of seasoning.

The Stars opened the season with an infield of R. C. Stevens, Bill Mazeroski, Jack Lohrke and Leo Rodriguez, while Prescott, Bernier and Del Greco were in the outfield. Bill Hall had won the catching job and veteran Red Munger was the pitcher. That lineup didn't last as the Stars lost their first four games and remained in the lower regions of the second division for the first six weeks.

The club was simply too inexperienced. Mazeroski was a fielding wizard but, at eighteen, was not ready to hit PCL pitching and was benched. His replacement, Jim Baumer, wasn't any better, and they were both sent out for further seasoning when the Pirates sent Curt Roberts as a replacement. Roberts had been the regular Pittsburgh second baseman in 1954 and was still considered a good prospect. Dick Smith, the club's 1954 shortstop, was returned at the same time.

Stevens was also very inexperienced, both in the field and at bat. He had much natural power, but tended to overswing much of the time and frequently struck out. When he made contact, which wasn't often in the early season, the ball travelled a long way.

Third baseman Rodriguez was injured early and was

optioned to Mexico City for seasoning upon his return. Bragan used Lohrke as his early replacement and then when Walls arrrived, took a long look at Del Greco at the position. Later he played Prescott and Bernier there before help arrived from Pittsburgh on June 15 in the person of George Freese. He was almost thirty and had been in the Brooklyn system before the Pirates drafted him. George was one of those good minor league players who never quite made it in the majors. But he was a solid player for the Stars and was especially helpful during their stretch drive.

The pitching was as unsettled as the infield. Although Munger and Garber pitched well from the beginning, the others struggled. Bragan used George Witt and Gonzalo "Cholly" Naranjo as starters, but they were very inexperienced. Each threw several nice games but they were frequently hit hard. They were both optioned to Lincoln in the Western League when additional pitching strength arrived.

Munger and Garber were outstanding, and their work kept the Stars from a complete collapse. The veteran redhead was thirty six when the season started, his best days thought to be well behind him. But like Johnny Lindell a few years previously, Munger revived his career with a knuckleball he perfected during spring training. The new pitch added much to his already fine slider and fastball. Although he didn't post his first victory until the season was three weeks old, he soon began winning with regularity.

Garber had been acquired from Denver along with Prescott after a fine season in the Western League. He was twenty-seven, a bit older than the other rookies, and his work made everyone wonder why he hadn't received a chance at the AAA level before. Garber had a good live fastball, knew how to set up the hitter to hit his pitch and was a real workhorse. He was willing to start or relieve and was frequently called upon with only two days rest between starts. Bragan had a lot of confidence in Garber and used him often as his number one reliever, even though George O'Donnell was having a fine year.

The club obtained needed pitching help when the Pirates returned Roger Bowman outright at the end of May and then sent Ben Wade along with George Freese for Lino Donoso on June 15. Earlier in May, the club had acquired righthander Joe Trimble from the Red Sox system. Bowman had failed to make the grade at Pittsburgh once again, but it was questionable whether he received a real opportunity. Wade had been an important member of Hollywood clubs a few years earlier and after indifferent success at Brooklyn and St. Louis, was acquired by the Pirates in early 1955. Now thirty three, Big Ben still had much life left in his arm. Trimble had just a fair fastball but had a great curve and fine control.

The Stars rallied with the additional pitching strength and a more stabilized infield. After being as far back as 14½ games in early June, the Stars went over .500 to stay on June 29. They enjoyed a fine July, and by August 5 the club was only three games back of the Rainiers. The race was very tight all season with little distance separating the first six clubs. Seattle led most of the way but had to fight off periodic threats by the Padres.

The Twinks owed their surge to the fine pitching of Munger and Garber with help from Joe Trimble, who won five straight decisions during this period. That they could get no closer was a result of inconsistency on the part of Bowman and Wade. After winning three of his first four decisions upon rejoining the Stars, Roger was hit hard and found it very difficult to win. Wade, too, was slumping after a good start. Bragan was relying heavily upon his relief corps of O'Donnell and Al Lyons, the PCL veteran signed after his release by San Diego in July.

A doubleheader sweep at San Diego behind Trimble and Bowman cut the Seattle lead to half a game August 28, and the Stars finally moved into first place on September 1 when Trimble pitched a 3-0 masterpiece at Los Angeles before a crowd of 18,007. It looked as if Hollywood was on its way to the championship.

But that was to be the high point of the season. The Angles turned around and defeated the Stars four straight, including a doubleheader sweep on September 4, 6-5 and 4-3. Garber was beaten in relief in the first game while Trimble's winning streak was stopped at eight The Stars were now four games behind as the Rainiers were defeating Portland five straight.

The pennant race was virtually over. The Stars stumbled in the final two series at Gilmore and were officially eliminated from the race the day before the season ended. The Padres finished one game ahead of the Stars by winning the season's final game at Gilmore, 6-5.

There being no playoffs in 1955, the Stars and Angels had agreed earlier to play a city series for the mythical championship of Los Angeles. Now there was a little more at stake with the clubs tied. A best of five game series was played with all games at Wrigley Field and the Stars did well by themselves winning the series three games to two and not surrendering a home run to Steve Bilko. The games featured two oddities. Shortstop Dick Smith hit three home runs in the five games to pace the offense. He had played 137 games during the regular season without collecting one! Pitcher Don Corella won the second game in relief and that was his only victory in a Hollywood uniform.

This was Bragan's finest job as the manager of the Stars. He controlled his temper and his antics on the field far better than ever before; only once was he ejected from a game and that in the season's finale. He demonstrated a great deal of managerial ability and by season's end was recognized as a very good strategist. A classic example of his original thinking took place in a game with San Diego. With a runner on second base and no one out, pitcher Bob Kerrigan was at bat in a sacrifice situation. Bragan brought Walls in from right field as an extra infielder. The big gap in the outfield was too tempting for Kerrigan who swung away and flied out to Del Greco in center field. The next batter hit what would have been a sacrifice fly had

Kerrigan bunted successfully, and the Stars won 5-4.

Another memorable event but not so flattering to Bragan occurred at Wrigley Field when the Hollywood skipper brought in nine consecutive pinch hitters for the pitcher before allowing Clarence Buheller to complete the turn at bat. "The umpires have made a farce of this game already — I just completed it," Bragan stormed.

The Stars might have won the 1955 pennant with more pitching. The biggest shock was Roger Bowman's failure to come close to his 1954 record. The left hander won only two games during the last two months of the season and finished 5-10. Motivation seemed to be a problem for Roger that year. "When Pittsburgh sent me back to Hollywood in May, I realized that was probably it. I just couldn't get myself going again after that," he says. It is unfortunate that Bowman did not get the opportunity to play for Bragan at Pittsburgh, for Bobby seemed to use him more effectively.

Hollywood had two twenty game winners that year in George Munger and Bob Garber. Munger was the best pitcher in the league. He finished 23-8 with a sparkling ERA of 1.85. This was the lowest in the PCL since Tommy Bridges of Portland had a 1.64 mark in 1947. Munger pitched five shutouts and seven other games in which he allowed only one run. Munger fit the classic definition of a stopper, completing 25 of his 35 starts. He defeated every club in the league at least twice and was especially effective against Seattle, allowing the champions a paltry two runs in 36 innings.

Garber was 20-16 and led the PCL in losses. He may have been overworked early in the year, for he seemed tired in the stretch. During the crucial series at Wrigley Field Garber lost three times, twice in relief. Nevertheless, Garber was an extremely effective pitcher through most of the year and earned a chance with the Pirates in 1956.

Curt Roberts led the club with a .321 average and played exceptionally well at second. Walls was the club's power man with 24 home runs and also led with 99 RBI's. Bobby

Del Greco had one of his best seasons, hitting .287 with 13 home runs while the Twinks had good performances in part time roles from George Freese and George Vico.

At the close of the season Fred Haney was notified by Pittsburgh officials that his contract would not be renewed for 1956. The new manager would be Bobby Bragan.

1955 STANDINGS

	W	L	PCT.
Seattle	95	77	.552
San Diego	92	80	.535
HOLLYWOOD	91	81	.529
Los Angeles	91	81	.529
Portland	86	86	.500
San Francisco	80	92	.465
Oakland	77	95	.448
Sacramento	76	96	.442

Bobby Delgreco

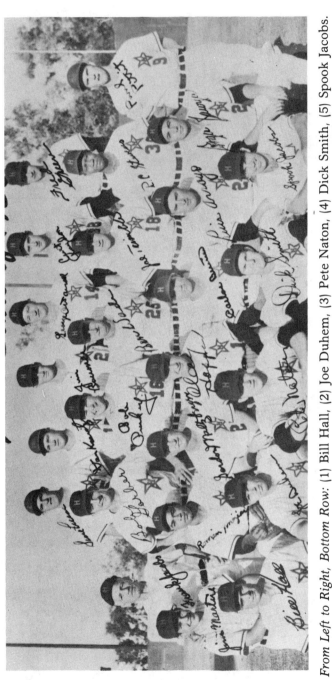

From Left to Right, Bottom Row: (1) Bill Hall, (2) Joe Duhem, (3) Pete Naton, (4) Dick Smith, (5) Spook Jacobs.
Second Row: (6) Jim Martins, Bat Boy, (7) Roman Mejias, (8) Gordon Maltzberger, Coach, (9) Clay Hopper, Mgr.,
(10) Carlos Bernier, (11) Luis Arroyo, (12) Roger Sawyer.
Third Row: (13) Frank Jacobs, Trainer, (14) Bob Garber, (15) Bob Purkey, (16) Ben Wade, (17) Joe Trimble,
(18) R. C. Stevens, (19) Paul Pettit.
Top Row: (20) Gene Freese, (21) Dan Kravitz, (22) Jim Baumer, (23) George O'Donnell, (24) Curt Raydon,
(25) Fred Green.

1956 – A NEW MANAGER AGAIN

THE LOS ANGELES ANGELS DOMINATED THE PCL in 1956. They had one of their best teams in history and finished sixteen games ahead of second place Seattle. There was no pennant race after the middle of July. Hollywood finished in fourth place, 22 games behind the Seraphs. The Stars began the season badly, improved after the Pirates had their May 15 cutdown and moved into the first division in June. But at no time were the Twinks in contention for the pennant.

This was the poorest Hollywood team since the pre-Haney days, and the small crowds reflected the fans' disinterest. Although the Stars abandoned their gate-devouring television policy, attendance dropped to 165,517. During the unseasonably cold spring that year week night crowds were often below one thousand paid. This was unheard of in the post war era.

The new Hollywood field boss was Clay Hopper, a long time manager in the Dodger organization. He had been quite successful at Montreal during the late 40's, winning several pennants with the Royals. In 1946 he was Jackie Robinson's first manager in Organized Baseball and earned Branch Rickey's eternal respect for his handling of the first black player of modern times. Hopper was always known as a Rickey man after that. He had a good reputation as a teacher and handler of young players which would serve him in good stead at Hollywood. In 1955 Hopper had managed Portland, so he was no stranger to the PCL.

The Anaheim training camp was dominated by young players as was now customary. Outfielders Dick Stuart, Joe Duhem and Howie Goss; catchers Bill Onuska, Pete Naton and Nick Koback; pitcher Chuck Churn – these were new names. Cholly Naranjo was back from Lincoln as were Paul Pettit and Jim Baumer from Mexico City and Bill Mazeroski from Williamsport. Experience was at a premium as only Carlos Bernier, Dick Smith and R. C. Stevens were returning regulars.

Hopper thought there was enough potential among the young players that if the Stars could hold their own until the Pirates sent reinforcements at major league cut down day, they could contend for the pennant. But he was the only one who was so optimistic.

The Stars opened with an infield of Pettit, Mazeroski, Smith and Gair Allie, while Bernier, Duhem and Gail Henley were in the outfield. Nick Koback was the opening day catcher with Ben Wade drawing the pitching assignment. He was expected to be the club's ace and was joined by Naranjo, Roger Sawyer, Don Dangleis and Curt Raydon as early starters.

The PCL directors continued to adjust the length of the schedule. This year the number of games was reduced to 168, and for the first time since 1938 a PCL franchise was moved to another city. The Oakland Oaks were shifted to Vancouver where they became the Mounties. Owner Brick Laws could not absorb his losses at Emeryville any longer and sold the club to Canadian interests.

For the first six weeks the Stars were at or in the vicinity of last place before making a move. Help was obtained on May 15 when the Pirates sent pitchers Bob Garber, Joe Trimble and Bob Purkey to Hollywood. The Stars remained in the nether regions of the league until early June when they began a twelve game winning streak which shot them into fourth place. They alternated between third and fourth for the rest of the season, usually remaining a few games above .500 but never posing much of a threat to Los Angeles, who began to run away from the rest of the league in early July.

Hopper believed in a running game and he had the Stars doing just that in 1956. It was just as well, for the club had little power. R. C. Stevens was the home run leader with 27, a goodly number, but he also struck out 92 times, frequently with men in scoring position, and finished at .262. But there were many speedsters on the club. Bernier, as usual, led the way. His 48 stolen bases were easily the highest total in the PCL and he stole more bases himself than either San Diego and Sacramento. Roman Mejias was next in line with 32. This highly underrated outfielder enjoyed a fine season at Gilmore, hitting .274 and 15 home runs. Outfield defense was not a problem with this club; Bernier, Mejias and Joe Duhem covered as much ground as any trio in the league.

The Star who garnered the most attention during the season first half was Bill Mazeroski. Vastly improved after his year at Williamsport, Maz was now a very aggressive hitter as well as a brilliant second baseman. Not yet twenty, Mazeroski was the club's batting leader at .306 when he was acquired by Pittsburgh in exchange for catcher Danny Kravitz, pitcher Luis Arroyo, second baseman Forest "Spook" Jacobs and third baseman Gene Freese. The wholesale move helped the Stars. Kravitz proved to be a workman-like catcher and filled in admirably for Bill Hall, who wasn't hitting that year. Arroyo had been an early standout with the Cardinals in 1955 but was ineffective over the last half of the season. The Pirates acquired him early in 1956, but he was of no help. The half season Arroyo spent at Hollywood seemed to turn him around. He was the club's ERA leader at 2.81 and finished 7-5. Jacobs was a good hitter but had no power. He enjoyed one of his very best years, hitting .341 and was the club's most popular player. Gene Freese was George's younger brother and a better player. He was a

243

good hitter but somewhat erratic in the field. Freese replaced Gair Allie at third when the latter was drafted into the Army after a fine first half of the season.

The Stars battled Portland for third place through the balance of the season and finally lost out in September as the club stopped hitting. Both Kravitz and Hall were injured during the last two weeks and the club used veteran Jack Paepke as the catcher. Jack had played on the championship clubs of 1949-50 and distinguished himself this year by both pitching and catching during the Labor Day doubleheader. The Stars finally fell into fourth for keeps on the next to last day of the season. Their final record of 85-83 was only one game better than fifth place Sacramento.

The Stars suffered from a weak bench all year, and the constant flow of players to and from Pittsburgh created an atmosphere of uncertainty. There were many good performances, but unfortunately most of them were for half a season or less. Although Jacobs and Mazeroski were above .300, no regular who played close to the full season was above that figure. Bernier hit .283, but had his usual troubles with management. He was fined and suspended by Hopper for three games just before the season ended.

The pitching honors were spread among several players. Garber complained of a sore arm when he was returned by the Pirates and spent some time on the disabled list. By the middle of July he seemed to be back to his 1955 form. From that point on he was the club's most reliable pitcher, posting an 11-6 mark. Ben Wade suffered through a miserable start, losing three games in the first week, but he improved after that and finished 13-18. Wade's five shutouts were tops on the club. Cholly Naranjo was 8-6 during the first half and was rushed to Pittsburgh, but he never developed into a good major league pitcher. Although he had a fine curve ball, his fastball was below average, not good enough to win in the big leagues.

George O'Donnell was the club's ace in the bullpen, appearing in over fifty games for the second straight year.

There wasn't anyone to back him up, however. Perhaps Hopper could have tried Arroyo, who was to go on to greater fame as a relief star for the Yankees during their championship years of the early 1960's.

The 1956 season closed in an unsettled manner. Gilmore Field was set to be taken over by CBS after the 1957 season. P. K. Wrigley had agreed to allow the Stars to play in Wrigley Field on a year to year basis should that happen, but only with the understanding that the Stars should find their own park. But that was uncertain at best. What did the future hold for the Hollywood franchise?

Events were to happen fast in 1957.

1956 STANDINGS

	W	L	PCT.
Los Angeles	107	61	.637
Seattle	91	77	.542
Portland	86	82	.512
HOLLYWOOD	85	83	.506
Sacramento	84	84	.500
San Francisco	77	88	.467
San Diego	72	96	.429
Vancouver	67	98	.406

Lino Donoso

(From the collection of Dick Dobbins)

Ben Wade

1957 – THE LAST TWINKLE

AS THE STARS BEGAN SPRING TRAINING FOR the 1957 season, there were few if any observers who suspected that they were watching the last edition of the ball club. But that was what it would be. The Stars would be no more after the season ended. Major league baseball was finally coming to Los Angeles.

No one expected the arrival of the big leagues so soon. Although rumors of an impending franchise transfer to Southern California had developed every summer since 1953, the consensus in 1957 was that such an event was several years away. Whenever the ownership of the also ran Senators or, possibly the Giants, had suffered enough losses, or perhaps when the major leagues decided to expand, that was when Los Angeles would have its major league team.

However, events were already well under way. As far back as August, 1955 Walter O'Malley, President and majority stockholder of the Brooklyn Dodgers, had announced that his team would not play in Ebbets Field beyond the 1957 season. The ball park had small parking facilities and limited seating with no possibility of expanding either; it was no longer adequate for major league baseball. Already fans were becoming fearful of attending games there because of the deteriorating neighborhood.

To show the Brooklyn politicians that he was serious, O'Malley contracted to play eight Dodger home games in 1956 at Roosevelt Stadium in Jersey City. This seemed to activate the politicos, for a Brooklyn Sports Authority was created by the New York State Legislature to study the feasibility of building another stadium for the team.

The location that O'Malley had in mind was in the heart of Brooklyn, a one hundred block area in the vicinity of Flatbush and Atlantic Avenue. A major Long Island Railway terminal was close by, and location was within easy driving distance from Queens and Nassau counties. It would have been an ideal location for a Brooklyn team. However, the project would have required many condemnation proceedings at high cost and ran into much resistance.

The controversy raged throughout 1956, as the Dodgers were on their way to their fourth National League pennant in five years. Attendance was 1,213,000, considerably better than it had been through much of the period, approximately a million or so fans a year. In contrast the Milwaukee Braves were drawing 2,046,000 in 1956. O'Malley feared that he would no longer be competitive if this gap in attendance continued. When the Atlantic project died because of the high cost estimates, the Dodger president began to look for alternative sites.

Los Angeles had always been appealing to O'Malley, and perhaps he more than any other baseball official realized the true potential of the Southern California market. In November 1956 O'Malley sold the Ebbets Field property to realtor Marvin Kratter with the proviso that the Dodgers could play there through 1959. Now he had operating capital should a move be necessary.

The first step that led to the Dodgers' move to Los Angeles took place on February 21, 1957, when O'Malley purchased the Angel franchise and Wrigley Field from P. K. Wrigley for approximately three million dollars and the Brooklyn farm club at Fort Worth. Now the Dodgers had a place to play should they move from Brooklyn.

Although O'Malley denied that the Dodgers were planning to move, Mr. Wrigley evidently thought otherwise for he stated that the sale would make it possible for Los Angeles to have a major league team in the very near future. What O'Malley told Wrigley in this regard is not known.

The PCL directors were concerned over the sale and there was some doubt that the transaction would be approved. Directors from the Northern Cities were especially concerned; they were fearful that a Dodger move would put them out of business. But O'Malley assured the directors that the Angels were intended to be the Brooklyn farm club in the PCL and the sale was approved on March 2.

Los Angeles officials did not feel that way, however; and Mayor Norris Poulson announced that it was his goal to persuade the Dodgers to move to Los Angeles. A number of studies had been made of potential stadium sites in the city and these were reactivated. Among the locations was the Chavez Ravine area, not far from downtown Los Angeles.

Shortly after the beginning of spring training Mayor Poulson and supervisor Kenneth Hahn flew to the Dodger camp at Vero Beach, Florida to meet with O'Malley. Upon their return to Los Angeles it was announced that nothing had been agreed upoon, but in view of later events it seems clear that the general outline of an understanding between the city and the Dodgers had been presented. The National League gave the Dodgers and Giants permission to move from New York on May 28. The Dodgers had already filed articles of incorporation in California a month previously.

The final proposition was not officially submitted to the Dodger president until September 16. It called for the transfer of the Chavez Ravine area to the Dodgers for $4,400,000. The city would also grade the site, the county would spend $2,700,000 for connecting roads to the free-ways, and the city would also buy Wrigley Field for $2,500,000. The proposal was approved by the Los Angeles

City Council and on October 8, 1957, the Brooklyn club directors and stockholders voted unanimously to move. The major leagues were on their way to the Pacific Coast.

All of this was still in the future as the Stars trained in Anaheim. The club had a new manager once again in the person of Clyde King. He was a former Brooklyn pitcher who had guided the Atlanta Crackers to the 1956 Southern Association championship. Like his predecessor, King had the reputation of being a Branch Rickey man.

The Pittsburgh farm system was now beginning to produce good players in earnest, and the young prospects who joined the Stars in camp that year looked very good. Most impressive were pitchers Bennie Daniels and George Witt. Young outfielder Bill Causion was the best player in camp. He was a good hitter with fine speed and soon won the center field position.

The most exciting rookie that year was outfielder Dick Stuart. A big, gangly slugger from San Carlos, California, Stuart had enjoyed a fabulous season at Lincoln in 1956. He hit sixty-six home runs to set an all time Western League record and drove in 171 runs as well. Although he was helped somewhat by a very friendly left field fence at Cy Sherman Field, Stuart was a bona fide power hitter and many of his blows were among the longest ever in the Western League. A brash likeable fellow, Stuart announced upon his arrival that he would lead the PCL in home runs and the Stars would win the pennant.

It looked as if Stuart's predictions would come true when the season opened. Installed as the right fielder, Stuart was hitless in the opener of a day-night doubleheader at San Diego but crashed two home runs to pace a 4-1 Hollywood victory at night. The next day he hit a shot over the right center field fence estimated to be over 500 feet, as the Stars won 14-1. He added two more the next day to insure George Witt's 4-1 victory. Although he went hitless in the Sunday doubleheader which the Stars swept, the fans had a new hero.

Unfortunately, Stuart's bubble soon burst. He was

striking out half of the time and not getting many hits besides. His fielding was atrocious. He was very immobile in the field and did not seem to have better than an average arm. Although the big fellow managed one more home run, at Wrigley Field on the Stars' first visit, King benched him on April 25. Paul Pettit took over in right field where he played for the balance of the year. Stuart was optioned to Atlanta on May 11 and eventually found himself back at Lincoln again. He resumed his destruction of Western League pitchers, learned to play first base, and was in the major leagues in 1958.

The Stars got off to an unusually fast start and led the league during much of May. They then suffered a mild slump during the last week of the month that carried into June. It was during this period that San Francisco and Vancouver passed the Stars, and they settled in third place for the balance of the season. Hollywood was never able to come closer than three games behind the leaders after that and ended the season seven games behind the champion Seals.

This was a much better team than the 1956 club, but in view of the exciting speculation on the Dodgers' imminent move to Los Angeles, the improvement went almost unnoticed. The club was much more stable. After the early shakedown of Pittsburgh optionees King was able to play a set lineup much of the time. The only exception was at first base. After going with R.C. Stevens during the first three months the club gave up on the powerful but erratic first baseman and sent him to Columbus in July. Tony Bartirome replaced him and was much more useful. Although he had no power, Bartirome was a consistent hitter with good speed. King used him as leadoff hitter where the Pittsburgh native responded with a .316 average.

The Hollywood pitching staff was outstanding in 1957. It had two fine starters in George Witt and Bennie Daniels, several pitchers who pitched well in spots—Curt Raydon, Don Rowe and Bob Garber, and an excellent bullpen led by Chuck Churn and Ben Wade. As a former pitcher himself, King knew how to handle this group and got the most out of each man.

Witt had the finest season of his career, winning 18 games and leading the PCL with 6 shutouts. At one stage in July and August the tall righthander went 50 2/3 innings without allowing a run. Witt's ERA of 2.24 was second in the league to veteran Morrie Martin of Vancouver. George had not enjoyed a season nearly as good in his previous professional career and in 1956 had experienced some arm problems at New Orleans. But in spring training he converted to the "no windup" style of pitching and the results were extraordinary. The new delivery cured his ailments and greatly improved his control.

Witt advanced to the parent Pirates in mid season of 1958 and led Pittsburgh to a surprising second place finish with his fine pitching. He compiled a 9-2 record with a sparkling 1.61 ERA and was the talk of the league in August and September. But that was the last success for the redhead. He developed an elbow problem in the spring of 1959 and was never again the same pitcher.

Daniels won 17 games and was also among the leaders with a 2.95 ERA. A fine athlete out of Compton High, Daniels had a good live, sinking fastball that frequently jumped out of the strike zone. When Bennie's control was good, he was extremely difficult to hit. Daniels was one of the finest fielding pitchers to ever wear a Hollywood uniform and was a good hitter as well. When the outfield corps was beset with injury King used Bennie in right field for several games.

Daniels was called up by Pittsburgh late in the 1957 season and in an ironic twist started the last game ever played in Ebbets Field.

Churn appeared in 67 games as the bullpen ace that year as he quelled many an enemy rally. He was such a willing worker and so effective that the club's bullpen hero of previous years, George O'Donnell, was shipped to Columbus because he wasn't getting enough work. Veteran Ben Wade also performed well in a relief role.

There were a number of memorable events during the Stars' last year in Hollywood. Utility infielder Dick Smith had six straight pinch hits to tie a PCL record. Paul Pettit drove in ten runs in a 20-2 slaughter of Seattle September 12. Pettit threw out pitcher Earl Harrist of Sacramento on a "single" to right May 8 – only Gus Zernial had done that at Gilmore Field. And left handed first baseman Tony Bartimore appeared in several games at third in late July when King had no one else to play the position.

As the season drew to a close, there was nostalgia mixed with anticipation among the Hollywood fans. The final game at Gilmore was played on September 5 and a crowd of 6,354 showed up to see Hugh Pepper pitch a 6-0 one hitter against the first place Seals, President Bob Cobb was given a standing ovation by the crowd, a gesture which brought tears to his eyes. He had given Hollywood fans a great deal of excitement for twenty years, and everyone would miss him.

The Stars were on the road for the last two weeks of the season. By this time it seemed clear that the Dodgers were coming to Los Angeles. The club played its last game as a Hollywood entity at Portland and won 5-4 behind Don Rowe.

The move of the New York teams to the Pacific Coast made it necessary for several PCL franchises to be transferred, and this was accomplished at the winter meetings in Colorado Springs. The Angel franchise was moved to Spokane, San Francisco to Phoenix and the Stars to Salt Lake City. With the loss of its two major cities the PCL dropped back to AAA classification and its major league aspirations were ended.

It was a sad day for Bob Cobb when he sold the franchise. Although the club was sold for approximately $150,000, a fine return on the original investment, money could not substitute for the joy in running the Hollywood baseball club. That was probably the most enjoyable job Cobb ever had.

And so the Stars returned to Salt Lake City from whence they originally came thirty years before.

1957 STANDINGS

	W	L	PCT.
San Francisco	101	67	.601
Vancouver	97	70	.581
HOLLYWOOD	94	74	.560
San Diego	89	79	.530
Seattle	87	80	.521
Los Angeles	80	88	.476
Sacramento	63	105	.375
Portland	60	108	.357

(From the collection of Dick Dobbins)

Clyde King – The last Hollywood Manager.

Two Hollywood greats in comfortable retirement in 1983. Babe Herman (L) and Mickey Heath.

EPILOGUE

LIFE AFTER THE STARS

CBS EXERCISED ITS OPTION ON THE GILMORE Field property after the 1957 season closed, and in 1958 the wreckers assaulted the friendly ball park on Beverly Boulevard. It was a sad day for all Hollywood fans, but it was also inevitable. Even had the Dodgers not come West when they did, the Stars would have been forced to abandon their playground in 1958. Perhaps it was just as well that the franchise expired at the same time as the park. It wouldn't have been quite the same in Wrigley Field.

The Pirates ended their thirty three year pennant drought by capturing the National League title in 1960. The Hollywood fans who were now converted to the Dodgers had mixed feelings over this event, for several of their old favorites played important roles in the Pittsburgh pennant drive. Dick Stuart and Bill Mazeroski enjoyed fine years, and Maz thrilled all of Pittsburgh with his game winning home run in the decisive seventh game of the World Series. Other former Stars on the club were pitchers George Witt, Bennie Daniels and Fred Green.

By 1966 the only Hollywood alumni still in active playing roles were Stuart and Mazeroski, and when the great Pirate second baseman called it a career at the close of the 1972 season baseball had seen the last of the Stars.

Clyde King, Monte Basgall and Mazeroski subsequently served in non-playing roles, but at the close of the 1983 season, only Basgall remained in uniform.

Today the Stars are just a memory but a very pleasant one. They were representative of an era in baseball history that is long over – that of the independent minor league club. The men who played at Hollywood remember their experiences as among the most rewarding of their careers. So do the fans.

There is no tangible evidence today that Gilmore Field ever existed. Much of the site is occupied by the mammoth CBS facilities parking lot. The trees that bordered the outfield fences provide a dim outline of where the field was. If you should stand in that parking lot someday, try to visualize what it must have been like thirty and forty years ago, when Gilmore Field was an exciting place to be.

BIBLIOGRAPHY

BOOKS

Mayer, Ronald A., *The 1937 Newark Bears, A Baseball Legend*, Union City, New Jersey, Wm. H. Wise & Company, 1980

Obojski, Robert, *Bush League*, New York, McMillan, 1975

Mead, William B., *Even The Browns*, Chicago, Contemporary Books, 1978

Schroeder, W. R., *The Pacific Coast League From 1903 To 1940*, Los Angeles, Helms Athletic Foundation, 1941

Linthurst, Randolph, *Newark Bears*, Trenton, N.J. Linthurst, 1978

Davids, L. Robert Ed., *Minor League Baseball Stars*, Career Records compiled by The Society For American Baseball Research, Washington, D. C., 1978.

Lange, Fred W., *History of Baseball in California And Pacific Coast Leagues, 1847-1938*, Oakland, Lange, 1938

Lieb, Frederick G., *The Detroit Tigers*, New York, Putnam's, 1946

Allen, Lee, *The Giants and the Dodgers*, New York, Putnam's, 1964

Heath, Minor W., *Baseball Before Money*, Unpublished Manuscript, 1981

Dykes, Jimmie & Dexter, Charles O., *You Can't Steal First Base*, Philadelphia, J. B. Lippincott & Co., 1967

Day, Laraine & Crichton, Kyle, *Day With The Giants*, Garden City, N.Y., Doubleday & Co., 1952

Lowenfish, Lee & Lupien, Tony, *The Imperfect Diamond*, Briarcliff Manor, N.Y., Stein & Day, 1980

Finch, Robert L.; Addington, L. H., Morgan, Ben M. Ed. *The Story of Minor League Baseball*, The National Association of Professional Baseball Leagues, Columbus, O, 1952

Daniels, Stephen M. *The Hollywood Stars*, Baseball Research Journal, Davids, L. Robert, Ed., Washington, D.C. 1980

Mann, Authur, *Branch Rickey—American In Action*, Boston, Houghton Mifflin Company, 1957

Henstel, Bruce, *Los Angeles—An Illustrated History*, New York, Alfred A. Knopf, 1980

Eckhouse, Morris & Mastroola, Carl, *This Date In Pittsburgh Pirates History*, Briarcliff Manor, N.Y., Stein & Day, 1980

Frommer, Harvey, *New York City Baseball, The Last Golden Age, 1947-1957*, New York, Macmillan Publishing Company, 1980

Beverage, Richard E. *The Angels—Los Angeles in the Pacific Coast League, 1919-57*, The Deacon Press, Placentia, Ca, 1981

NEWSPAPERS

Los Angeles *Times*, 1926-57
Los Angeles *Examiner*, 1926-57
San Francisco *Chronicle*, 1926-57
Sacramento *Bee*, 1926-57
The Sporting News, St. Louis, 1926-57

RECORD BOOKS

Spaulding Official Baseball Guide, 1920-40
Reach Official Baseball Guide, 1915-40
Spaulding—Reach Official Baseball Guide, 1941
The Sporting News Baseball Guide and Record Book, 1942-43
The Sporting News Official Baseball Guide, 1944-58
Pacific Coast League Record Book, 1956-57

APPENDIX

Hollywood Stars – Team and Individual Records

1926 – 1957

1926 - 6th PLACE (94-107)
MANAGER: OSCAR VITT

		G	AB	AVG	HR	RBI
1B	ROY LESLIE	119	399	.258	6	50
2B	JOHNNY KERR	198	705	.272	16	75
3B	OSCAR VITT	110	341	.252	1	25
SS	DUDLEY LEE	165	558	.228	0	42
LF	JOHNNY FREDERICK	186	667	.277	8	63
CF	FRANK ZOELLER	163	585	.268	7	56
RF	LEFTY O'DOUL	180	659	.338	20	116
C	JOHN PETERS	143	403	.290	3	53
C	LES COOK	93	226	.208	0	18
1B	FRITZ COUMBE	101	323	.250	7	28
INF	MACK HILLIS	43	142	.260	1	13
3B	CHARLIE GOOCH	120	404	.262	0	36
OF	LES SHEEHAN	116	395	.306	5	46

		G	IP	W	L	ERA	SHUTOUTS
P	FRANK SHELLENBACK	34	230	16	12	2.97	7
P	JOHN SINGLETON	42	235	10	13	3.18	2
P	HARRY O'NEILL	36	166	9	9	3.20	0
P	DICK McCABE	35	239	15	19	3.28	0
P	PHIL MULCAHY	40	192	7	12	3.38	1
P	GEORGE HOLLERSON	27	133	9	7	3.52	1
P	HANK HULVEY	34	150	13	10	3.90	1
P	CURT FULLERTON	44	230	10	17	4.34	2
P	BILL MURPHY	11	55	0	3	4.58	0

1927 - 6th PLACE (92-104)

MANAGER: OSCAR VITT

		G	AB	AVG	HR	RBI
1B	MICKEY HEATH	106	330	.282	9	51
2B	JOHNNY KERR	189	660	.276	18	91
3B	CHARLIE GOOCH	134	437	.252	1	40
SS	DUDLEY LEE	190	689	.242	2	39
LF	BABE TWOMBLEY	158	521	.309	0	54
CF	PAT McNULTY	106	362	.312	0	43
RF	JOHNNY FREDERICK	180	623	.305	9	93
C	DENNY MURPHY	116	351	.293	7	53
C	SAM AGNEW	75	203	.296	6	34
C	LES COOK	55	125	.232	0	11
1B	JIM McDOWELL	74	240	.242	5	30
3B	TOM HOLLEY	63	165	.230	3	18
3B	COTTON TIERNEY	34	104	.231	0	13
OF	LES SHEEHAN	117	361	.288	6	44
OF	JIM SWEENEY	68	231	.251	6	24

		G	IP	W	L	ERA	SHUTOUTS
P	HANK HULVEY	35	225	17	14	2.97	2
P	FRANK SHELLENBACK	34	265	19	12	3.05	4
P	BILL MURPHY	34	191	14	8	3.39	3
P	DICK McCABE	42	196	11	16	3.63	3
P	BUD TEACHOUT	18	103	6	6	3.84	0
P	CURT FULLERTON	44	263	13	19	3.93	1
P	PHIL MULCAHY	49	208	6	13	4.24	0
P	ART JACOBS	30	136	3	9	4.96	0

1928 - SPLIT SEASON

FIRST HALF: 2nd PLACE (53-39)
SECOND HALF: 3rd PLACE (59-40)
                        112-79

MANAGER: OSCAR VITT

		G	AB	AVG	HR	RBI
1B	MICKEY HEATH	191	662	.307	19	109
2B	JOHNNY KERR	192	775	.301	16	82
3B	JULIE WERA	89	294	.303	3	45
SS	DUDLEY LEE	191	802	.273	5	77
LF	WALT REHG	78	261	.306	3	47
CF	CLEO CARLYLE	126	440	.289	14	72
RF	BABE TWOMBLEY	187	697	.314	0	75
C	JOHNNY BASSLER	127	373	.300	2	33
C	SAM AGNEW	88	252	.321	4	38
3B	LEO OSTENBERG	61	221	.294	8	35
3B	TOM HOLLEY	63	153	.261	3	18
OF	PAT McNULTY	47	139	.266	1	20
OF	ELMER SMITH	55	207	.309	14	47
OF	TONY BOROJA	58	169	.308	1	13
OF	BOBBY ROTH	67	226	.283	1	37

		G	IP	W	L	ERA	SHUTOUTS
P	CURT FULLERTON	32	169	10	12	3.09	1
P	FRANK SHELLENBACK	38	272	23	11	3.13	3
P	GORDON RHODES	40	229	17	10	3.26	4
P	DICK McCABE	37	224	16	10	3.93	1
P	HANK HULVEY	38	226	14	9	4.42	0
P	PHIL MULCAHY	33	104	4	5	4.67	0
P	JOHNNY COUCH	10	53	2	3	4.67	1
P	WALT KINNEY	38	210	17	8	4.67	1
P	BILL MURPHY	26	95	5	6	4.83	0

1929 - SPLIT SEASON

FIRST HALF: 4th PLACE (52-47)
SECOND HALF: 1st PLACE (61-42)
                         113-89
MANAGER: OSCAR VITT

		G	AB	AVG	HR	RBI
1B	MICKEY HEATH	201	680	.349	38	156
2B	HOWARD BURKETT	141	408	.245	5	52
3B	RUSS ROLLINGS	198	738	.324	6	86
SS	DUDLEY LEE	205	848	.262	4	71
LF	ELIAS FUNK	150	547	.384	13	125
CF	CLEO CARLYLE	195	666	.347	20	136
RF	BILL RUMLER	140	503	.386	26	120
C	JOHNNY BASSLER	107	299	.251	0	37
C	ROWDY SYPHER	51	95	.306	0	11
C	HANK SEVEREID	79	263	.415	9	72
2B	MIKE MALONEY	96	292	.236	1	34
OF	WALT REHG	80	200	.305	2	38
OF	BILL ALBERT	89	203	.286	2	30
OF	HARRY GREEN	71	190	.279	9	45

		G	IP	W	L	ERA	SHUTOUTS
P	AUGIE JOHNS	44	201	17	10	3.89	1
P	FRANK SHELLENBACK	46	335	26	12	3.97	1
P	BUZZ WETZEL	45	269	17	15	4.04	2
P	WALT KINNEY	41	203	12	12	4.25	2
P	GEORGE HOLLERSON	45	247	13	13	4.40	1
P	JOE MARTICORENA	45	145	10	9	5.77	1
P	DICK McCABE	19	62	1	4	5.81	0
P	HANK HULVEY	49	240	14	11	6.07	1

1930 - SPLIT SEASON
FIRST HALF: 2nd PLACE (54-46)
SECOND HALF: 1st PLACE (65-35)
                        119-81
MANAGER: OSCAR VITT

		G	AB	AVG	HR	RBI
1B	MICKEY HEATH	174	546	.324	37	136
2B	OTIS BRANNAN	191	742	.307	18	130
3B	MIKE GAZELLA	171	650	.303	11	94
SS	DUDLEY LEE	187	717	.275	3	57
LF	JESS HILL	115	480	.356	18	71
CF	CLEO CARLYLE	172	616	.326	12	97
RF	DAVE BARBEE	100	427	.333	31	115
C	HANK SEVEREID	129	376	.367	13	93
C	JOHNNY BASSLER	123	348	.365	0	71
INF	LOU CATINA	77	184	.212	0	10
OF	BILL RUMLER	95	346	.353	14	82
OF	HARRY GREEN	123	431	.329	14	80

		G	IP	W	L	ERA	SHUTOUTS
P	JIM TURNER	36	258	21	9	3.80	1
P	VANCE PAGE	41	172	8	11	3.87	0
P	AUGIE JOHNS	42	195	12	11	4.38	1
P	FRANK SHELLENBACK	36	252	19	7	4.64	0
P	HANK HULVEY	38	171	11	10	4.89	2
P	GORDON RHODES	20	117	9	2	5.23	1
P	EMIL YDE	39	179	13	11	5.33	0
P	BUZZ WETZEL	44	200	13	10	5.58	0
P	GEORGE HOLLERSON	49	203	13	10	6.03	0

1931 - SPLIT SEASON
FIRST HALF: 1st PLACE   (57-34)
SECOND HALF: 5th PLACE   (47-49)
                         ‾‾‾‾‾‾
                         104-83

MANAGER: OSCAR VITT

		G	AB	AVG	HR	RBI
1B	JACK SHERLOCK	169	614	.279	10	99
2B	OTIS BRANNAN	145	555	.283	7	85
3B	MIKE GAZELLA	174	653	.314	6	77
SS	DUDLEY LEE	161	651	.275	3	55
LF	JESS HILL	159	600	.318	19	97
CF	CLEO CARLYLE	135	490	.320	10	89
RF	DAVE BARBEE	168	650	.332	47	166
C	JOHNNY BASSLER	103	316	.354	0	43
C	HANK SEVEREID	94	308	.347	17	65
INF	LOU CATINA	61	167	.246	1	24
OF	MARTY CALLAGHAN	112	372	.304	1	54
OF	HARRY GREEN	54	176	.239	2	16
OF	AL McNEELEY	51	154	.299	0	17

		G	IP	W	L	ERA	SHUTOUTS
P	FRANK SHELLENBACK	36	306	27	7	2.85	5
P	BUZZ WETZEL	19	128	7	6	3.87	0
P	JIM TURNER	45	292	17	15	4.28	0
P	EMIL YDE	39	210	14	16	4.32	2
P	VANCE PAGE	31	201	17	8	4.34	1
P	AUGIE JOHNS	33	89	4	5	5.17	0
P	ELMER BRAY	33	166	6	11	5.42	0
P	GEORGE HOLLERSON	13	61	4	4	5.90	0
P	LOU McEVOY	16	66	4	5	6.68	0

HOLLYWOOD STARS SEASON STATISTICS
1926 - 1957

1932 - 2nd PLACE (106-83)
MANAGER: OSCAR VITT

		G	AB	AVG	HR	RBI
1B	JACK SHERLOCK	185	674	.292	11	114
2B	OTIS BRANNAN	177	697	.311	17	111
3B	MIKE GAZELLA	129	474	.232	5	42
SS	DUDLEY LEE	163	611	.265	1	44
LF	MARTY CALLAGHAN	140	511	.311	0	42
CF	CLEO CARLYLE	181	673	.346	16	106
RF	AL McNEELEY	148	553	.284	11	82
C	JOHNNY BASSLER	156	443	.357	1	66
C	TED MAYER	68	175	.246	4	32
INF	ALAN STRANGE	110	354	.277	2	40
OF	BOB MEUSEL	64	228	.329	4	26
OF	LOU MARTIN	34	130	.269	3	14
OF	GEORGE QUELLICH	47	175	.269	5	30

		G	IP	W	L	ERA	SHUTOUTS
P	TOM SHEEHAN	31	181	13	6	3.03	7
P	FRANK SHELLENBACK	36	322	26	10	3.14	0
P	MYLES THOMAS	36	229	14	18	3.66	0
P	EMIL YDE	35	226	17	9	3.94	1
P	FRED ORTMAN	14	82	5	4	4.07	2
P	VANCE PAGE	40	258	13	19	4.23	0
P	AUGIE JOHNS	16	52	1	1	4.31	0
P	JIM TURNER	40	194	11	10	4.61	1

1933 - 3rd PLACE (107-80)

MANAGER: OSCAR VITT

		G	AB	AVG	HR	RBI
1B	RAY JACOBS	159	564	.284	36	125
2B	OTIS BRANNAN	188	717	.303	14	108
3B	FRED HANEY	176	719	.317	2	65
SS	ALAN STRANGE	133	490	.324	6	81
LF	DOUG TAITT	103	378	.336	15	67
CF	CLEO CARLYLE	158	584	.320	9	94
RF	CED DURST	180	730	.318	14	80
C	JOHNNY BASSLER	122	330	.336	0	50
C	FRANK TOBIN	47	138	.254	3	11
C	LLOYD SUMMERS	65	162	.235	1	15
P-1B	DAN CROWLEY	37	93	.290	5	21
INF	JOE BERKOWITZ	83	266	.305	1	26
OF	LOU MARTIN	51	144	.299	3	24
OF	VINCE DIMAGGIO	74	302	.348	10	57

		G	IP	W	L	ERA	SHUTOUTS
P	ARCHIE CAMPBELL	51	311	22	15	4.08	2
P	TOM SHEEHAN	38	271	21	13	4.25	3
P	FRANK SHELLENBACK	38	314	21	12	4.53	1
P	VANCE PAGE	45	293	20	15	4.54	2
P	BUZZ WETZEL	42	177	14	10	4.92	1
P	GEORGE BUCHANAN	14	54	2	5	5.33	0
P	DICK SCHULTZE	12	50	2	2	5.45	0

1934 - SPLIT SEASON

FIRST HALF: 5th PLACE (39-45)
SECOND HALF: 2nd PLACE (58-43)
                         97-86

MANAGER: OSCAR VITT

		G	AB	AVG	HR	RBI
1B	RAY JACOBS	178	597	.288	24	112
2B	JOE BERKOWITZ	112	373	.279	3	23
3B	FRED HANEY	179	702	.306	1	76
SS	JIM LEVEY	183	718	.256	7	63
LF	VINCE DIMAGGIO	166	587	.288	17	91
CF	CLEO CARLYLE	122	459	.272	4	58
RF	SMEAD JOLLEY	171	631	.360	23	133
C	JOHNNY BASSLER	123	308	.351	0	55
C	WILLARD HERSHBERGER	114	332	.307	3	46
2B	BOBBY DOERR	67	201	.259	0	11
OF-1B	CED DURST	125	438	.299	4	61
OF	FERN BELL	43	145	.283	8	30

		G	IP	W	L	ERA	SHUTOUTS
P	JOE SULLIVAN	39	288	25	11	2.88	1
P	TOM SHEEHAN	37	237	16	14	3.69	2
P	FRANK SHELLENBACK	34	229	14	12	4.17	3
P	JACK HILE	28	79	1	6	4.21	0
P	WALLY HEBERT	37	170	11	11	4.23	0
P	ARCHIE CAMPBELL	42	191	12	13	4.81	1
P	JIM DENSMORE	44	230	14	11	4.84	0
P	VANCE PAGE	11	67	2	4	5.41	0

1935 - SPLIT SEASON
FIRST HALF: 4th PLACE (36-34)
SECOND HALF: 8th PLACE (37-65)
                        73-99
MANAGER: FRANK SHELLENBACK

		G	AB	AVG	HR	RBI
1B	RAY JACOBS	115	402	.296	13	69
2B	BOBBY DOERR	172	647	.317	4	74
3B	JIM LEVEY	130	532	.278	2	47
SS	GEORGE MYATT	135	530	.311	1	33
LF	VINCE DIMAGGIO	174	659	.278	24	112
CF	CED DURST	167	639	.324	6	72
RF	SMEAD JOLLEY	159	599	.372	29	128
C	GENE DESAUTELS	129	426	.265	6	55
C	JIM KERR	66	193	.269	4	31
1B	GEORGE McDONALD	68	212	.255	0	23
INF	EDDIE MULLIGAN	51	134	.269	0	16
INF	JOE BERKOWITZ	71	222	.275	0	21
OF	VAN WIRTHMAN	57	131	.260	1	9

		G	IP	W	L	ERA	SHUTOUTS
P	FRANK SHELLENBACK	26	200	14	9	3.42	0
P	BERLYN HORNE	29	158	13	7	4.10	2
P	ED WELLS	39	264	9	20	4.33	0
P	ARCHIE CAMPBELL	42	241	12	17	4.51	0
P	WALLY HEBERT	39	219	10	17	4.94	1
P	HERMAN PILLETTE	21	159	12	9	5.09	0
P	JACK HILE	33	148	1	7	5.24	0

HOLLYWOOD STARS SEASON STATISTICS
1926 - 1957

1938 - 7th PLACE (79-99)
MANAGER: WADE KILLEFER

		G	AB	AVG	HR	RBI
1B	ROY MORT	167	605	.266	1	73
2B	DON JOHNSON	121	389	.221	2	28
3B	JOE COSCARART	155	564	.271	6	69
SS	TOM CAREY	157	629	.297	3	65
LF	GEORGE PUCCINELLI	87	298	.305	22	59
CF	FRENCHY UHALT	166	635	.332	5	65
RF	CED DURST	107	407	.314	4	37
C	JOE ANNUNZIO	39	109	.239	1	11
C	BILL BRENZEL	123	410	.251	0	52
C	CHICK OUTEN	52	103	.320	0	13
INF	JOE HOOVER	93	288	.257	3	26
INF	BILL McWILLIAMS	45	130	.192	0	10
OF	FERN BELL	44	187	.305	5	30
OF	BILL NORMAN	82	242	.293	12	47
OF	VIC METTLER	81	241	.249	0	18

		G	IP	W	L	ERA	SHUTOUTS
P	JOHN BABICH	39	275	19	17	3.27	4
P	LOU TOST	39	220	11	16	3.48	4
P	LEROY HERRMANN	16	63	3	3	4.14	0
P	OTHO NITCHOLAS	39	217	14	13	4.15	2
P	JIM CRANDALL	29	81	4	5	4.56	0
P	STEWART BOLEN	32	208	12	17	4.67	1
P	RALPH HUTCHINSON	15	58	2	3	4.81	0
P	WAYNE OSBORNE	37	246	12	18	5.01	1
P	BOOM BOOM BECK	12	50	2	7	7.56	0

1939 - 6th PLACE (82-94)

MANAGER: WADE KILLEFER

		G	AB	AVG	HR	RBI
1B	LEN GABRIELSON	86	315	.276	1	34
2B	BILL CISSELL	167	696	.269	3	83
3B	BOB KAHLE	113	405	.247	6	43
SS	JOE HOOVER	137	457	.298	6	72
LF	GEORGE PUCCINELLI	114	413	.298	16	70
CF	FRENCHY UHALT	147	585	.284	2	54
RF	SPENCER HARRIS	138	383	.339	6	58
C	BILL BRENZEL	101	275	.262	1	33
C	CLIFF DAPPER	88	209	.316	1	32
C	JIM CRANDALL	49	112	.188	0	5
1B	BABE HERMAN	90	350	.317	13	71
3B	HARL MAGGART	43	99	.242	3	12
INF	TIM MARBLE	37	106	.227	1	9
INF	FRANK MOREHOUSE	53	202	.302	2	17
OF	JIM TYACK	70	214	.290	4	40
OF	BILL NORMAN	75	231	.260	10	45
OF	ERNIE ORSATTI	37	77	.273	0	4
OF	GEORGE MANDISH	39	157	.312	2	22

		G	IP	W	L	ERA	SHUTOUTS
P	RUGGER ARDIZOIA	38	235	14	9	3.99	1
P	BILL FLEMING	46	234	12	16	4.00	4
P	CHARLIE MONCRIEF	49	83	7	7	4.10	0
P	JOHNNY BITTNER	35	237	13	14	4.14	1
P	BOB MUNCRIEF	37	169	11	11	4.32	1
P	WAYNE OSBORNE	42	277	16	17	4.61	1
P	LOU TOST	33	121	5	10	4.98	0

1940 - 6th PLACE (84-94)

MANAGER: BILL SWEENEY

		G	AB	AVG	HR	RBI
1B	BILL SWEENEY	85	313	.268	4	50
2B	BILL CISSELL	162	629	.289	4	76
3B	BOB KAHLE	171	641	.312	2	83
SS	JOE HOOVER	154	583	.250	3	49
LF	RUPERT THOMPSON	151	447	.210	5	53
CF	FRENCHY UHALT	170	651	.269	1	52
RF	BABE HERMAN	148	469	.307	9	80
C	BILL BRENZEL	77	255	.294	3	35
C	CLIFF DAPPER	79	209	.249	2	17
C	VINCE MONZO	66	181	.238	1	20
1B	BILL GRAY	68	230	.226	4	27
OF	JACK ROTHROCK	68	229	.249	1	36
OF	BILL MATHESON	44	116	.233	3	15
OF	GEORGE MANDISH	66	202	.272	2	16

		G	IP	W	L	ERA	SHUTOUTS
P	BILL FLEMING	35	231	17	12	2.77	2
P	JOHNNY BITTNER	33	158	10	9	3.42	1
P	WAYNE OSBORNE	43	262	18	17	4.06	2
P	LOU TOST	46	135	4	6	4.07	0
P	RUGGER ARDIZOIA	45	264	14	20	4.09	2
P	HI BITHORN	43	181	10	17	4.37	2
P	FRED GAY	37	171	6	6	4.69	1

1941 - 4th PLACE (85-91)
MANAGER: BILL SWEENEY

		G	AB	AVG	HR	RBI
1B	BILL GRAY	90	325	.283	3	45
2B	HAM SCHULTE	173	676	.280	0	62
3B	BOB KAHLE	176	693	.319	5	95
SS	JOE HOOVER	164	531	.235	8	62
LF	JOHNNY DICKSHOT	175	608	.298	10	86
CF	FRENCHY UHALT	148	534	.288	2	44
RF	JOHNNY BARRETT	149	517	.313	4	66
C	CLIFF DAPPER	125	433	.277	8	63
C	BILL BRENZEL	77	228	.268	4	22
1B	BABE HERMAN	110	272	.346	11	63
1B	BILL SWEENEY	48	121	.273	1	16
OF	HARRY ROSENBERG	120	420	.286	1	55

		G	IP	W	L	ERA	SHUTOUTS
P	FRED GAY	38	144	11	7	3.31	0
P	HI BITHORN	41	228	17	15	3.59	2
P	LOU TOST	47	243	13	10	3.85	1
P	FRANK DASSO	43	230	15	15	3.91	3
P	JOHNNY BITTNER	45	215	12	14	4.19	1
P	WAYNE OSBORNE	33	207	12	12	4.22	0
P	ROY JOINER	34	126	2	12	4.79	1
P	ALEX WELDON	22	58	2	1	4.96	0

1942 - 7th PLACE (75-103)

MANAGER: OSCAR VITT

		G	AB	AVG	HR	RBI
1B	BILL GARBE	112	355	.265	2	36
2B	HAM SCHULTE	107	368	.247	1	24
3B	BOB KAHLE	161	634	.263	0	62
SS	JOE HOOVER	149	590	.327	11	62
LF	FRANK KALIN	127	450	.304	13	79
CF	FRENCHY UHALT	173	669	.275	1	40
RF	JOHNNY DICKSHOT	175	623	.303	11	87
C	BILL ATWOOD	106	300	.253	4	26
C	BILL BRENZEL	98	287	.226	1	20
1B-OF	BABE HERMAN	85	149	.322	5	42
1B	CHARLIE SYLVESTER	75	250	.232	0	27
INF	DEL YOUNG	133	425	.249	2	37

		G	IP	W	L	ERA	SHUTOUTS
P	BILL THOMAS	25	95	9	5	1.70	2
P	JOHNNY BITTNER	28	174	13	9	2.48	0
P	CHARLIE ROOT	30	215	11	14	3.18	1
P	MANNY PEREZ	41	227	14	15	3.33	6
P	WALTER HILCHER	28	141	5	9	3.51	0
P	FRED GAY	36	229	8	19	3.69	0
P	ROY JOINER	37	234	12	18	3.85	2
P	BILL BEVENS	16	58	2	5	4.64	1
P	WAYNE OSBORNE	7	33	1	2	5.75	0

1943 - 5th PLACE (TIED 73-82)

MANAGER: CHARLIE ROOT

		G	AB	AVG	HR	RBI
1B	BUTCH MORAN	156	492	.284	4	64
2B	BILL KNICKERBOCKER	68	236	.284	0	26
3B	HARRY CLEMENTS	156	612	.306	0	51
SS	TOD DAVIS	103	362	.221	2	37
LF	JOHNNY DICKSHOT	158	583	.352	13	99
CF	BROOKS HOLDER	149	543	.273	6	62
RF	ROY YOUNKER	132	414	.280	13	67
C	BILL BRENZEL	88	271	.247	2	26
C	JIM HILL	62	157	.229	1	9
INF	KENNY RICHARDSON	111	310	.258	6	43
INF	JIMMY ADAIR	66	208	.240	0	22
2B	ART LILLY	65	189	.206	0	10
OF	BABE HERMAN	81	147	.354	4	22
OF	MARV GUDAT	36	92	.207	0	1

		G	IP	W	L	ERA	SHUTOUTS
P	CY BLANTON	24	150	9	9	2.70	0
P	CHARLIE ROOT	25	166	15	5	3.09	2
P	EDDIE ERAUTT	20	115	5	9	3.29	1
P	EARL ESCALANTE	21	83	4	7	3.90	1
P	BILL THOMAS	52	249	11	21	3.90	3
P	RON SMITH	44	168	12	9	3.91	1
P	PAT McLAUGHLIN	47	113	4	6	4.22	0
P	ROY JOINER	32	174	11	11	5.28	0

1944 - 6th PLACE (83-86)
MANAGER: CHARLIE ROOT

		G	AB	AVG	HR	RBI
1B	BUTCH MORAN	141	521	.315	2	65
2B	KENNY RICHARDSON	159	536	.252	7	62
3B	BUCK FAUSETT	94	381	.315	0	35
SS	TOD DAVIS	169	604	.248	4	77
LF	FRANK KELLEHER	130	487	.329	29	121
CF	BROOKS HOLDER	161	583	.280	6	54
RF	DEL JONES	110	367	.281	0	20
C	JIM HILL	112	375	.253	2	35
C-OF	ROY YOUNKER	106	299	.237	3	27
INF	RAY OLSEN	92	302	.232	5	35
INF	HARRY CLEMENTS	37	148	.243	1	15
OF	BABE HERMAN	78	107	.346	0	23
OF	JOE GONZALES	52	119	.294	1	15
OF-1B	LES POWERS	83	239	.280	3	32

		G	IP	W	L	ERA	SHUTOUTS
P	JOHN INTLEKOFER	40	145	11	6	2.92	3
P	CY BLANTON	14	68	5	5	3.18	1
P	CHARLIE ROOT	21	87	3	5	3.20	0
P	CLINT HUFFORD	36	137	8	6	3.61	1
P	RON SMITH	46	213	15	11	3.63	0
P	JOE MISHASEK	39	209	16	10	3.79	1
P	ALEX WELDON	34	125	6	9	3.89	1
P	NEWT KIMBALL	11	62	4	4	3.92	0
P	EARL ESCALANTE	41	200	10	15	4.10	1
P	JIM SHARP	29	134	5	9	4.90	0

1945 - 8th PLACE (73-110)

MANAGER: BUCK FAUSETT

		G	AB	AVG	HR	RBI
1B	BUTCH MORAN	169	625	.302	6	101
2B	KENNY RICHARDSON	157	469	.301	14	85
3B	BUCK FAUSETT	167	644	.315	2	60
SS	JOHN CAVALLI	60	229	.271	1	28
LF	BEN CANTRELL	148	502	.281	3	69
CF	BROOKS HOLDER	109	312	.256	5	41
RF	MEL STEINER	122	339	.221	3	27
C	JIM HILL	143	465	.284	1	47
C	HARRY KRAUSE	63	136	.309	2	20
INF	HUGH WILLINGHAM	121	359	.256	10	63
INF	MIKE CHOZEN	37	140	.200	0	15
INF	VERN REYNOLDS	80	258	.225	0	22
OF	ED STEWART	63	251	.323	0	34
OF	LES POWERS	118	397	.287	4	56

		G	IP	W	L	ERA	SHUTOUTS
P	NEWT KIMBALL	42	301	19	21	3.44	4
P	STEVE LeGAULT	22	98	4	6	4.04	1
P	RON SMITH	44	281	15	20	4.29	0
P	JOE MISHASEK	43	252	17	16	5.14	2
P	BOB WILLIAMS	26	131	7	10	5.36	1
P	JOHN INTLEKOFER	34	100	1	8	5.94	0
P	JOHN MARSHALL	34	146	5	12	6.10	1
P	EARL PORTER	16	53	2	4	7.98	0
P	JIM SHARP	18	59	1	7	8.39	0

1946 - 3rd PLACE (95-88)

MANAGER: BUCK FAUSETT
                    JIMMY DYKES

		G	AB	AVG	HR	RBI
1B	TONY LUPIEN	170	633	.295	9	77
2B	GABBY STEWART	139	479	.280	4	58
3B	BUCK FAUSETT	84	252	.258	0	22
SS	ALF ANDERSON	142	550	.264	0	31
LF	FRANK KALIN	121	389	.311	11	60
CF	CULLY RIKARD	144	456	.325	8	68
RF	TOMMY O'BRIEN	119	348	.276	17	73
C	AL UNSER	150	475	.254	13	68
C	BUD SHEELY	38	80	.200	0	4
INF	WOODY WILLIAMS	31	114	.272	0	7
INF	JOHN CAVALLI	99	331	.211	1	24
INF	KENNY RICHARDSON	73	236	.246	5	37
OF	FRANK KELLEHER	91	297	.286	18	54
OF-1B	BUTCH MORAN	105	305	.285	1	33
OF	BEN GUINTINI	28	104	.260	2	6
OF	ED STEWART	83	246	.285	2	32

		G	IP	W	L	ERA	SHUTOUTS
P	RON SMITH	35	112	7	6	2.49	0
P	ART CUCCURULLO	38	180	7	11	2.70	0
P	EDDIE ERAUTT	44	290	20	14	2.76	8
P	ALDON WILKIE	21	142	9	7	2.85	1
P	MANNY PEREZ	36	199	7	13	2.94	2
P	XAVIER RESCIGNO	27	155	11	9	3.19	3
P	FRANK DASSO	36	146	12	5	3.27	2
P	JOHNNY BITTNER	29	97	4	7	3.34	0
P	NEWT KIMBALL	24	74	3	5	3.77	0
P	PAUL GREGORY	31	63	8	5	4.57	0

1947 - 6th PLACE (88-98)
MANAGER: JIMMY DYKES

		G	AB	AVG	HR	RBI
1B	TONY LUPIEN	186	696	.341	21	110
2B	FRED VAUGHAN	104	380	.300	12	56
3B	DON ROSS	142	476	.307	11	67
SS	CARL COX	141	570	.293	3	54
LF	FRANK KELLEHER	121	427	.314	21	93
CF	JIM DELSING	153	572	.316	5	53
RF	AL LIBKE	141	506	.310	10	81
C	CLINT CAMERON	112	265	.272	3	38
C	AL UNSER	89	230	.265	2	29
C	BUD SHEELY	74	153	.248	0	24
INF	WOODY WILLIAMS	40	130	.231	0	13
INF	GABBY STEWART	89	267	.273	1	35
INF	TOD DAVIS	119	380	.234	6	44
OF	GUS ZERNIAL	120	372	.344	12	77
OF	ANDY SKURSKI	112	335	.260	4	32

		G	IP	W	L	ERA	SHUTOUTS
P	ED ALBOSTA	25	140	11	6	3.47	1
P	RUGGER ARDIZOIA	28	212	11	10	3.48	0
P	FRANK SEWARD	17	37	2	1	3.89	0
P	AL YAYLIAN	38	111	5	7	4.05	0
P	FRANK DASSO	7	46	1	6	4.08	0
P	JOE KRAKAUSKAS	39	244	11	17	4.35	1
P	XAVIER RESCIGNO	25	150	11	9	4.38	0
P	PINKY WOODS	28	179	13	10	4.47	4
P	HUGH ORPHAN	28	102	4	8	4.59	1
P	RON SMITH	11	63	5	2	5.00	0
P	CLINT HUFFORD	37	122	7	6	5.16	0
P	PAUL GREGORY	26	51	0	7	6.18	0

1948 - 6th PLACE (84-104)

MANAGER: JIMMY DYKES
          LOU STRINGER 8-28-48
          MULE HAAS 9-20-48

		G	AB	AVG	HR	RBI
1B	RIP RUSSELL	114	382	.288	10	43
2B	LOU STRINGER	175	651	.333	7	99
3B	DON ROSS	128	416	.313	4	65
SS	TOD DAVIS	122	381	.252	12	55
LF	GUS ZERNIAL	186	737	.322	40	156
CF	JIM DELSING	122	463	.333	6	56
RF	FRANK KELLEHER	121	439	.333	25	107
C	JIM GLADD	114	358	.246	7	35
C	LOU KAHN	90	277	.296	2	37
1B	CHUCK STEVENS	38	140	.321	1	19
INF	GENE HANDLEY	127	442	.321	2	50
SS	CARL COX	54	170	.224	1	16
OF	AL WHITE	32	124	.275	0	10
OF	ANDY SKURSKI	120	360	.258	3	36
OF-1B	AL LIBKE	90	238	.231	2	33

		G	IP	W	L	ERA	SHUTOUTS
P	GORDON MALTZBERGER	27	93	7	8	3.00	0
P	PETE GEBRIAN	32	197	11	12	3.84	2
P	VERN KENNEDY	38	183	9	12	3.93	1
P	RUGGER ARDIZOIA	35	228	13	11	4.10	2
P	JOE KRAKAUSKAS	40	157	5	7	4.18	0
P	PINKY WOODS	44	279	15	20	4.52	0
P	ED OLIVER	26	91	5	2	4.75	0
P	EDGAR SMITH	11	49	3	4	5.33	0
P	BILL BUTLAND	44	111	7	8	5.59	0
P	ED ALBOSTA	34	117	4	9	5.85	0

1949 - 1st PLACE (109-78)

MANAGER: FRED HANEY

		G	AB	AVG	HR	RBI
1B	CHUCK STEVENS	183	679	.297	10	82
2B	GENE HANDLEY	181	520	.294	1	45
3B	JIM BAXES	184	641	.287	24	108
SS	JOHNNY O'NEIL	150	458	.218	0	41
LF	HERB GORMAN	154	507	.310	10	110
CF	IRV NOREN	180	678	.330	29	130
RF	FRANK KELLEHER	176	609	.253	29	90
C	MIKE SANDLOCK	118	379	.243	1	54
C	AL UNSER	90	269	.271	5	45
2B	GEORGE FALLON	58	184	.218	1	17
SS	GEORGE GENOVESE	102	251	.259	1	25
OF	ANDY SKURSKI	73	176	.273	4	25

		G	IP	W	L	ERA	SHUTOUTS
P	WILLARD RAMSDELL	34	267	18	12	2.60	2
P	JACK SALVESON	42	148	11	7	3.00	2
P	GORDON MALTZBERGER	46	232	18	10	3.34	1
P	PINKY WOODS	49	275	23	12	4.12	4
P	ART SCHALLOCK	31	167	12	9	4.20	2
P	JIM HUGHES	15	67	3	4	4.29	0
P	GLEN MOULDER	35	193	14	10	4.38	1
P	ED OLIVER	25	70	2	3	4.50	0
P	JEAN PIERRE ROY	22	68	2	4	4.50	0
P	WALT OLSEN	23	67	4	2	5.78	0

1950 - 3rd PLACE (104-96)

MANAGER: FRED HANEY

		G	AB	AVG	HR	RBI
1B	CHUCK STEVENS	171	605	.288	12	88
2B	GENE HANDLEY	160	548	.290	1	42
3B	JIM BAXES	131	408	.243	31	76
SS	BUDDY HICKS	149	507	.239	7	48
LF	FRANK KELLEHER	186	589	.270	40	135
CF	ED SAUER	174	566	.260	9	65
RF	HERB GORMAN	163	534	.305	13	96
C	MIKE SANDLOCK	140	411	.297	2	32
C	CLIFF DAPPER	82	192	.245	3	23
C	JACK PAEPKE	57	167	.228	4	22
SS	JOHNNY O'NEIL	83	236	.263	0	18
INF	MURRAY FRANKLIN	151	507	.260	8	59
OF	BILL ANTONELLO	58	164	.238	2	30
OF	CLINT CONATSER	99	212	.231	7	27
OF	BOB BUNDY	41	165	.321	4	20
OF	GEORGE SCHMEES	41	121	.174	2	9

		G	IP	W	L	ERA	SHUTOUTS
P	JACK SALVESON	30	165	15	4	2.84	2
P	HERB KARPEL	18	74	1	5	3.28	0
P	KEN LEHMAN	33	158	10	11	3.47	1
P	GORDON MALTZBERGER	52	172	13	13	3.61	1
P	BEN WADE	40	248	14	13	3.67	4
P	PINKY WOODS	32	184	10	11	3.72	3
P	PETE MONDORFF	43	130	7	7	3.81	0
P	LEE ANTHONY	53	198	13	9	3.95	2
P	ART SCHALLOCK	38	128	5	7	4.09	0
P	GLEN MOULDER	23	142	7	8	4.50	1
P	KEWPIE BARRETT	15	68	5	4	6.09	0

1951 - 2nd PLACE (93-74)
MANAGER: FRED HANEY

		G	AB	AVG	HR	RBI
1B	CHUCK STEVENS	144	489	.292	10	67
2B	GENE HANDLEY	141	524	.271	0	39
3B	LOU STRINGER	143	525	.284	11	64
SS	GEORGE GENOVESE	109	384	.211	0	19
LF	FRANK KELLEHER	146	470	.253	28	94
CF	DINO RESTELLI	76	270	.281	10	46
RF	GEORGE SCHMEES	135	485	.328	26	100
C	MIKE SANDLOCK	90	311	.248	3	38
C	EDDIE MALONE	30	82	.305	2	18
C	CLIFF DAPPER	50	151	.219	3	22
1B	DALE COOGAN	30	103	.223	6	14
3B	MURRAY FRANKLIN	110	311	.257	13	49
SS	JOHNNY O'NEIL	76	218	.271	0	15
OF	HERB GORMAN	80	262	.275	8	53
OF	CLINT CONATSER	93	247	.231	9	42
OF	JOHNNY LINDELL	75	178	.292	9	24

		G	IP	W	L	ERA	SHUTOUTS
P	BEN WADE	30	200	16	6	2.61	4
P	JOHNNY LINDELL	26	190	12	9	3.03	3
P	JACK SALVESON	36	219	15	10	3.16	0
P	ART SCHALLOCK	20	127	11	5	3.40	2
P	WALLY HOOD	13	85	4	4	3.81	0
P	GORDON MALTZBERGER	41	101	7	8	3.83	0
P	VIC LOMBARDI	28	162	10	11	3.94	1
P	PINKY WOODS	28	162	12	9	4.06	2
P	ROY WELMAKER	21	60	2	3	4.80	1
P	HERB KARPEL	27	52	1	4	5.71	0
P	BOB CHESNES	10	41	2	2	6.24	0

HOLLYWOOD STARS SEASON STATISTICS
1926 - 1957

1952 - 1st PLACE (109-71)
MANAGER: FRED HANEY

		G	AB	AVG	HR	RBI
1B	CHUCK STEVENS	142	490	.278	2	57
2B	MONTY BASGALL	149	478	.279	8	63
3B	JACK PHILLIPS	101	353	.300	9	53
SS	DICK COLE	178	602	.286	8	73
LF	CARLOS BERNIER	171	652	.301	9	79
CF	TOM SAFFELL	154	495	.273	4	57
RF	TED BEARD	127	390	.269	11	53
C	MIKE SANDLOCK	111	374	.286	0	31
C	JIM MANGAN	50	138	.297	5	24
C	EDDIE MALONE	51	136	.279	4	29
3B	LOU STRINGER	45	155	.271	5	28
INF	GENE HANDLEY	131	456	.274	0	46
OF-P	ERV DUSAK	36	91	.253	1	14
OF	FRANK KELLEHER	82	222	.239	11	33
OF-1B	DICK WILSON	48	120	.233	3	16
OF-P	JOHNNY LINDELL	74	174	.213	8	25

		G	IP	W	L	ERA	SHUTOUTS
P	PAUL LA PALME	9	56	6	1	1.29	3
P	MEL QUEEN	29	205	14	9	2.41	5
P	JOHNNY LINDELL	37	282	24	9	2.52	4
P	RED MUNGER	14	64	4	3	2.67	0
P	LEE ANTHONY	22	66	4	1	3.00	1
P	LARRY SHEPARD	35	107	6	4	3.11	1
P	JIM WALSH	36	172	10	9	3.19	2
P	HARRY FISHER	11	47	2	4	3.64	0
P	PAUL PETTIT	31	197	15	8	3.70	2
P	RED LYNN	29	72	6	3	3.75	0
P	PINKY WOODS	29	160	11	9	3.88	3
P	JOE MUIR	13	52	3	4	5.19	0

1953 - 1st PLACE (106-74)

MANAGER: BOBBY BRAGAN

		G	AB	AVG	HR	RBI
1B	DALE LONG	172	599	.272	35	116
2B	MONTY BASGALL	162	578	.249	10	77
3B	GENE HANDLEY	137	428	.259	1	35
SS	JACK PHILLIPS	147	515	.270	16	77
LF	LEE WALLS	178	593	.268	10	83
CF	TOM SAFFELL	170	630	.273	13	61
RF	TED BEARD	134	402	.286	17	60
C	EDDIE MALONE	109	303	.261	9	39
C	BOBBY BRAGAN	98	303	.251	4	28
1B	CHUCK STEVENS	108	274	.230	5	35
INF	DON DAHLKE	81	198	.237	1	10
OF	BOB BUNDY	35	102	.324	2	15
OF	FRANK KELLEHER	109	249	.329	15	65

		G	IP	W	L	ERA	SHUTOUTS
P	JOE MUIR	21	70	5	2	2.33	0
P	GORDON MALTZBERGER	29	49	5	5	3.10	0
P	JIM WALSH	41	190	16	9	3.13	3
P	RED MUNGER	37	166	12	10	3.37	5
P	BILL MacDONALD	24	84	5	2	3.42	0
P	GEORGE O'DONNELL	45	281	20	12	3.61	4
P	HARRY FISHER	33	155	10	10	3.65	2
P	MEL QUEEN	27	144	8	7	3.69	2
P	RED LYNN	53	143	10	4	3.72	0
P	LLOYD HITTLE	38	131	7	9	3.79	1

1954 - 2nd PLACE (101-68)
MANAGER: BOBBY BRAGAN

		G	AB	AVG	HR	RBI
1B	DALE LONG	129	410	.280	23	68
2B	MONTE BASGALL	145	457	.252	4	59
3B	JACK PHILLIPS	160	577	.300	17	88
SS	DICK SMITH	136	517	.294	0	51
LF	CARLOS BERNIER	119	431	.313	6	41
CF	TOM SAFFELL	166	567	.279	8	58
RF	LEE WALLS	162	601	.290	16	93
C	BOBBY BRAGAN	76	182	.258	2	19
C	EDDIE MALONE	73	158	.241	1	22
C	JIM MANGAN	43	103	.262	1	5
C	LARRY DORTON	49	98	.204	0	12
INF	JACK LOHRKE	132	418	.263	8	52
OF	BOBBY DEL GRECO	40	96	.240	1	10
OF	FRANK KELLEHER	95	191	.246	10	38

		G	IP	W	L	ERA	SHUTOUTS
P	RED MUNGER	38	218	17	8	2.32	5
P	LINO DONOSO	46	205	19	8	2.37	4
P	ROGER BOWMAN	46	258	22	13	2.51	6
P	FORREST MAIN	41	64	2	3	2.52	0
P	ED WOLFE	19	92	7	4	2.65	1
P	GEORGE O'DONNELL	18	58	3	1	2.65	1
P	MEL QUEEN	36	200	16	8	3.19	2
P	JIM WALSH	47	168	10	7	3.21	2
P	BOB HALL	18	121	4	9	3.35	0

1955 - 3rd PLACE (91-81)

MANAGER: BOBBY BRAGAN

		G	AB	AVG	HR	RBI
1B	R. C. STEVENS	116	316	.241	9	44
2B	CURT ROBERTS	123	452	.321	8	49
3B	JACK LOHRKE	144	338	.251	3	36
SS	DICK SMITH	137	493	.282	0	34
LF	CARLOS BERNIER	168	580	.279	12	73
CF	BOBBY DEL GRECO	159	481	.287	13	73
RF	LEE WALLS	160	568	.283	24	99
C	BILL HALL	119	339	.257	1	47
C	BOBBY BRAGAN	72	201	.254	2	21
1B	GEORGE VICO	66	166	.283	8	30
INF	GEORGE FREESE	79	235	.302	10	40
OF	BOBBY PRESCOTT	143	381	.276	9	71

		G	IP	W	L	ERA	SHUTOUTS
P	RED MUNGER	36	272	23	8	1.85	5
P	BOB GARBER	48	292	20	16	2.84	3
P	LINO DONOSO	15	58	4	3	3.24	0
P	JOE TRIMBLE	37	135	11	4	3.27	2
P	BEN WADE	24	123	7	8	3.30	0
P	GEORGE O'DONNELL	59	129	9	7	3.41	0
P	ROGER BOWMAN	26	131	5	10	3.70	3
P	NELSON KING	20	58	2	3	3.70	0
P	GEORGE WITT	17	52	3	5	4.30	0
P	CHOLLY NARANJO	22	104	4	10	4.40	1

1956 - 4th PLACE (85-83)

MANAGER: CLAY HOPPER

		G	AB	AVG	HR	RBI
1B	R. C. STEVENS	125	427	.262	27	72
2B	SPOOK JACOBS	81	302	.341	0	24
2B	BILL MAZEROSKI	80	284	.306	9	36
3B	GAIR ALLIE	69	219	.292	4	21
3B	GENE FREESE	68	223	.274	11	36
SS	DICK SMITH	146	505	.269	2	48
LF	JOE DUHEM	139	449	.256	13	68
CF	CARLOS BERNIER	159	626	.283	3	57
RF	ROMAN MEJIAS	166	594	.274	15	71
C	BILL HALL	91	253	.198	3	24
C	DANNY KRAVITZ	39	117	.265	5	21
1B-OF	PAUL PETTIT	114	284	.236	10	45
INF	JIM BAUMER	101	288	.264	6	34

		G	IP	W	L	ERA	SHUTOUTS
P	LUIS ARROYO	22	115	7	5	2.81	2
P	CHOLLY NARANJO	19	118	8	6	3.05	3
P	GEORGE O'DONNELL	51	94	10	5	3.15	0
P	FRED WATERS	14	72	4	3	3.25	2
P	BOB PURKEY	20	118	6	8	3.36	0
P	ROGER SAWYER	44	146	6	4	3.38	0
P	BOB GARBER	24	129	11	6	3.76	1
P	BEN WADE	37	184	13	18	4.05	5
P	CURT RAYDON	21	100	5	5	4.23	0
P	JOE TRIMBLE	22	124	4	11	4.49	1
P	FRED GREEN	33	82	5	4	4.72	0

1957 - 3rd PLACE (94-74)

MANAGER: CLYDE KING

		G	AB	AVG	HR	RBI
1B	R. C. STEVENS	76	240	.225	11	32
2B	SPOOK JACOBS	135	526	.295	0	34
3B	JIM BAUMER	138	486	.300	14	76
SS	LEO RODRIGUEZ	145	536	.287	5	63
LF	CARLOS BERNIER	126	445	.290	3	49
CF	BILL CAUSION	152	552	.301	13	80
RF	PAUL PETTIT	158	542	.284	20	102
C	BILL HALL	132	453	.276	6	62
C	PETE NATON	52	151	.232	5	28
1B	TONY BARTIROME	71	253	.316	0	22
INF	DICK SMITH	121	351	.299	1	32
OF	JOE DUHEM	119	393	.265	6	43
1B	DICK STUART	23	72	.236	6	17

		G	IP	W	L	ERA	SHUTOUTS
P	GEORGE WITT	30	185	18	7	2.24	6
P	CHUCK CHURN	67	136	9	7	2.78	0
P	BENNIE DANIELS	31	229	17	8	2.95	3
P	BEN WADE	39	164	9	10	3.30	0
P	CURT RAYDON	32	169	10	10	3.30	3
P	FRED WATERS	39	122	5	7	3.56	0
P	BOB GARBER	42	154	10	8	3.56	2
P	HUGH PEPPER	28	136	5	9	4.50	2
P	DON ROWE	28	109	8	6	4.69	1

	BATTING AVERAGE *			HITS	
YEAR	PLAYER	AVERAGE	YEAR	PLAYER	HITS
1926	LEFTY O'DOUL	.338	1926	LEFTY O'DOUL	223
1927	PAT MCNULTY	.312	1927	JOHNNY FREDERICK	190
1928	BABE TWOMBLEY	.314	1928	JOHNNY KERR	233
1929	BILL RUMLER	.386	1929	RUSS ROLLINGS	239
1930	HANK SEVEREID	.367	1930	OTIS BRANNAN	208
1931	JOHNNY BASSLER	.354	1931	DAVE BARBEE	216
1932	JOHNNY BASSLER	.357	1932	CLEO CARLYLE	233
1933	JOHNNY BASSLER	.336	1933	CEDRIC DURST	232
1934	SMEAD JOLLEY	.360	1934	SMEAD JOLLEY	227
1935	SMEAD JOLLEY	.372	1935	SMEAD JOLLEY	223
1938	FRENCHY UHALT	.332	1938	FRENCHY UHALT	211
1939	SPENCER HARRIS	.339	1939	BILL CISSELL	187
1940	BOB KAHLE	.312	1940	BOB KAHLE	200
1941	BABE HERMAN	.346	1941	BOB KAHLE	221
1942	JOE HOOVER	.327	1942	JOE HOOVER	193
1943	JOHNNY DICKSHOT	.352	1943	JOHNNY DICKSHOT	205
1944	FRANK KELLEHER	.329	1944	BUTCH MORAN	164
1945	BUCK FAUSETT	.315	1945	BUCK FAUSETT	203
1946	CULLY RIKARD	.325	1946	TONY LUPIEN	187
1947	GUS ZERNIAL	.344	1947	TONY LUPIEN	237
1948	LOU STRINGER	.333	1948	GUS ZERNIAL	237
1949	IRV NOREN	.330	1949	IRV NOREN	224
1950	HERB GORMAN	.305	1950	CHUCK STEVENS	174
1951	GEORGE SCHMEES	.328	1951	GEORGE SCHMEES	159
1952	CARLOS BERNIER	.301	1952	CARLOS BERNIER	196
1953	FRANK KELLEHER	.329	1953	TOM SAFFELL	172
1954	CARLOS BERNIER	.313	1954	LEE WALLS	174
1955	CURT ROBERTS	.321	1955	CARLOS BERNIER	162
1956	CARLOS BERNIER	.293	1956	CARLOS BERNIER	177
1957	BILL CAUSION	.301	1957	BILL CAUSION	166

* 100 GAMES OR MORE

DOUBLES				TRIPLES	
YEAR	PLAYER	DOUBLES	YEAR	PLAYER	TRIPLES
1926	JOHNNY KERR	38	1926	JOHNNY KERR	6
1927	JOHNNY FREDERICK	40	1927	BABE TWOMBLEY	5
1928	JOHNNY KERR	46	1928	MICKEY HEATH	12
1929	MICKEY HEATH	44	1929	CLEO CARLYLE	12
1930	MIKE GAZELLA	44	1930	JESS HILL	13
1931	MIKE GAZELLA	47	1931	JESS HILL	9
1932	CLEO CARLYLE	54	1932	CLEO CARLYLE	9
1933	OTIS BRANNAN	44	1933	FRED HANEY,	
1934	SMEAD JOLLEY	49		CLEO CARLYLE	7
1935	SMEAD JOLLEY	44	1934	SMEAD JOLLEY	7
			1935	BOBBY DOERR	8
1938	FRENCHY UHALT	39			
1939	BILL CISSELL	38	1938	FRENCHY UHALT	11
1940	BABE HERMAN	45	1939	FRENCHY UHALT	13
1941	BOB KAHLE	41	1940	BABE HERMAN	7
1942	JOE HOOVER	34	1941	JOHNNY BARRETT	14
1943	JOHNNY DICKSHOT	31	1942	FRANK KALIN	11
1944	FRANK KELLEHER,		1943	HARRY CLEMENTS	8
	BUTCH MORAN	34	1944	BROOKS HOLDER	8
1945	BUTCH MORAN	56	1945	BUCK FAUSETT	6
1946	TONY LUPIEN	37	1946	CULLY RIKARD,	
1947	TONY LUPIEN	38		TONY LUPIEN	9
1948	LOU STRINGER	50	1947	TONY LUPIEN,	
1949	CHUCK STEVENS,			JIM DELSING	12
	HERB GOPMAN	41	1948	GENE HANDLEY	8
1950	HERB GORMAN	39	1949	IRV NOREN,	
1951	GEORGE SCHMEES	34		HERB GORMAN	6
1952	CHUCK STEVENS	31	1950	ED SAUER	7
1953	DALE LONG	34	1951	GEORGE SCHMEES	17
1954	JACK PHILLIPS	35	1952	CARLOS BERNIER	9
1955	BOBBY DELGRECO	26	1953	TED BEARD	13
1956	DICK SMITH	24	1954	TOM SAFFELL	10
1957	BILL CAUSION	36	1955	BILL HALL	9
			1956	CARLOS BERNIER	15
			1957	BILL HALL	6

HOME RUNS			RUNS BATTED IN		
YEAR	PLAYER	HOME RUNS	YEAR	PLAYER	RUNS BATTED IN
1926	LEFTY O'DOUL	20	1926	LEFTY O'DOUL	116
1927	JOHNNY KERR	18	1927	JOHNNY FREDERICK	93
1928	MICKEY HEATH	19	1928	MICKEY HEATH	109
1929	MICKEY HEATH	38	1929	MICKEY HEATH	156
1930	MICKEY HEATH	37	1930	MICKEY HEATH	136
1931	DAVE BARBEE	47	1931	DAVE BARBEE	166
1932	OTIS BRANNAN	17	1932	JACK SHERLOCK	114
1933	RAY JACOBS	36	1933	RAY JACOBS	125
1934	RAY JACOBS	24	1934	SMEAD JOLLEY	133
1935	SMEAD JOLLEY	29	1935	SMEAD JOLLEY	128
1938	GEORGE PUCCINELLI	22	1938	ROY MORT	73
1939	GEORGE PUCCINELLI	16	1939	BILL CISSELL	83
1940	BABE HERMAN	9	1940	BOB KAHLE	83
1941	BABE HERMAN	11	1941	BOB KAHLE	95
1942	FRANK KALIN	13	1942	JOHNNY DICKSHOT	87
1943	JOHNNY DICKSHOT,		1943	JOHNNY DICKSHOT	99
	ROY YOUNKER	13	1944	FRANK KELLEHER	121
1944	FRANK KELLEHER	29	1945	BUTCH MORAN	101
1945	KENNY RICHARDSON	14	1946	TONY LUPIEN	77
1946	FRANK KELLEHER	18	1947	TONY LUPIEN	110
1947	FRANK KELLEHER,		1948	GUS ZERNIAL	156
	TONY LUPIEN	21	1949	IRV NOREN	130
1948	GUS ZERNIAL	40	1950	FRANK KELLEHER	135
1949	FRANK KELLEHER,		1951	GEORGE SCHMEES	100
	IRV NOREN	29	1952	CARLOS BERNIER	79
1950	FRANK KELLEHER	40	1953	DALE LONG	116
1951	FRANK KELLEHER	28	1954	LEE WALLS	93
1952	FRANK KELLEHER,		1955	LEE WALLS	99
	TED BEARD	11	1956	R.C.STEVENS	72
1953	DALE LONG	35	1957	PAUL PETTIT	102
1954	DALE LONG	23			
1955	LEE WALLS	24			
1956	R.C.STEVENS	27			
1957	PAUL PETTIT	20			

HOLLYWOOD STARS
BATTING AND PITCHING LEADERS
1926-1957

YEAR	GAMES WON PLAYER	GAMES WON	YEAR	GAMES LOST PLAYER	GAMES LOST
1926	FRANK SHELLENBACK	16	1926	CURT FULLERTON	17
1927	FRANK SHELLENBACK	19	1927	CURT FULLERTON	19
1928	FRANK SHELLENBACK	23	1928	CURT FULLERTON,	
1929	FRANK SHELLENBACK	26		FRANK SHELLENBACK	11
1930	JIM TURNER	21	1929	BUZZ WETZEL	15
1931	FRANK SHELLENBACK	27	1930	VANCE PAGE	12
1932	FRANK SHELLENBACK	26	1931	EMIL YDE	16
1933	ARCHIE CAMPBELL	22	1932	VANCE PAGE	19
1934	JOE SULLIVAN	25	1933	VANCE PAGE,	
1935	FRANK SHELLENBACK	14		ARCHIE CAMPBELL	15
---			1934	TOM SHEEHAN	14
1938	JOHNNY BABICH	19	1935	ED WELLS	20
1939	WAYNE OSBORNE	16	---		
1940	WAYNE OSBORNE	18	1938	WAYNE OSBORNE	18
1941	HI BITHORN	17	1939	WAYNE OSBORNE	17
1942	MANNY PEREZ	14	1940	RUGGER ARDIZOIA	20
1943	CHARLIE ROOT	15	1941	HI BITHORN,	
1944	RON SMITH,			FRANK DASSO	15
	JOE MISHASEK	16	1942	FRED GAY	19
1945	NEWT KIMBALL	19	1943	BILL THOMAS	21
1946	EDDIE ERAUTT	20	1944	EARL ESCALANTE	14
1947	PINKY WOODS	13	1945	NEWT KIMBALL	21
1948	PINKY WOODS	15	1946	EDDIE ERAUTT	14
1949	PINKY WOODS	23	1947	JOE KRAKAUSKAS	17
1950	JACK SALVESON	15	1948	PINKY WOODS	20
1951	BEN WADE	16	1949	WILLARD RAMSDELL,	
1952	JOHNNY LINDELL	24		PINKY WOODS	12
1953	GEORGE O'DONNELL	20	1950	BEN WADE,	
1954	ROGER BOWMAN	22		GORDON MALTZBERGER	13
1955	GEORGE MUNGER	23	1951	VIC LOMBARDI	11
1956	BEN WADE	13	1952	MEL QUEEN,	
1957	GEORGE WITT	18		JOHNNY LINDELL,	
				JIM WALSH,	
				PINKY WOODS	9
			1953	GEORGE O'DONNELL	12
			1954	ROGER BOWMAN	13
			1955	BOB GARBER	16
			1956	BEN WADE	18
			1957	BEN WADE,	
				CURT RAYDON	10

THESE MEN DID DOUBLE DUTY

PLAYERS WHO SERVED WITH BOTH
THE LOS ANGELES ANGELS AND
THE HOLLYWOOD STARS

PLAYER	YEARS WITH HOLLYWOOD	YEARS WITH LOS ANGELES
CLIFF ABERSON	1950	1948-49
LEE ANTHONY	1950-52	1948-49
JOHNNY BASSLER	1928-35	1919-20
JIM BAXES	1949-50	1957
FERN BELL	1934,38,42	1942
GEORGE BUCHANAN	1933	1933
HOWARD BURKETT	1928-29	1929
ARCHIE CAMPBELL	1933-35	1937
DON CARLSEN	1951	1949
CLEO CARLYLE	1928-34	1935-37
TOD DAVIS	1943-44, 47-48	1951-53
CEDRIC DURST	1933-35,38	1924
BILL FLEMING	1939-40	1946-47
MURRAY FRANKLIN	1949-51	1953
GEORGE FREESE	1955	1956
LOU GARLAND	1931	1934-35
MIKE GAZELLA	1930-32	1933
GORDON GOLDSBERRY	1944-45, 47-48	1949
MARV GUDAT	1943	1933-38
FRED HANEY	1933-34	1919-20, 29-32
LEROY HERRMANN	1938	1931-33
GOLDY HOLT	1935	1936
BERLYN HORNE	1935	1929-30
JIM HUGHES	1948-49	1957
JOHN INTLEKOFER	1944-45	1933-34
RAY JACOBS	1933-35	1925-31
DON JOHNSON	1938-40	1948
ROY JOINER	1941-43	1935
NEWT KIMBALL	1944-46	1934-35
RED LYNN	1952-53	1942-43, 46-49
EDDIE MALONE	1951-54	1947-49
GORDON MALTZBERGER	1933-34, 48-51, 53-54	1932
BILL MCWILLIAMS	1938	1937
CHARLIE MONCRIEF	1939-40	1920-33
BUTCH MORAN	1943-46	1949
BOB MUNCRIEF	1939	1950
BOBBY MURRAY	1929	1929
VANCE PAGE	1930-34	1942
ELMER PHILLIPS	1926	1925-26
WILLARD RAMSDELL	1949	1952-53
KENNY RICHARDSON	1943-46	1936-37
CHARLIE ROOT	1942-44	1924-25
JACK ROTHROCK	1940	1939-40
RIP RUSSELL	1948	1936-38, 43-45
TOM SAFFELL	1952-54	1957
JACK SALVESON	1949-51	1936-38

THESE MEN DID DOUBLE DUTY (CONTINUED)

PLAYERS WHO SERVED WITH BOTH
THE LOS ANGELES ANGELS AND
THE HOLLYWOOD STARS

PLAYER	YEARS WITH HOLLYWOOD	YEARS WITH LOS ANGELES
ED SAUER	1950-51	1946-48
BILL SCHUSTER	1952	1941-44,46-49
GORDON SLADE	1938	1939
GABBY STEWART	1946-47	1942
LOU STRINGER	1948,51,57	1939-40,47
RALPH STROUD	1926	1926
DOUG TAITT	1933	1925
FAY THOMAS	1943	1933-34,36-41
BABE TWOMBLEY	1927-28	1922-25
JIM TYACK	1939	1932,45-46
BEN WADE	1950-51,55-57	1948
AUGIE WALSH	1932	1929-30
BUZZ WETZEL	1928-31,33	1931-32
HUGH WILLINGHAM	1945	1944
DICK WILSON	1944,52	1949

```
                    HOLLYWOOD STARS
                    SEASON STATISTICS
                    1926-1957
                    -------------------
                    MOST VALUABLE PLAYERS

1926    LEFTY O' DOUL          1943    JOHNNY DICKSHOT
1927    JOHNNY KERR            1944    FRANK KELLEHER
1928    JOHNNY KERR            1945    BUCK FAUSETT
1929    MICKEY HEATH           1946    ALF ANDERSON
1930    OTIS BRANNAN           1947    TONY LUPIEN
1931    FRANK SHELLENBACK      1948    LOU STRINGER
1932    JOHNNY BASSLER         1949    IRV NOREN
1933    FRED HANEY             1950    GENE HANDLEY
1934    FRED HANEY             1951    JOHNNY LINDELL
1935    BOBBY DOERR            1952    JOHNNY LINDELL
.....                          1953    DALE LONG
1938    FRENCHY UHALT          1954    JACK PHILLIPS
1939    BILL CISSELL           1955    RED MUNGER
1940    BOB KAHLE              1956    SPOOK JACOBS*
1941    HAM SCHULTE            1957    BILL HALL
1942    JOE HOOVER
```

* IN 1956 THE AWARD WAS CALLED"MOST POPULAR PLAYER"

```
            THE UNOFFICIAL HOLLYWOOD STARS ALL TIME TEAM
            -------------------------------------------
                    (MY VERSION, WHAT'S YOURS?)

        1B      MICKEY HEATH
        2B      GENE HANDLEY
        3B      BOB KAHLE
        SS      DUDLEY LEE
        OF      CLEO CARLYLE
        OF      FRANK KELLEHER
        OF      CARLOS BERNIER
        C       JOHNNY BASSLER
        P       FRANK SHELLENBACK
        P       PINKY WOODS

                ----------
```

NUMBERS ON THE BACKS OF PLAYERS WERE UNKNOWN IN THE PCL BEFORE 1932,
BUT BY 1934 ALL UNIFORMS WERE SO EQUIPPED. BELOW IS A LISTING OF THE
HOLLYWOOD NUMBERS AND SOME OF THE PLAYERS WHO WORE THEM. SOME STARS CHANGED
THEIR NUMBER EVERY YEAR WHILE WITH THE CLUB, AND THE NUMBER SHOWN MIGHT NOT
BE THE ONE YOU REMEMBER.

UNIFORM NUMBER	WORN BY	UNIFORM NUMBER	WORN BY
1	BILL SWEENEY, JIMMY DYKES, OSCAR VITT	18.	TOM SAFFELL, FRED GAY.
2	FRED HANEY, BOBBY BRAGAN	19.	EDDIE ERAUTT.
3.	TONY LUPIEN, CHUCK STEVENS	20.	GORDON MALTZBERGER.
4.	GENE HANDLEY, HAM SCHULTE.	21.	FRENCHY UHALT,
5.	JIM BAXES, LOU STRINGER, BOBBY DOERR.		FRANK SHELLENBACK.
6.	BOB KAHLE, JOHNNY O'NEIL	22.	GUS ZERNIAL.
7.	FRANK KELLEHER, JOHNNY DICKSHOT	23.	CLYDE KING.
8.	JOE HOOVER.	24.	WILLARD RAMSDELL.
9.	BABE HERMAN, LEE WALLS, PAUL PETTIT	25.	GLENN WRIGHT, MEL QUEEN.
10.	BUTCH MORAN.	26.	MARTY KRUG, DICK COLE
11.	IRV NOREN, HERB GORMAN.	27.	FRENCHY UHALT.
12.	LOU TOST, JACK SALVESON, GEORGE WITT.	28.	JOHN FITZPATRICK.
13.	------------	30.	KENNY RICHARDSON.
14.	BILL BRENZEL, CLEO CARLYLE, HI BITHORN.	31.	BEN WADE.
15.	MONTY BASGALL, CLIFF DAPPER.	34.	PINKY WOODS.
16.	JOHNNY BASSLER, JOHNNY BITTNER.	36.	JOHNNY LINDELL.
17.	CHARLIE ROOT, RUGGER ARDIZOIA.	38.	CARLOS BERNIER.
		40.	ROGER BOWMAN.

NAME	YEARS	RECORD	PCT.
ED ALBOSTA	1947-48	15-15	.500
HARRY ANDERSON	1931	1-2	.333
LEE ANTHONY	1950-52	17-12	.586
RUGGER ARDIZOIA	1939-40		
	1947-48	52-50	.510
LUIS ARROYO	1956	7-5	.583
JOHN BABICH	1938	19-17	.528
BILL BARISOFF	1942	0-1	.000
KEWPIE BARRETT	1950	5-4	.556
WALTER BECK	1938	2-7	.222
CHARLIE BEENE	1955	0-1	.000
BILL BEVENS	1942	2-5	.286
DICK BISHOP	1948	1-1	.500
HI BITHORN	1939-40,		
	1947	27-33	.450
JOHN BITTNER	1939-42,		
	1946	52-53	.495
CY BLANTON	1943-44	14-14	.500
STU BOLEN	1938	12-17	.414
RAY BONNELLY	1928	1-1	.500
GRANT BOWLER	1935	0-5	.000
ROGER BOWMAN	1954-55	27-23	.540
ED BRANDT	1939	2-3	.400
ELMER BRAY	1931	6-11	.353
GEORGE BUCHANAN	1933	2-5	.286
GEORGE BYRD	1946	0-1	.000
ARCHIE CAMPBELL	1933-35	45-45	.500
JACK CANO	1934-35	1-3	.250
GUY CANTRELL	1935	2-5	.286
JOE CARBONARO	1950	0-1	.000
LLOYD CARDEN	1955	0-1	.000
PUG CAVET	1929	0-1	.000
GEORGE CASTER	1947	2-1	.667
ED CHAPMAN	1939	1-2	.333
BOB CHESNES	1951	2-2	.500
CHUCK CHURN	1956-57	9-8	.529
DON CORELLA	1954	0-1	.000
JACK COSTA	1933	1-1	.500
JOHN COUCH	1928	2-3	.400
JIM CRANDALL	1938	4-5	.444
DAN CROWLEY	1933	0-1	.000
ART CUCCURULLO	1946	7-11	.389
WES CURTIS	1952	0-1	.000
DON DANGLEIS	1956	1-1	.500
BENNIE DANIELS	1957	17-8	.680
GEORGE DARROW	1939	1-3	.333

NAME	YEARS	RECORD	PCT.
FRANK DASSO	1941,46,		
	1947	28-26	.519
JIM DENSMORE	1934	14-11	.560
PETE DONOHUE	1933	1-2	.333
LINO DONOSO	1954-56	25-13	.658
ZIP DUMOVICH	1933	0-2	.000
ERV DUSAK	1952	0-1	.000
EARL EMBREE	1944-45	0-4	.000
EDDIE ERAUTT	1942-43,		
	1946	25-26	.490
EARL ESCALANTE	1943-44,		
	1946	17-25	.405
BUCK FAUSETT	1945	0-1	.000
HARRY FISHER	1952-54	12-15	.444
LEO FITTERER	1926-27	3-2	.600
BILL FLEMING	1939-40	29-28	.509
CURT FULLERTON	1926-28	34-49	.410
BOB GARBER	1955-57	41-30	.577
FRED GAY	1940-42,		
	1946	26-32	.448
PETE GEBRIAN	1948	11-12	.478
JIM GOODWIN	1948	0-1	.000
HANK GORNICKI	1946	1-0	1.000
JOHN CORSICA	1949	0-2	.000
PUDGY GOULD	1931	3-4	.429
FRED GREEN	1956	5-4	.556
PAUL GREGORY	1946-47	8-12	.400
AL GRUNWALD	1956	0-1	.000
BOB HALL	1954	4-9	.308
DON HANSKI	1944	0-2	.000
WALLY HEBERT	1934-35	21-28	.429
LEROY HERRMANN	1938	3-3	.500
WHITEY HILCHER	1942	5-9	.357
JACK HILE	1934-35	2-13	.133
LLOYD HITTLE	1953-54	7-10	.412
CAL HOGUE	1955	1-0	1.000
GEORGE HOLLERSON	1926-27		
	1929-31	39-37	.513
AL HOLLINGSWORTH	1947	1-3	.250
WALLY HOOD	1951	4-4	.500
BERLYN HORNE	1935	13-7	.650
CLINT HUFFORD	1944-47	15-12	.556
JIM HUGHES	1949-50	4-4	.500
HANK HULVEY	1926-30	69-54	.561
RALPH HUTCHINSON	1938	2-3	.400
JOHN INTLEKOFER	1944-45	12-14	.462

NAME	YEARS	RECORD	PCT.	NAME	YEARS	RECORD	PCT.
HOOKS IOTT	1948	3-5	.375	CHOLLY NARANJO	1955-56	12-16	.429
ART JACOBS	1927-28	3-10	.231	OLOV NELSON	1955	1-2	.333
AUGIE JOHNS	1929-32	34-27	.557	OTHO NITCHOLAS	1938	14-13	.519
ROY JOINER	1941-43	25-41	.379	WALT NOTHE	1949	1-0	1.000
GORDON JONES	1929	3-2	.600	GEORGE O'DONNELL	1953-57	43-26	.623
HERB KARPEL	1950-51	2-9	.182	ED OLIVER	1948-49	7-5	.583
CHET KEHN	1950	1-0	1.000	WALT OLSON	1949	4-2	.667
VERN KENNEDY	1948	9-12	.429	JOHN O'NEILL	1926	9-9	.500
DON KILDOO	1957	1-1	.500	HUGH ORPHAN	1947	4-8	.333
NEWT KIMBALL	1944-46	26-30	.464	FOREST ORRELL	1948	1-3	.250
NELSON KING	1955	2-3	.400	FRED ORTMAN	1932	5-4	.556
WALTER KINNEY	1928-29, 1932	29-20	.592	WAYNE OSBORNE	1938-42	59-65	.476
				JACK PAEPKE	1949	0-3	.000
JOE KRAKAUSKAS	1947-48	16-24	.400	VANCE PAGE	1930-34	60-57	.513
ARNIE LANDECK	1951	1-1	.500	GEORGE PAYNTER	1947	2-1	.667
PAUL LAPALME	1952	6-1	.857	MONTE PEARSON	1941	0-1	.000
STEVE LEGAULT	1945	4-6	.400	HUGH PEPPER	1956-57	7-10	.412
KEN LEHMAN	1950	10-11	.476	MANNY PEREZ	1942,46	21-28	.429
JOHN LINDELL	1950-52	36-19	.655	LEN PERME	1947	2-1	.667
ROYCE LINT	1952	1-2	.333	DEWITT PERRY	1932	1-1	.500
VIC LOMBARDI	1951	10-11	.476	PAUL PETTIT	1952	15-8	.652
RED LYNN	1952-53	16-7	.696	RAY PHEBUS	1939	0-1	.000
AL LYONS	1955	2-2	.500	ELMER PHILLIPS	1926	3-2	.600
BILL MACDONALD	1953-54	5-3	.625	AL PIECHOTA	1941	1-3	.250
FORREST MAIN	1954	2-3	.400	HERMAN PILLETTE	1935	12-9	.571
JOHN MALLOY	1926	0-1	.000	WALLY PITTS	1955	0-1	.000
GORDON MALTZ-BERGER	1934,47-51,53-54	50-46	.521	EARL POPTER	1945	2-4	.333
				WILLIS PRAUL	1927	0-1	.000
JOHN MARSHALL	1945	5-12	.294	DON PULFORD	1943	2-0	1.000
JOE MARTICORENA	1929	10-9	.526	BOB PURKEY	1955	6-8	.429
DICK MCCABE	1926-29	43-49	.467	MEL QUEEN	1952-55	39-25	.609
LOU MCEVOY	1931	4-5	.444	JACK QUINN	1934	1-1	.500
PAT MCLAUGHLIN	1943	4-6	.400	WILLARD RAMSDELL	1949	18-12	.600
RUSS MESSERLY	1943,46	1-4	.200	CURT RAYDON	1956-57	15-15	.500
JOHN MILJUS	1932-33	4-4	.500	JACK REGER	1945	0-1	.000
JOE MISHASEK	1944-46	33-27	.550	XAVIER RESCIGNO	1946-47	22-19	.537
CHARLIE MONCRIEF	1939-40	8-8	.500	GORDON RHODES	1928,30	26-12	.684
PETE MONDORFF	1950	7-7	.500	BOB RODRIGUEZ	1944	0-1	.000
GLEN MOULDER	1949-50	21-18	.538	AL ROMPLE	1947	0-1	.000
JOE MUIR	1952-53	7-6	.538	CHARLIE ROOT	1942-44	29-29	.500
PHIL MULCAHY	1926-28	16-29	.356	DON ROWE	1957	8-6	.571
BOB MUNCRIEF	1939	11-11	.500	JEAN PIERRE ROY	1949-50	4-6	.400
GEORGE MUNGER	1952-55	56-29	.659	JACK SALVESON	1949-51	41-21	.661
BILL MURPHY	1926-28	19-17	.528	WARREN SANDEL	1952	1-0	1.000
ALEX MUSTAIKIS	1940	2-4	.333	ROGER SAWYER	1956	6-4	.600
				ART SCHALLOCK	1949-51	28-21	.571

NAME	YEARS	RECORD	PCT.	NAME	YEARS	RECORD	PCT.
DON SCHULTZ	1957	1-0	1.000	PINKY WOODS	1947-53	84-72	.538
DICK SCHULTZE	1933-34	2-4	.333	AL YAYLIAN	1946-48	6-8	.429
TOM SEATS	1949	1-0	1.000	LEN YOCHIM	1955	0-1	.000
FRANK SEWARD	1947	2-1	.667	EMIL YDE	1930-32	44-37	.543
JIM SHARP	1944-45	6-16	.273				
PAT SHEA	1927	1-2	.333				
TOM SHEEHAN	1932-34	51-32	.614				
FRANK SHELLENBACK	1926-1935	205-104	.663				
LARRY SHEPARD	1952-54	10-6	.625				
JOHN SINGLETON	1926	11-13	.458				
EDGAR SMITH	1948	3-4	.429				
PAUL SMITH	1939-40	2-3	.400				
DICK SMITH	1953	1-0	1.000				
RON SMITH	1943-47	54-48	.529				
FRED STROBEL	1952,54	3-3	.500				
RALPH STROUD	1926	0-2	.000				
JOE SULLIVAN	1934	25-11	.694				
BUD TEACHOUT	1927	6-6	.500				
FAY THOMAS	1943	0-2	.000				
MYLES THOMAS	1932	14-18	.438				
BILL THOMAS	1942-43	20-26	.435				
QUENTIN THOMPSON	1941	0-1	.000				
LOU TOST	1938-41	33-42	.440				
JOE TRIMBLE	1955-56	15-15	.500				
JIM TURNER	1930-32	49-34	.590				
BUD TUTTLE	1935	0-1	.000				
GENE VALLA	1928	0-2	.000				
BEN WADE	1950-51, 1955-57	59-55	.518				
AUGIE WALSH	1932	3-3	.500				
JIM WALSH	1952-54	36-25	.590				
FRED WATERS	1953,56-1957	9-11	.450				
ED WEILAND	1942	0-1	.000				
ALEX WELDON	1941-42, 1944-45	10-14	.417				
ED WELLS	1935	9-20	.310				
ROY WELMAKER	1951-53	5-5	.500				
BUZZ WETZEL	1928-31, 1931,33	54-42	.563				
ALDON WILKIE	1946	9-7	.563				
CARL WILLIAMS	1944	0-1	.000				
BOB WILLIAMS	1945	7-10	.412				
GEORGE WITT	1955,57	21-12	.636				
ED WOLFE	1954	7-4	.636				

FOLLOWING IS A LISTING OF PLAYERS WHO APPEARED IN AT LEAST ONE REGULAR
SEASON GAME WITH THE STARS. ALTHOUGH EVERY EFFORT HAS BEEN MADE TO INSURE
COMPLETENESS, IT IS POSSIBLE THAT A FEW NAMES HAVE BEEN OMITTED. THE AUTHOR
ACCEPTS RESPONSIBILITY FOR ANY ERRORS AND APOLOGIZES TO THOSE STARS NOT INCLUDED.

NAME-POSITION-IST YEAR WITH STARS   NAME-POSITION-IST YEAR WITH STARS
---- -------- --------------------   ---- -------- --------------------

-A-

CLIFF ABERSON	OF 1950	RAY BONNELLY	P 1928
JIMMY ADAIR	INF 1943	JOE BONOWITZ	OF 1929
DICK ADAMS	1B 1947	RAY BOONE	INF 1948
SAM AGNEW	C 1926	TONY BOROJA	OF 1928
BILL ALBERT	OF 1929	CARL BOUTON	INF 1926
ED ALBOSTA	P 1947	GRANT BOWLER	P 1935
CAIR ALLIE	3B 1956	ROGER BOWMAN	P 1954
ALF ANDERSON	SS 1946	BOBBY BRAGAN	C 1954
HARRY ANDERSON	P 1931	ED BRANDT	P 1939
IVY PAUL ANDREWS	P 1940	BILL BRANDT	P 1946
STAN ANDREWS	C 1946	OTIS BRANNAN	2B 1930
JOE ANNUNZIO	C 1938	ELMER BRAY	P 1931
LEE ANTHONY	P 1950	BILL BRENZEL	C 1938
BILL ANTONELLO	OF 1950	BEV BROWN	P 1935
GARRETT ARBELBIDE	OF 1933	GEORGE BUCHANAN	P 1933
RUGGER ARDIZOIA	P 1939	CLARENCE BUHELLER	OF 1955
LUIS ARROYO	P 1956	BOB BUNDY	OF 1949
BILL ATWOOD	C 1942	NICK BUONARICO	C 1944
-----		HOWARD BURKETT	INF 1929
-B-		BILL BUTLAND	P 1948
JOHN BABICH	P 1938	GEORGE BYRD	P 1946
DAVE BARBEE	OF 1930	---	
BILL BARISOFF	P 1942	-C-	
LES BARNES	PH 1944	MARTY CALLAGHAN	OF 1933
JOHNNY BARRETT	OF 1941	CLINT CAMERON	C 1947
KEWPIE BARRETT	P 1950	ARCHIE CAMPBELL	P 1933
TONY BARTIROME	1B 1957	JACK CANO	P 1933
MONTE BASGALL	2B 1952	BEN CANTRELL	OF 1945
JOHNNY BASSLER	C 1928	GUY CANTRELL	P 1935
JIM BAUMER	INF 1956	BOB CANTRELL	P 1944
JIM BAXES	3B 1949	JOE CAPBONARO	P 1950
TED BEARD	OF 1952	LLOYD CARDEN	P 1955
WALTER BECK	P 1938	TOM CAREY	SS 1938
CHARLIE BEENE	P 1955	DON CARLSEN	P 1951
GUS BELL	OF 1952	CLEO CARLYLE	OF 1928
FERN BELL	OF 1934	BILL CARNEY	OF 1942
JOE BERKOWITZ	INF 1933	LOU CATINA	INF 1930
TONY BERNARDO	OF 1927	BILL CAUSION	OF 1957
CARLOS BERNIER	OF 1952	JOHN CAVALLI	INF 1945
BILL BEVENS	P 1942	PUG CAVET	P 1929
DICK BISHOP	P 1948	GEORGE CASTER	P 1947
HI BITHORN	P 1940	ED CHAPMAN	P 1939
JOHN BITTNER	P 1939	BOB CHESNES	P 1951
CY BLANTON	P 1943	ROY CHESTERFIELD	P 1929
STU BOLEN	P 1938	MYER CHOZEN	INF 1944

NAME-POSITION-1ST YEAR WITH STARS		NAME-POSITION-1ST YEAR WITH STARS	
-C- (CONTINUED)			
CHUCK CHURN	P 1956	ERV DUSAK	P/OF 1952
HARRY CLEMENTS	3B 1943	---	
ELMER CLOW	INF 1953	**-E-**	
CLIFF COGGIN	P 1954	EARL EMBREE	P 1944
SID COHEN	P 1933	EDDIE ERAUTT	P 1942
DICK COLE	SS 1952	EARL ESCALANTE	P 1943
CLINT CONATSER	OF 1950	---	
JOE CONNOLLY	OF 1926	**-F-**	
DALE COOGAN	1B 1952	GEORGE FALLON	INF 1949
LES COOK	C 1926	BUCK FAUSETT	3B 1944
DON CORELLA	P 1954	HARRY FISHER	P 1952
JACK COSTA	P 1933	LEO FITTERER	P 1928
JOHN COUCH	P 1928	BILL FLEMING	P 1939
STAN COULLING	P 1949	MURRAY FRANKLIN	INF 1949
FRITZ COUMBE	OF/1B 1926	HERMAN FRANKS	C 1933
CARL COX	INF 1939	JOHNNY FREDERICK	OF 1926
JIM CRANDALLL	C/P 1938	GENE FREESE	3B 1956
CONNIE CREEDON	OF 1943	GEORGE FREESE	3B 1955
DAN CROWLEY	P/1B 1933	BOB FROST	C 1943
ART CUCCURULLO	P 1946	CURT FULLERTON	P 1926
WES CURTIS	P 1952	ELIAS FUNK	OF 1929
---		---	
-D-		**-G-**	
DON DAHLKE	INF 1953	BILL GABLER	1B 1956
DON DANGLEIS	P 1956	LEN GABRIELSON	1B 1939
BENNIE DANIELS	P 1957	BILL CARBE	1B 1942
CLIFF DAPPER	C 1939	BOB GARBER	P 1955
GEORGE DARROW	P 1939	GEORGE GARDNER	P 1933
FRANK DASSO	P 1941	JERRY GARDNER	PH 1956
TOD DAVIS	SS 1943	LOU GARLAND	P 1931
HUBERT DAWSON	INF 1943	FRED GAY	P 1940
RENO DEBENEDETTI	3B 1954	MIKE GAZELLA	3B 1930
ROD DEDEAUX	SS 1939	PETE GEBRIAN	P 1948
BOBBY DEL GRECO	OF 1954	GEORGE GENOVESE	INF 1948
JIM DELSING	OF 1947	ROSS GILHOUSEN	OF 1934
JIM DENSMORE	P 1934	JIM GLADD	C 1947
GENE DESAUTELS	C 1935	GORDON GOLDSBERRY	1B 1944
JOHN DESKIN	PH 1953	AL GONZALES	INF 1945
JACK DEVINCENZI	OF 1942	JOE GONZALES	OF 1944
JOHNNY DICKSHOT	OF 1941	CHARLIE GOOCH	INF 1927
VINCE DIMAGGIO	OF 1933	JIM GOODWIN	P 1948
JOE DOBBINS	INF 1943	HERB GORMAN	OF 1949
BOBBY DOERR	2B 1934~	HANK GORNICKI	P 1946
PETE DONOHUE	P 1933	JOHN GORSICA	P 1949
LINO DONOSO	P 1954	PUDGY GOULD	P 1931
LARRY DORTON	C 1955	TONY GOVERNOR	OF 1930
JOE DUHEM	OF 1956	BILL GRAY	1B 1940
ZIP DUMOVICH	P 1933	FRED GREEN	P 1956
BOB DURETTO	P 1945	HARRY GREEN	OF/1B 1929
CED DURST	OF/1B 1933	PAUL GREGORY	P 1946

HOLLYWOOD STARS
ALL TIME PLAYER INDEX
1926-1957

NAME-POSITION-1ST YEAR WITH STARS				NAME-POSITION-1ST YEAR WITH STARS		
-G-(CONTINUED)				**-I-**		
JOHN GROHAVEC	INF	1945				
AL GRUNWALD	P	1956		HOOKS IOTT	P	1948
SIG GRYSKA	INF	1940				
MARV GUDAT	OF	1943		**-J-**		
BEN GUINTINI	OF	1946				
				ART JACOBS	P	1927
-H-				SPOOK JACOBS	2B	1956
BOB HALL	P	1954		JOHN JACOBS	OF	1928
BILL HALL	C	1955		RAY JACOBS	1B	1939
GENE HANDLEY	INF	1948		DAVE JASKA	INF	1955
FRED HANEY	3B	1933		MILT JOFFE	OF	1948
ANDY HANSEN	P	1954		AUGIE JOHNS	P	1929
CHUCK HANSEN	C	1945		DON JOHNSON	INF	1938
DON HANSKI	P	1944		BILL JOHNSON	INF	1942
SPENCER HARRIS	OF	1939		ROY JOINER	P	1941
CHRIS HARTJE	C	1938		SMEAD JOLLEY	OF	1934
MICKEY HEATH	1B	1927		DEL JONES	OF	1943
WALLY HEBERT	P	1934		GORDON JONES	P	1929
GARY HEGEDORN	P	1953		JOHN JONES	OF	1930
GAIL HENLEY	OF	1956				
BABE HERMAN	OF/1B	1939		**-K-**		
LEROY HERRMANN	P	1938				
WILLARD HERSHBERGER	C	1934		BOB KAHLE	3B	1939
BUDDY HICKS	SS	1950		LOU KAHN	C	1948
WHITEY HILCHER	P	1942		FRANK KALIN	OF	1942
DANNY HILE	P	1943		HERB KARPEL	P	1950
JACK HILE	P	1934		CHET KEHN	P	1950
JIM HILL	C	1943		FRANK KELLEHER	OF	1944
JESS HILL	OF	1930		VERN KENNEDY	P	1948
MACK HILLIS	SS	1926		JIM KERR	C	1935
HAL HIRSHON	OF	1947		JOHNNY KERR	2B	1926
LLOYD HITTLE	P	1953		DON KILDOO	P	1957
CAL HOGUE	P	1955		JOHN KILLEEN	P	1931
BROOKS HOLDER	OF	1943		NEWT KIMBALL	P	1944
GEORGE HOLLERSON	P	1928		NELSON KING	P	1955
TOM HOLLEY	INF	1927		WALTER KINNEY	P	1928
AL HOLLINGSWORTH	P	1947		LEO KINTANA	INF	1939
GOLDY HOLT	INF	1935		BILL KNICKERBOCKER	2B	1943
BOB HONOR	OF	1956		EARL KNUDSON	P	1943
WALLY HOOD	P	1951		NICK KOBACK	C	1956
JOE HOOVER	SS	1938		CLEM KOSHOREK	SS	1953
BERLYN HORNE	P	1935		JOE KRAKAUSKAS	P	1947
ROY HOUSE	C	1940		HARRY KRAUSE	C	1945
LEE HOWARD	INF	1946		DANNY KRAVITZ	C	1956
CLINT HUFFORD	P	1944				
JIM HUGHES	P	1949		**-L-**		
HANK HULVEY	P	1926		PAUL LAPALME	P	1952
KEN HUMPHREY	OF	1954		AL LEAP	INF	1949
RALPH HUTCHINSON	P	1938		DUDLEY LEE	SS	1926

NAME-POSITION-1ST YEAR WITH STARS   NAME-POSITION-1ST YEAR WITH STARS

-L- (CONTINUED)

STEVE LEGAULT	P	1945	AL MCNEELEY	OF	1931
KEN LEHMAN	P	1950	PAT MCNULTY	OF	1927
EDDIE LEISHMAN	INF	1930	BILL MCWILLIAMS	INF	1938
STEVE LEMBO	C	1949	ROMAN MEJIAS	OF	1956
ROY LESLIE	OF	1926	RUSS MESSERLY	P	1943
JIM LEVEY	INF	1934	VIC METTLER	OF	1938
AL LIBKE	OF	1946	BOB MEUSEL	OF	1932
BILL LILLARD	SS	1941	JOHN MILJUS	P	1932
ART LILLY	INF	1943	JACK MILLER	P	1943
LEN LINDBORG	P	1954	BILL MILLER	P	1938
JOHN LINDELL	OF/P	1950	JOE MISHASEK	P	1943
HOWARD LINDIMORE	INF	1926	BOB MISTELE	OF	1944
ROYCE LINT	P	1952	CHARLIE MONCRIEF	P	1939
WALT LIPSHIN	P	1935	PETE MONDORFF	P	1950
JACK LOHRKE	INF	1954	VINCE MONZO	C	1943
VIC LOMBARDI	P	1951	NEAL MONTANK	P	1945
DALE LONG	1B	1953	BOB MOORE	OF	1943
DICK LOPEMAN	INF	1955	BUTCH MORAN	1B	1943
JAKE LORENTZEN	P	1930	FRANK MOREHOUSE	INF	1939
ED LOWELL	1B	1927	ROY MORT	1B	1938
TONY LUPIEN	1B	1946	MARV MOUDY	P	1930
RED LYNN	P	1952	GLEN MOULDER	P	1949
AL LYONS	P	1955	JOE MUIR	P	1952
			PHIL MULCAHY	P	1926
	---		EDDIE MULLIGAN	3B	1935
	-M-		BOB MUNCRIEF	P	1939
BILL MACDONALD	P	1953	GEORGE MUNGER	P	1952
HARL MAGGART	INF	1938	DENNY MURPHY	C	1927
FORREST MAIN	P	1954	BILL MURPHY	P	1926
JOHN MALLOY	P	1926	APT MURRAY	P	1956
EDDIE MALONE	C	1953	BOBBY MURRAY	INF	1929
MIKE MALONEY	INF	1929	ALEX MUSTAIKIS	P	1940
GORDON MALTZBERGER	P	1934	GEORGE MYATT	SS	1935
GEORGE MANDISH	OF	1939	OTTO MYERS	OF	1944
JIM MANGAN	C	1952		---	
TIM MARBLE	INF	1938		-N-	
PHIL MARLOW	OF	1930		---	
HARRY MARNIE	OF	1942	CLARENCE NACHAND	OF	1938
CLARENCE MARSHALL	P	1953	CHOLLY NARANJO	P	1955
JOHN MARSHALL	P	1945	PETE NATON	C	1957
JOE MARTICORENA	P	1929	CHARLIE NEAL	PR	1952
LOU MARTIN	OF	1932	RON NECCIAI	P	1955
BILL MATHESON	OF	1940	OLOV NELSON	P	1956
TED MAYER	C	1932	OTHO NITCHOLAS	P	1938
BILL MAZEROSKI	2B	1955	IRV NOREN	OF	1949
DICK MCCABE	P	1926			
HUBIE MCCONNELL	C	1942			
GEORGE MCDONALD	1B	1935			
JIM MCDOWELL	1B	1927			
LOU MCEVOY	P	1931			
PAT MCLAUGHLIN	P	1943			

NAME-POSITION-1ST YEAR WITH STARS   NAME-POSITION-1ST YEAR WITH STARS

-N- (CONTINUED) | | | -P- (CONTINUED)

Name	Pos	Year	Name	Pos	Year
BILL NORMAN	OF	1938	HERMAN PILLETTE	P	1935
WALT NOTHE	P	1949	WALLY PITTS	P	1955
FRANK NOVOSEL	OF	1932	VERN PIVER	UTL	1956
AL NYSTROM	P	1943	EARL PORTER	P	1945
			ERNIE POTOCAR	C	1944
-O-			JOHN POWERS	OF	1954
			LES POWERS	OF/1B	1944
EDDIE O'BRIEN	INF	1957	WILLIS PRAUL	P	1927
TOM O'BRIEN	OF	1946	JIM PRENDERGAST	P	1938
GEORGE O'DONNELL	P	1953	DAN PRENTICE	PH	1957
FRANK O'DOUL	OF	1926	BOBBY PRESCOTT	OF	1955
JOHN O'KEEFE	INF	1953	GEORGE PUCCINELLI	OF	1938
ED OLIVER	P	1948	DON PULFORD	P	1943
RAY OLSEN	INF	1944	BOB PURKEY	P	1956
WALT OLSEN	P	1949			
JOHN O'NEIL	INF	1949	-Q-		
JOHN O'NEILL	P	1926			
BILL ONUSKA	C	1956	MEL QUEEN	P	1952
HUGH ORPHAN	P	1947	GEORGE QUELLICH	OF	1932
FOREST ORRELL	P	1948	JACK QUINN	P	1934
ERNIE ORSATTI	OF	1939			
FRED ORTMAN	P	1932	-R-		
WAYNE OSBORNE	P	1938			
ALBERTO OSORIO	P	1953	JOHN RAGER	P	1945
LEO OSTENBERG	INF	1928	WILLARD RAMSDELL	P	1949
CHICK OUTEN	C	1938	CLINT RAPER	P	1941
			CURT RAYDON	P	1956
-P-			BOB REASH	OF	1948
			CHARLIE REDLING	P	1930
JACK PAEPKE	P/C	1949	GUS REDMAN	C	1926
VANCE PAGE	P	1930	JACK REGER	P	1945
EMIL PANKO	OF	1957	WALT REHG	OF	1929
HENRY PATTERSON	OF	1933	XAVIER RESCIGNO	P	1946
GEORGE PAYNTER	P	1947	DINO RESTELLI	OF	1951
MONTE PEARSON	P	1941	VERN REYNOLDS	INF	1945
HUGH PEPPER	P	1956	GORDON RHODES	P	1928
MANNY PEREZ	P	1942	FRAN RICE	OF	1954
LEN PERME	P	1947	KEN RICHARDSON	INF	1943
DEWITT PERRY	P	1932	CULLY RIKARD	OF	1946
JOHN PETERS	C	1926	WALLY RITTER	P	1929
PAUL PETTIT	P/OF	1952	CURT ROBERTS	2B	1955
RAY PHEBUS	P	1939	HENRY ROBINSON	INF	1943
BUDDY PHILLIPS	C	1947	LEO PODRIGUEZ	INF	1956
ELMER PHILLIPS	P	1926	BOB RODRIGUEZ	P	1944
JACK PHILLIPS	INF	1952	RUSS ROLLINGS	3B	1929
AL PIECHOTA	P	1941	AL ROMPLE	P	1947
LEN PIEROTTI	INF	1926	CHARLIE ROOT	P	1942
VINCE PIGNATIRO	OF	1935	HARRY ROSENBERG	OF	1941

NAME-POSITION-1ST YEAR WITH STARS	NAME-POSITION-1ST YEAR WITH STARS

-R-(CONTINUED)

Name	Pos	Year	Name	Pos	Year
DON ROSS	INF	1947	ANDY SKURSKI	OF	1947
BOB ROTH	OF	1928	GORDON SLADE	INF	1938
JACK ROTHROCK	OF	1940	EDGAR SMITH	P	1948
DON ROWE	P	1957	ELMER SMITH	OF	1927
JEAN PIERRE ROY	P	1949	JACK D. SMITH	INF	1945
HARRY RUBY	INF	1935	PAUL SMITH	P	1940
BOB RUCK	PH	1956	DICK SMITH	INF	1954
BILL RUMLER	OF	1929	DICK SMITH	P	1953
GLEN RUSSELL	1B	1948	RON SMITH	P	1943
			JOE STANLEY	P	1929

-S-

Name	Pos	Year	Name	Pos	Year
			ED STEELE	OF	1952
			MEL STEINER	OF	1945
ATHOS SADA	OF	1934	CHUCK STEVENS	1B	1948
TOM SAFFELL	OF	1952	R. C. STEVENS	1B	1955
JACK SALVESON	P	1949	ED STEWART	OF	1945
ROBERTO SANCHEZ	SS	1955	GABBY STEWART	INF	1946
WARREN SANDEL	P	1952	JOHN STILLWELL	P	1949
MIKE SANDLOCK	C	1949	LIN STORTI	2B	1944
ED SAUER	OF	1950	ALAN STRANGE	INF	1932
ROGER SAWYER	P	1956	LOU STRINGER	INF	1947
DEAN SCARBOROUGH	INF	1947	FRED STROBEL	P	1952
ART SCHALLOCK	P	1949	RALPH STROUD	P	1926
HAL SCHIMLING	C	1945	DICK STUART	OF	1957
GEORGE SCHMEES	OF	1950	JOE SULLIVAN	P	1934
HAM SCHULTE	2B	1941	LLOYD SUMMERS	C	1934
DON SCHULTZ	P	1957	GEORGE SUSCE	C	1934
BARNEY SCHULTZ	P	1953	RAY SWARTZ	INF	1954
DICK SCHULTZE	P	1933	JIM SWEENEY	OF	1927
BILL SCHUSTER	INF	1952	BILL SWEENEY	1B	1940
TOM SEATS	P	1949	CHARLIE SYLVESTER	1B/OF	1942
JOHN SEGRIST	OF	1926	ROWDY SYPHER	C	1926
HANK SEVEREID	C	1929			

-T-

Name	Pos	Year	Name	Pos	Year
FRANK SEWARD	P	1947	DOUG TAITT	OF	1933
JIM SHARP	P	1945	BUD TEACHOUT	P	1927
SOLON SHAW	P	1954	FAY THOMAS	P	1943
PAT SHEA	P	1927	MYLES THOMAS	P	1932
LES SHEEHAN	OF	1926	BILL THOMAS	P	1942
TOM SHEEHAN	P	1933	RUPERT THOMPSON	OF	1940
BUD SHEELY	C	1946	QUENTIN THOMPSON	P	1941
BILL SHEETS	C	1948	COTTON TIERNEY	INF	1927
FRANK SHELLENBACK	P	1926	FRANK TOBIN	C	1933
LARRY SHEPARD	P	1952	LOU TOST	P	1938
JOHN SHERLOCK	1B	1931	AL TREICHEL	P	1944
ED SIBLER	OF	1940	JOE TRIMBLE	P	1955
MKIE SICHKO	OF	1949	JIM TURNER	P	1930
ANDY SIERRA	INF	1946	BUD TUTTLE	P	1935
JOHN SINGLETON	P	1926	BABE TWOMBLEY	OF	1928
STEVE SITEK	P	1944			

NAME-POSITION-1ST YEAR WITH STARS			NAME-POSITION-1ST YEAR WITH STARS		
-T- (CONTINUED)					
JIM TYACK	OF	1939	GEORGE WOPINEK	SS	1954
---			---		
-U-			-Y-		
BERNIE UHALT	OF	1938	AL YAYLIAN	P	1946
AL UNSER	C	1944	LEN YOCHIM	P	1955
---			DEL YOUNG	INF	1942
-V-			ROY YOUNKER	C/OF	1943
GENE VALLA	P	1928	EMIL YDE	P	1930
ROLAND VAN SLATE	P	1945	---		
FRED VAUGHAN	2B	1947	-Z-		
LOU VEZELICH	OF	1947			
GEORGE VICO	1B	1954	CHARLIE ZABY	OF	1933
OSCAR VITT	3B	1926	AL ZARILLA	OF	1955
JOHN VUXICH	OF	1933	GUS ZERNIAL	OF	1947
---			FRANK ZOELLER	OF	1926
-W-			---		
BEN WADE	P	1950			
BOB WADE	P	1955			
BOB WAKEFIELD	OF	1949			
ROWE WALLERSTEIN	P	1945			
LEE WALLS	OF	1953			
AUGIE WALSH	P	1932			
JIM WALSH	P	1952			
JACK WARREN	C	1947			
BILLY JO WATERS	P	1953			
FRED WATERS	P	1953			
RALPH WATSON	INF	1945			
ED WEILAND	P	1942			
FRANK WELCH	OF	1928			
ALEX WELDON	P	1941			
ED WELLS	P	1935			
ROY WELMAKER	P	1941			
JULIE WERA	3B	1928			
DARYL WESTERFELD	C	1955			
BUZZ WETZEL	P	1928			
FRANK WETZEL	OF	1930			
AL WHITE	OF	1948			
JO JO WHITE	OF	1949			
ALDON WILKIE	P	1946			
CARL WILLIAMS	P	1944			
MERLIN WILLIAMS	P	1948			
BOB WILLIAMS	P	1945			
WOODY WILLIAMS	INF	1946			
HUGH WILLINGHAM	INF	1945			
DICK WILSON	OF	1952			
VAN WIRTHMAN	OF	1935			
GEORGE WITT	P	1955			
ED WOLFE	P	1954			
DON WOLIN	SS	1940			
PINKY WOODS	P	1947